SPELLING 1500:

A PROGRAM

Second Edition

SPELLING 1500: A PROGRAM

Second Edition

J. N. Hook

UNIVERSITY OF ILLINOIS AT URBANA

Harcourt Brace Jovanovich, Inc.
New York   Chicago   San Francisco   Atlanta

ISBN: 0-15-583211-5

Library of Congress Catalog Card Number: 76-9569

Printed in the United States of America

Author's Note

I am grateful to Donald J. Goodman, of Muskegon, Michigan, Community College, for suggesting the use of test-word cassettes, for describing a regrouping of units like the one I have given, and for recommending words to be added. I also thank other instructors and a number of students who during the past several years have sent their comments to the publisher or to me. Their words of praise have been heartwarming and their suggestions helpful.

J. N. Hook
Waveland, Indiana

To the Student

Spelling 1500: A Program will help you to master the spelling of many troublesome words. It uses a variety of approaches, since different words pose different problems. The approaches you will find here include the following:

- **programed learning**   Learning to spell is less a group effort than an individual effort; programed learning helps the individual—you—to learn what you most need to know.

- **grouping of words with similar trouble spots**   You will find words like *monkeys*, *turkeys*, and *valleys* together, for example.

- **pairing**   It is economical to learn *prominEnce* at the same time that you learn *prominEnt*.

- **pronunciation**   Many spelling errors are caused by nonstandard pronunciation; in such cases *Spelling 1500* teaches you to hear and say the word in a standard way in order to see and write it in standard spelling.

- **mnemonic devices (memory aids)**   These include special typography, like *stationAry* and *stAnd*, or such sentences as "He took my *advice* about a *device* to catch *mice* on the *ice.*"

- **rhyme**   For instance, you will relate *drowned*, often misspelled, with *crowned*, seldom misspelled.

- **rationality**   Reasons for oddities are given whenever possible; for example, *dyeing* keeps the *e* to prevent confusion with *dying*.

- **definition**   In one part of most units, you will recall and write the word when given its definition (and you may incidentally add a few words to your vocabulary).

- **use in context**   In at least one part of most units you will see each word in context, and you will often be asked to compose a short sentence using the word.

- **attention to etymology**   When you learn, for example, that *colonel* is derived from the Italian *colonello*, you will have a better chance of remembering the spelling.

Suggestions for Individual Use

Your instructor may let you know how he or she wants you to use *Spelling 1500*. However, if you are free to use it as you wish, you may want to consider these suggestions.

- A friend dictates the words in the Diagnostic Test (which you should *not* study in advance). You then work through the units corresponding to the words you miss. For instance, if you miss Word 2, you study Unit 2, and so on. Thus you will learn not only the word you missed but a number of other similarly troublesome words, and you will remember them easily by associating them.

- When you misspell a word in your writing, or if you recall a word that occasionally gives you trouble, look in the Word List to see whether the word is included in *Spelling 1500*. If it is, study the entire unit that contains that word.

- In completing the units, conceal each answer until you have written your own. (It is easy to cheat, but you will not learn to spell if you do.) Check immediately to see whether your written answer is correct. To do so, simply look at the answer frame that has the same number as the question frame.

- If you are a poor speller, you may need to study many of the eighty-five units. As a rule, though, you should not do more than one or two units at one sitting. It is much more effective to *proceed slowly and thoughtfully* through a single unit than to rush unthinkingly through several units. If you average one unit a day and really *master* it, you can become a good speller in less than three months. Even a unit once a week will greatly increase your proficiency in a few months.

- After you learn the spelling of a word that you formerly misspelled, try consciously to use it a few times in letters or other writing, to strengthen your hold on it.

- After completing all the units that you believe you need, have a friend pronounce the words in the Mastery Test (which you should *not* study in advance). If you miss any of the words, restudy the units that correspond to the misspelled words.

To the Instructor

Since the first edition of *Spelling 1500: A Program* was written, about one hundred pieces of spelling research have been reported in *Research in Education*. Although many of these studies apply mainly to teaching elementary-school children, a fair number have applicability to teaching more mature students. In general these studies confirm that a variety of approaches such as that in *Spelling 1500* is more productive than a single repetitive kind of attack. Particularly these recent studies have reinforced awareness of how important it is to group words according to common linguistic (graphemic) characteristics instead of offering merely random lists.

In the Preface to the original edition of this book I commented on the efficacy of programed learning and the inductive method in teaching spelling. The intervening years have further confirmed the usefulness of these strategies in mastering such mechanical matters as punctuation, capitalization, and spelling. So the Second Edition of this spelling book continues the use of inductive methods in the format of programed instruction.

In that earlier Preface I commented also on the psychological base of *Spelling 1500*, saying that we remember most easily those things that we can associate. Association helps us to see relationships or patterns and to understand how each element fits into a pattern. For example, it is easier to remember the sequence 1 3 5 7 9 11 13 15 than it is to remember 3 7 13 11 15 1 9 5. The first sequence follows an established pattern; the second is a random mixture. In the Second Edition, I still place much emphasis on this principle of association—teaching, for instance, in one unit nothing but adverbs ending in *-ally*, nothing but contractions in another, nothing but *-ible* words at one time and *-able* words at a different time.

The Second Edition of *Spelling 1500* differs from the original edition mainly in these ways:

- I have added units on words from home economics; business and secretarial work; carpentry, masonry, and plumbing; and mechanical and electrical work.

- Other changes bring the total of added words to about 180. (I have retained the title *Spelling 1500* to preserve the identity of the book. Actually, since some of the underlying principles apply to hundreds of unlisted words, the spelling of several times fifteen hundred words is taught directly or indirectly.) Here and there I have compressed a little to save space, but almost none of the words in the first edition have been deleted.

- I have regrouped the units. The first 43 units, headed "Spellings That Are Predictable," show the student that English spelling is less haphazard than is often believed; hundreds, even thousands, of words do follow reasonably predictable patterns. Units 44–70, "Words Best Learned in Groups," concern less predictable spellings, such as the *-or* endings of various nouns—spellings that may most easily be remembered by associating the grouped words with one another. Finally, Units 71–85, "Spellings with Low Predictability," present rather odd spellings, like *aisle, ecstasy,* and *psychology,* and offer various aids to retention.

Suggestions for Class Use

- In general, little class time should be devoted to discussion or drill in spelling, because the English or other academic program is crammed with material for which class discussion is more profitable. Improvement in spelling ultimately depends on individual effort.

- You may want to dictate the words in the Diagnostic Test, let students exchange and correct papers, and then assign to each student for independent work the units that correspond to the words he or she missed. Or you might record the test words on a cassette and use a paraprofessional to mark the tests. You may instruct students to master each week one (or perhaps two or three) of the units thus assigned. If necessary, answer sheets may be turned in as proof that the work has been done, although they need not be graded and certainly are not needed with serious students. At the end of a term or a year, students may take the Mastery Test to measure their improvement. At that time they should note which words they missed so that they can restudy the corresponding units.

- When a student misspells a word in a composition or on a test, you may ask him or her to see whether the word is treated in *Spelling 1500*. If it is, you may require the student to study the unit containing that word—but usually you should assign no more than two units as a follow-up to a single piece of writing.

- For teachers who do want to devote class time to spelling, a valuable procedure is to offer as a pretest, say on Monday, the list of words at the beginning of one of the units. During the week each student completes the unit individually; then the same list is given as a retest, perhaps on Friday. The order of units treated in this way is optional. Students who make no errors in the pretest need not take the retest.

- On some occasions the whole class may work through a unit on a word group that has proved generally troublesome to them. They may discuss the words in the list, use them in sentences, write them, or suggest other words with the same characteristics.

- Although I believe that for psychological reasons it is best to separate the *–able*'s from the *–ible*'s, the *–eous*'s from the *–ious*'s, and so on, some instructors feel otherwise and prefer to teach together these somewhat-alikes. For those instructors I supply these possible regroupings:
    Different spellings for the schwa sound: Units 44, 45, 52, 58
    Words with *–ible* or *–able*: Units 46, 51
    Words with *–eous, –ous, –uous,* or *–ious*: Units 24, 30, 37, 53
    Words with *–ise* or *–yze* or *–ize*: Units 23, 36
    Words with *–ar* or *–or*: Units 35, 47
    Words with *–al, –le,* or *–el*: Units 48, 50, 59
    Keeping or dropping final *e*: Units 4, 5, 11, 12
    Double letters: Units 2, 21, 22, 34, 49, 55

Diagnostic Test

Note to the student: When your test has been graded, record the number that precedes each word you missed. Word 1 corresponds to Unit 1, Word 2 to Unit 2, and so on. At the rate of one or two units a week, study the units that correspond to the words you missed. Mastering each unit is more important than covering many units.

1. quality
2. bookkeeper
3. monkeys
4. careful
5. severely
6. loveliness
7. ladies (*as in* two ladies)
8. disappear
9. believe
10. accidentally
11. coming
12. valuable
13. frolicked
14. athlete
15. candidate
16. quantity
17. studying
18. hundred
19. disgusted
20. destroy
21. dropped
22. occurred
23. devise
24. courteous
25. proceed
26. conference
27. confident
28. insistent
29. circumference
30. boisterous
31. potatoes
32. bushes
33. cemetery
34. embarrass
35. grammar
36. analyze
37. continuous
38. eighty
39. defendant
40. aren't
41. men's (*as in* men's work)
42. fourth (*as in* the fourth word)
43. *m*'s (*as in* There are two *m*'s in *remember*.)
44. definite
45. optimist
46. flexible
47. governor
48. testimonial
49. omission
50. angle
51. acceptable
52. narrative
53. delicious
54. villain
55. commemorate
56. cylinder
57. diphthong
58. comedy
59. personnel
60. analyses (plural)
61. appositive
62. simile
63. saxophone
64. respiration
65. legislative
66. decimal
67. pasteurize
68. mortar
69. acquisition
70. carburetor
71. develop
72. maintenance
73. debt
74. column
75. wrangle (to quarrel)
76. their (*as in* their house)
77. its (*as in* The dog lost its bone.)
78. here (*as in* Here you are.)
79. sergeant
80. almost
81. aisle (*as in* a theater)
82. etc. (*abbreviation meaning* and so forth)
83. restaurant
84. souvenir
85. February

Mastery Test

Note to the student: When your test has been graded, you may want to compare the results with the results on the Diagnostic Test. Also, note the number that precedes each word you missed on this test and then study or restudy the corresponding unit.

1. question
2. drunkenness
3. turkeys
4. careless
5. sincerely
6. loneliness
7. babies (*as in* two babies)
8. disappoint
9. receive
10. artistically
11. hoping
12. admirable
13. picnicked
14. attacked
15. government
16. probably
17. pumpkin
18. perform
19. divide
20. partner
21. shipping
22. preferred
23. advise
24. beauteous
25. succeed
26. reference
27. evident
28. resident
29. superintendent
30. disastrous
31. tomatoes
32. churches
33. imaginary
34. aggressive
35. separate
36. hypnotize
37. strenuous
38. straight (*as in* a straight line)
39. repentance
40. weren't
41. women's (*as in* women's clothing)
42. twentieth
43. *n*'s (*as in* There are three *n*'s in *announce*.)
44. scarcity
45. article
46. sensible
47. doctor
48. substantial
49. profession
50. pickle
51. dependable
52. miracle
53. suspicious
54. Britain (*as in* Great Britain)
55. accumulate
56. mystery
57. pamphlet
58. operate
59. angel
60. syntheses (plural)
61. apostrophe
62. pentameter
63. orchestra
64. sterilization
65. judicial
66. perpendicular
67. meringue
68. galvanize
69. requisition
70. differential
71. lightning (*as in* lightning flashes)
72. pronunciation
73. meant
74. solemn
75. wrinkle
76. there (*as in* There you are.)
77. it's (*as in* It's five o'clock.)
78. hear (*as in* I hear you.)
79. knowledge
80. already
81. colonel (an army officer)
82. absurd
83. kindergarten
84. vegetable
85. Wednesday

Contents

PART ONE

Spellings That Are Predictable

UNIT 1 · Never a *q* without a *u*

WORDS TREATED

acquire	consequently	etiquette	quiet	quotation	tranquil
adequate	delinquent	quality	quit	quote	
conquered	eloquent	question	quite	sequel	
conqueror	equally	questionnaire	quiz	subsequent	

1

In a way, this unit is the easiest in all that you may study in *Spelling 1500*. The unit title above tells you what we shall be considering. It means that no properly spelled word in the English language has a *q* unless the *q* is followed by a _____ (What letter?).

---

2   quote   quotation

We will look at a few of the *q* words that sometimes cause trouble.

Copy: If you *quote* someone's exact words, you should use *quotation* marks.

1

u

---

3   quit   quite   quality

Copy: He refused to *quit*, although the *quality* of his work was not *quite* as good as he wished.

2

If you *quote* someone's exact words, you should use *quotation* marks.

---

4   quiz   question   questionnaire

Note the single *z* in *quiz* and the double *n* in *questionnaire*.

Copy: One *question* in the *questionnaire* concerned a *quiz* we took last week.

3

He refused to *quit*, although the *quality* of his work was not *quite* as good as he wished.

---

5   quiet   conquered   conqueror

Copy: The *quiet conqueror* also *conquered* the hearts of many fair ladies.

4

One *question* in the *questionnaire* concerned a *quiz* we took last week.

---

6   eloquent   delinquent   subsequent   consequently

Copy: At a *subsequent* trial, the *delinquent* gave an *eloquent* speech and *consequently* was freed.

_____

_____

7   tranquil   etiquette   equally

Copy: After both were equipped with books of *etiquette*, they became *equally tranquil*.

_____

_____

8   sequel   adequate   acquire

Copy: I *acquired* a typewriter and wrote an *adequate sequel* to my story.

_____

_____

9

Write in full each unfinished word in the following passage, choosing from those we have studied the one that best fits the meaning.

One [ques] _____ about [eti] _____ was given on the [qui] _____: "Is it [qui] _____ correct for a girl on a bus to give her seat to an elderly man?" I [quo] _____ the exact words because I do not believe they are [ade] _____. If on [subse] _____ investigation we found that the elderly man really needed the seat more than the girl did, I'd vote yes.

10

Follow the instructions for Frame 9.

In the [tran] _____ little town of Altamont, the great [con] _____ settled down, resolved to lead a [qui] _____ life. No longer, he thought, would he have to listen to selfish but [elo] _____ pleaders. No longer need he worry about [delin] _____ taxes. He could [qui] _____ being concerned about poorly equipped troops. [Conse] _____, he anticipated an easy, uneventful future. He felt no need to [ac] _____ great wealth.

5

The *quiet conqueror* also *conquered* the hearts of many fair ladies.

6

At a *subsequent* trial, the *delinquent* gave an *eloquent* speech and *consequently* was freed.

7

After both were equipped with books of *etiquette*, they became *equally tranquil*.

8

I *acquired* a typewriter and wrote an *adequate sequel* to my story.

9

question
etiquette
quiz
quite
quote
adequate
subsequent

11

Follow the instructions for Frame 9.

The [se] _____ to this novel is poorer in [qua] _____, although it was [e] _____ [ly] well received by the public. A [quest] _____ that was sent to a cross section of readers showed how completely LaRoux had [con] _____ the earlier hostility to his writing. A representative [quo] _____ _____ from one of the reviews declared, "LaRoux is the greatest living writer."

12

Choosing the most appropriate word studied in this unit, match each definition below. The first letters are supplied.

a. short examination, [qui] _____
b. as a result, [conse] _____
c. entirely, [qui] _____
d. rules for polite behavior, [eti] _____
e. one who wins, [con] _____
f. something that follows, e.g., a story, [se] _____
g. obtain, [ac] _____

13

Follow the instructions for Frame 12.

a. stopped; gave up, [qui] _____
b. something that is asked, [ques] _____
c. peaceful, [tran] _____
d. distinctive trait, [qual] _____
e. one who fails to do what law or duty demands, [del] _____
f. persuasive; fluent, [elo] _____
g. to repeat the exact words of, [quo] _____

14

Follow the instructions for Frame 12.

a. not noisy, [qui] _____
b. to the same degree, [eq] _____
c. sufficient, [ade] _____
d. defeated, [con] _____
e. list of brief inquiries, [ques] _____
f. later; following, [sub] _____
g. someone's words repeated exactly, [quo] _____

10

tranquil
conqueror
quiet
eloquent
delinquent
quit
Consequently
acquire

11

sequel
quality
equally
questionnaire
conquered
quotation

12

a. quiz
b. consequently
c. quite
d. etiquette
e. conqueror
f. sequel
g. acquire

13

a. quit
b. question
c. tranquil
d. quality
e. delinquent
f. eloquent
g. quote

15

Study each word that you misspelled in Frames 9–14. Note the *qu* and any other trouble spot. Write each missed word correctly three times. Check your answers against the list above Frame 1.

14

a. quiet
b. equally
c. adequate
d. conquered
e. questionnaire
f. subsequent
g. quotation

UNIT 2 • Words built on or with other words

WORDS TREATED

agreeable	characteristic	different	furtherance	mountainous	surely
agriculture	characterize	drunkenness	gardener	personal	unnecessary
assessment	criticism	equipment	handkerchief	really	whereas
bookkeeper	criticize	extraordinary	heroine	recommend	
breakfast	delivery	forestry	irreligious	roommate	

---

1   bookkeeper

This unit concerns twenty-eight of the many hundreds of English words that consist either of two words put together without change or of one basic word to which a prefix or a suffix is added.
a. What two words do you see in *bookkeeper*? _____, _____
b. Explain why *bookkeeper* has two *k*'s.

_____

c. Write *bookkeeper*. _____

1

a. book, keeper
Model:
b. The *k* of *book* and the *k* of *keeper* are both kept.
c. bookkeeper

2

a. When the word *hand* and the word *kerchief* are combined, the result is _____ (What word?).
b. When *room* and *mate* are combined, the result is _____ (What word?).
c. The first meal of the day must *break* the *fast* of the night. When *break* and *fast* are combined, the result is _____ (What word?).

1

a. handkerchief
b. roommate
c. breakfast

3

a. When the prefix *un* is added to *necessary*, both *n*'s are kept. Write *unnecessary*. _____
b. Write the combination of *ir* and *religious*. _____
c. Write the combination of *agri* and *culture*. _____
d. Write the combination of *re* and *commend*. _____

2

a. handkerchief
b. roommate
c. breakfast

4

a. When the suffix *–ness* is added to *drunken*, both *n*'s are kept. Write *drunkenness*. _____
b. Write the combination of *garden* and *–er*. _____
c. Write the combination of *hero* and *–ine*. _____
d. Write the combination of *deliver* and *–y*. _____
e. Write the combination of *forest* and *–ry*. _____

5

a. Write the combination of *character* and *–istic*. _____
b. Write the combination of *character* and *–ize*. _____
c. Write the combination of *critic* and *–ism*. _____
d. Write the combination of *critic* and *–ize*. _____
e. Write the combination of *real* and *–ly*. _____

6

a. Write the combination of *extra* and *ordinary*. _____
b. Write the combination of *agree* and *–able*. _____
c. Write the combination of *further* and *–ance*. _____
d. Write the combination of *mountain* and *–ous*. _____
e. Write the combination of *sure* and *–ly*. _____

7

a. Write the combination of *differ* and *–ent*. _____
b. Write the combination of *equip* and *–ment*. _____
c. Write the combination of *assess* and *–ment*. _____
d. Write the combination of *person* and *–al*. _____
e. Write the combination of *where* and *–as*. _____

8

Write in full the unfinished words, choosing from those studied in this unit.

a. The [hero] _____ took her [hand] _____ and wiped her forehead.
b. My [room] _____ is an [agree] _____ person.
c. A modern [garden] _____ needs much [equip] _____ _____.
d. [For] _____ is one branch of [agri] _____ _____.

3

a. unnecessary
b. irreligious
c. agriculture
d. recommend

4

a. drunkenness
b. gardener
c. heroine
d. delivery
e. forestry

5

a. characteristic
b. characterize
c. criticism
d. criticize
e. really

6

a. extraordinary
b. agreeable
c. furtherance
d. mountainous
e. surely

7

a. different
b. equipment
c. assessment
d. personal
e. whereas

9

Follow the instructions for Frame 8.

a. An [extra] _____ [critic] _____ was made of my story.

b. His [drunken] _____ is his greatest [person] _____ defect.

c. They [critic] _____ him because he is _____ [religious].

d. [Whe] _____ there [sur] _____ is a need for lower taxes, there may not be a need for lower salaries.

8

a. heroine, handkerchief
b. roommate, agreeable
c. gardener, equipment
d. Forestry, agriculture

10

Follow the instructions for Frame 8.

a. The [book] _____ paid for my [break] _____ _____.

b. We _____ [commend] a [differ] _____ approach to the problem.

c. An [assess] _____ is _____ [necessary] at this time.

9

a. extraordinary, criticism
b. drunkenness, personal
c. criticize, irreligious
d. Whereas, surely

11

Follow the instructions for Frame 8.

a. [Mountain] _____ country is not [real] _____ suitable for most farming.

b. The chief [character] _____ of our [deliver] _____ service is speed.

c. [Further] _____ of a sound financial policy did not [character] _____ his administration.

10

a. bookkeeper, breakfast
b. recommend, different
c. assessment, unnecessary

12

Spell in full the word required by each definition. The first letters have been supplied.

a. female hero, [he] _____
b. typical, [char] _____
c. describe, [char] _____
d. intoxication, [drunk] _____
e. one who gardens, [gar] _____
f. not religious, [ir] _____
g. study and care of forests, [for] _____
h. art of judging, [crit] _____
i. farming, [ag] _____

11

a. mountainous, really
b. characteristic, delivery
c. Furtherance, characterize

13

Follow the instructions for Frame 12.

a. to judge as a critic, [crit] _____
b. not necessary, [un] _____
c. pleasant, [agr] _____
d. unusual, [extr] _____
e. act of furthering, [fur] _____
f. small cloth, [han] _____
g. having mountains, [mount] _____
h. fellow lodger, [room] _____
i. because, [whe] _____

12

a. heroine
b. characteristic
c. characterize
d. drunkenness

e. gardener
f. irreligious
g. forestry
h. criticism
i. agriculture

14

Follow the instructions for Frame 12.

a. first meal, [bre] _____
b. accountant, [book] _____
c. sending of a purchase, [del] _____
d. not the same, [dif] _____
e. apparatus, [equip] _____
f. private, [pers] _____
g. advise, [rec] _____
h. amount assessed, [as] _____
i. indeed, certainly, [re] _____
j. indeed, certainly, [su] _____

13

a. criticize
b. unnecessary
c. agreeable
d. extraordinary

e. furtherance
f. handkerchief
g. mountainous
h. roommate
i. whereas

15

Study each word you missed in Frames 8–14. Note the trouble spots carefully. Write each missed word correctly three times. Check your spellings against the list above Frame 1.

14

a. breakfast
b. bookkeeper
c. delivery
d. different
e. equipment

f. personal
g. recommend
h. assessment
i. really
j. surely

UNIT 3 · *Keys* and *monkeys*

WORDS TREATED

alleys	monkeyed	volleyed
attorneys	monkeys	volleys
chimneys	turkeys	
donkeys	valleys	

1

One boy and another boy were practicing basketball.

In other words, two _____ (What?) were practicing basketball.

2

The coach had taught the boys a defensive play and an offensive play which he wanted them to practice.

They spent their time practicing these two _____ (What?).

1

boys

---

3   boy + s = boys   play + s = plays

Look at the word *boy* and the word *play*. The letter before the *y* in each word is a _____ (*consonant* or *vowel?*).

2

plays

4

When we add *s* to a word like *boy* or *play*, which ends with a vowel plus *y*, we _____ (*change* or *do not change?*) the *y* to anything else.

3

vowel

5

boyish   played   player   playful

The examples above show that when we add any other suffix to a word like *boy* or *play*, we treat the word just as we did in *boys* and *plays*. That is, we _____ (*change* or *do not change?*) the *y* to anything else.

4

do not change

6

Of course you would never misspell a word like *boys* or *played,* but some other words that follow the same principle are often misspelled. These are words that end in *ey.*

Do *key* and *monkey* both end in a vowel plus *y*, like *boy* and *play*? _____

5

do not change

7

Spell each incomplete word correctly in full.

a. Buyers of new automobiles are given two sets of [k]_____.
b. See those [monk] _____ in the trees.
c. We wasted our time. We just [monk] _____ around.

6

yes

---

8   alley   turkey

Like *boy, play, key,* and *monkey,* the words *alley* and *turkey* end in a vowel plus *y.*

a. Write the plural of *alley:* two _____.
b. Write the plural of *turkey:* a flock of _____.

9   valley   volley

Valley and *volley* are two more words that end in a vowel plus *y.* Write in full the unfinished words.

a. These tribes live in three deep [va] _____ between the mountain ranges.
b. Two [vo] _____ of shots rang out.
c. Cannon to left of them,
   Cannon to right of them,
   [Vo] _____ed and thundered.

10   donkeys   attorneys   chimneys

Donkey, attorney, and *chimney* are three more words that fit our rule about not changing the *y* if a vowel is just before it. Write the plural of the one of these words that is most suitable for each blank.

a. _____ have long ears.
b. Black smoke was pouring from several _____.
c. Lawyers are sometimes called _____.

11

Write the plurals of the following words.

a. an alley, several _____
b. a monkey, two _____
c. that turkey, those _____
d. this attorney, these _____

12

Write the required forms of the following words.

a. a green valley, some green _____
b. that chimney, those _____
c. to volley the ball. We _____ yesterday.
d. this donkey, these _____

7

a. keys
b. monkeys
c. monkeyed

8

a. alleys
b. turkeys

9

a. valleys
b. volleys
c. Volleyed

10

a. Donkeys
b. chimneys
c. attorneys

11

a. alleys
b. monkeys
c. turkeys
d. attorneys

13

For each definition below, write a synonym that we have studied in this unit.

a. large fowls, _____

b. lawyers, _____

c. tree-climbing animals, _____

d. low lands between mountains, _____

e. smokestacks, _____

f. pack animals, _____

g. narrow streets, _____

h. sharp series, as of gunfire, _____

14

Look carefully at each word you missed in Frames 7–13. Write its correct spelling three times. Check your spellings against the list above Frame 1.

12

a. valleys

b. chimneys

c. volleyed

d. donkeys

13

a. turkeys	e. chimneys
b. attorneys	f. donkeys
c. monkeys	g. alleys
d. valleys	h. volleys

UNIT 4 · Keeping final *e* (I)

WORDS TREATED

absolutely	arrangement	completely	immensely	Exceptions:	judgment
achievement	careful	excitement	lonely	acknowledgment	truly
advertisement	careless	extremely	nineteen	argument	
announcement	comparatively	forehead	ninety	duly	

1   announce   care   extreme   nine

a. Each of the four words above ends in _____ (What letter?).

b. In the four words above, the final *e* is _____ (*pronounced* or *silent*?).

2   –ment   –less   –ly   –ty

Each of the four suffixes above may be added to a number of English words. Each suffix begins with a _____ (*consonant* or *vowel*?).

1

a. *e*

b. silent

3   announce + –ment = announcement

       care + –less = careless

       extreme + –ly = extremely

       nine + –ty = ninety

The examples above show that when we add a suffix beginning with a consonant (like –*ment*) to a word ending with a silent *e* (like *announce*), the *e* is _____ (What?).

2

consonant

4 Write *announcement, careless, extremely,* and *ninety.* _____, _____, _____, _____	**3** kept
5 Write the following combinations: a. *achieve* + *–ment* = _____ b. *arrange* + *–ment* = _____ c. *excite* + *–ment* = _____ d. *advertise* + *–ment* = _____	**4** announcement careless extremely ninety
6 Write the following combinations: a. *lone* + *–ly* = _____ b. *immense* + *–ly* = _____ c. *absolute* + *–ly* = _____ d. *comparative* + *–ly* = _____	**5** a. achievement b. arrangement c. excitement d. advertisement
7 Write the following combinations: a. *complete* + *–ly* = _____ b. *fore* + *–head* = _____ c. *care* + *–ful* = _____ d. *nine* + *–teen* = _____	**6** a. lonely b. immensely c. absolutely d. comparatively
8 Five common words are exceptions to the principle we are studying and must simply be memorized. They are *duly, truly, argument, acknowledgment,* and *judgment* (although *acknowledgment* and *judgment* may also be correctly spelled with an *e*). Copy: I love you *truly,* I love you *duly,* But when we have an *argument* I insist upon *acknowledgment* Of the rightness of my *judgment,* darling Julie. _____ _____ _____ _____	**7** a. completely b. forehead c. careful d. nineteen

9

Write in full each incomplete word, choosing the most suitable one from those studied in this unit.

During the [exci] _____, all but one of the twenty students reached safety. These [nin] _____ [teen] were [absol] _____ horrified to discover that one girl had been hit on the [for] _____ and was lying, [comple] _____ unconscious, on a second-floor ledge. Using good [judg] _____, Marshall ran for a ladder.

10

Follow the instructions for Frame 9.

a. Being [du] _____ sworn, the defendant answered each question in an [extre] _____ [car] _____ manner, as if he were indifferent to his fate.

b. We are [immen] _____ pleased to have completed this [arrang] _____.

c. Being a [car] _____ worker, he could usually be proud of his [achiev] _____.

11

Follow the instructions for Frame 9.

a. This is an [advert] _____ for a new tool.

b. Mr. Grover was a [lon] _____ old man of nin_____.

c. This knife is [compar] _____ dull.

d. Following the [announ] _____, they got into an [argu] _____.

e. I love you [tru] _____.

12

Match each definition with a word we studied in this unit. The first letters have been supplied.

a. public notice, [ann] _____

b. accomplishment, [ach] _____

c. lonesome, [lon] _____

d. very, [ext] _____

e. done with care, [car] _____

f. act of arranging, [arr] _____

8

I love you *truly*, I love you *duly*,
But when we have an *argument*
I insist upon *acknowledgment*
Of the rightness of my *judgment*,
  darling Julie.

9

excitement
nineteen
absolutely
forehead
completely
judgment

10

a. duly, extremely, careless
b. immensely, arrangement
c. careful, achievement

11

a. advertisement
b. lonely, ninety
c. comparatively
d. announcement, argument
e. truly

13

Follow the instructions for Frame 12.

a. state of being excited, [exc] _____

b. hugely, [imm] _____

c. 90, [nin] _____

d. 19, [nin] _____

e. upper part of face, [for] _____

f. in due measure, [du] _____

g. honestly, [tru] _____

12

a. announcement

b. achievement

c. lonely

d. extremely

e. careful

f. arrangement

14

Follow the instructions for Frame 12.

a. completely, [abs] _____

b. verbal attempt to sell, [adv] _____

c. opinion, [jud] _____

d. in comparison, [comp] _____

e. debate, [arg] _____

f. entirely, [com] _____

g. heedless; sloppy, [car] _____

h. recognition, [ack] _____

13

a. excitement

b. immensely

c. ninety

d. nineteen

e. forehead

f. duly

g. truly

15

Study carefully each word you misspelled in Frames 9–14. Note the trouble spots, especially those involving an *e*. Write each missed word correctly three times. Check your spellings against the list above Frame 1.

14

a. absolutely

b. advertisement

c. judgment

d. comparatively

e. argument

f. completely

g. careless

h. acknowledgment

UNIT 5 · Keeping final *e* (II)

WORDS TREATED

appropriately	involvement	likeness	resourceful	sincerely
definitely	legitimately	merely	safety	therefore
immediately	leisurely	obstinately	scarcely	useful
infinitely	likely	peaceful	severely	useless

---

1   definite   there   involve   like

a. Each of the four words above ends in _____ (What letter?).

b. In the four words above, the final *e* is _____ (*pronounced* or *silent*?).

2 **–ly** **–fore** **–ment** **–ness** Each of the four suffixes above may be added to a number of English words. Each suffix begins with a _____ (*consonant* or *vowel?*).	**1** a. *e* b. silent

3   definite + –ly = definitely
    there + –fore = therefore
    involve + –ment = involvement
    like + –ness = likeness
 	
The examples above show that when we add a suffix beginning with a consonant (like *–ly*) to a word ending with silent *e* (like *definite*), the *e* is _____ (What?).
	2
	
	consonant

4 Write *definitely, therefore, involvement,* and *likeness.* _____, _____, _____, _____	**3** kept
5 Write the following combinations: a. *immediate* + *–ly* = _____ b. *leisure* + *–ly* = _____ c. *like* + *–ly* = _____ d. *scarce* + *–ly* = _____	**4** definitely therefore involvement likeness
6 Write the following combinations: a. *appropriate* + *–ly* = _____ b. *infinite* + *–ly* = _____ c. *mere* + *–ly* = _____ d. *legitimate* + *–ly* = _____	**5** a. immediately b. leisurely c. likely d. scarcely
7 Write the following combinations: a. *obstinate* + *–ly* = _____ b. *severe* + *–ly* = _____ c. *sincere* + *–ly* = _____ d. *resource* + *–ful* = _____	**6** a. appropriately b. infinitely c. merely d. legitimately
8 Write the following combinations: a. *peace* + *–ful* = _____ b. *safe* + *–ty* = _____ c. *use* + *–ful* = _____ d. *use* + *–less* = _____	**7** a. obstinately b. severely c. sincerely d. resourceful

9

Write in full each incomplete word, choosing the most suitable one from those studied in this unit.

The captain [immed] _____ decided that the mutineers must be [sever] _____ punished. The [saf] _____ of his ship, it seemed [lik] _____, depended upon it. Being a [resourc] _____ person, [ther] _____, he did not [mer] _____ toss the men into the brig.

10

Follow the instructions for Frame 9.

a. Because we were [defin] _____ early, we strolled in a [leis] _____ fashion.

b. The senator's [involv] _____ in this scandal is [scarc] _____ conceivable, for he has always acted [legit] _____.

c. My friend looked at the photograph and said [sinc] _____, "That is a good [lik] _____."

11

Follow the instructions for Frame 9.

a. Although he was not [approp] _____ dressed, he [obstin] _____ insisted on going to the party.

b. This heating pad is [us] _____ in an [infin] _____ large number of ways.

c. It was [us] _____ to try to explain to the savages that our mission was [peac] _____.

12

Match each definition with a word we studied in this unit. The first letters have been supplied.

a. for that reason, [th] _____

b. simply; only, [me] _____

c. honestly, [sin] _____

d. a resembling, [lik] _____

e. of no use, [us] _____

f. not warlike, [pe] _____

8

a. peaceful
b. safety
c. useful
d. useless

9

immediately
severely
safety
likely
resourceful
therefore
merely

10

a. definitely, leisurely
b. involvement, scarcely, legitimately
c. sincerely, likeness

11

a. appropriately, obstinately
b. useful, infinitely
c. useless, peaceful

13

Follow the instructions for Frame 12.

a. boundlessly, [inf] _____
b. of value, [us] _____
c. hardly, [sc] _____
d. state of being concerned in, [inv] _____
e. quick-witted, [resour] _____
f. probably, [lik] _____
g. lack of danger, [saf] _____

12

a. therefore
b. merely
c. sincerely
d. likeness
e. useless
f. peaceful

14

Follow the instructions for Frame 12.

a. suitably, [app] _____
b. stubbornly, [obs] _____
c. certainly, [def] _____
d. without hurry, [le] _____
e. harshly, [sev] _____
f. at once, [imm] _____
g. legally, [legit] _____

13

a. infinitely
b. useful
c. scarcely
d. involvement
e. resourceful
f. likely
g. safety

15

Study carefully each word you misspelled in Frames 9–14. Note the trouble spots, especially those involving an *e*. Write each missed word correctly three times. Check your spellings against the list above Frame 1.

14

a. appropriately
b. obstinately
c. definitely
d. leisurely
e. severely
f. immediately
g. legitimately

UNIT 6 · Adding suffixes to words like *angry*

WORDS TREATED

accompaniment	easier	hungrily	liveliness	pitiful	studious
angrily	emptiness	laziness	loneliness	prettier	variable
beautiful	friendliness	likelihood	lovelier	prettily	worrisome
busily	happier	liveliest	loveliness	reliability	
business	holiness	livelihood	luckily	reliable	

1   angry   beauty   happy   lazy

a. Each of the words above ends in __ (What letter?).
b. The letter just before the final *y* in each of the four words at the top of this frame is a _____ (*vowel* or *consonant*?).

18

2
    angry + –ly = angrily
    beauty + –ful = beautiful
    happy + –er = happier
    lazy + –ness = laziness

Notice that we have added a suffix to each of the words that end in a consonant plus *y*.

    When we add a suffix to a word ending in a consonant plus *y*, we change the *y* to _____ (What letter?).

3

Write the words resulting from the following combinations.

a. *busy + –ly =* _____
b. *lucky + –ly =* _____
c. *hungry + –ly =* _____
d. *pretty + –ly =* _____

4

a. Add *–ness* to each of these words: *holy, lonely, lively, lovely, friendly, empty.* _____, _____, _____

    _____, _____, _____,

    _____

b. Write the word based upon *busy* that means buying and selling, or commercial activity. _____

5

a. Add *–est* to *lively.*

    _____

b. Add *–er* to *easy, lovely, pretty.*

    _____, _____, _____

c. Add *–ous* to *study.*

    _____

d. Add *–able* to *vary* and *rely.*

    _____, _____

6

a. Add *–ment* to *accompany.*

    _____

b. Add *–ful* to *pity.*

    _____

c. Add *–ability* to *rely.*

    _____

d. Add *–some* to *worry.*

    _____

e. Add *–hood* to *lively* and *likely.*

    _____, _____

1

a. *y*
b. consonant

2

i

3

a. busily
b. luckily
c. hungrily
d. prettily

4

a. holiness, loneliness, liveliness, loveliness, friendliness, emptiness
b. business

5

a. liveliest
b. easier, lovelier, prettier
c. studious
d. variable, reliable

7

a. The principle that we are studying applies to several hundred English words. It does *not* apply to words like *study* + *-ing* because if we changed that *y* to an *i*, we would have, awkwardly, _____ (How many?) *i*'s together.

b. Our principle does not apply, either, to words like *monkey* + *-s* because in *monkey* the letter before the *y* is not a _____ (*consonant* or *vowel*?).

(Words like *studying* and *monkeys* are treated in Units 3 and 17.)

6

a. accompaniment
b. pitiful
c. reliability
d. worrisome
e. livelihood, likelihood

8

Write in full words studied in this unit that complete these sentences:

a. The [lone] _____ of a forest ranger's life did not bother him.
b. Darby made a huge profit from his [bus] _____.
c. She is the [live] _____ of the three girls.
d. The [friendl] _____ of the natives surprised us.
e. The dog looked [hung] _____ at the bone.

7

a. two
b. consonant

9

Follow the instructions for Frame 8.

a. Louise sang with a banjo [accompan] _____.
b. In all [likel] _____, you will pass.
c. I marvel at the [lovel] _____ of maple trees in autumn.
d. A child was playing [bus] _____ in the sandbox.
e. I sensed the deep religiousness, the [hol] _____, of this man.

8

a. loneliness
b. business
c. liveliest
d. friendliness
e. hungrily

10

Follow the instructions for Frame 8.

a. Cruncher earned his [livel] _____ in a secret way.
b. The tasks were annoying and [worr] _____.
c. The weather forecaster said "[var] _____ cloudiness" for today.
d. You can depend upon him. He is [rel] _____.
e. The dog growled [ang] _____.

9

a. accompaniment
b. likelihood
c. loveliness
d. busily
e. holiness

11

Follow the instructions for Frame 8.

a. Harry brought me a [beaut] _____ corsage.

b. Your work is [eas] _____ than mine.

c. The [empt] _____ of his life increased after the death of his wife.

d. Today is even [love] _____ than yesterday.

e. [Luck] _____, I still had a dime.

10

a. livelihood

b. worrisome

c. variable

d. reliable

e. angrily

12

Follow the instructions for Frame 8.

a. I have never seen a more [pit] _____ sight.

b. You are even [prett] _____ than I realized.

c. Joe had many friends who teased him because he was so [stud] _____ .

d. Hans was a steady worker. His [rel] _____ was soon noticed by his foreman.

e. The [live] _____ of the music set my foot to tapping.

11

a. beautiful

b. easier

c. emptiness

d. lovelier

e. Luckily

13

Match the following synonyms with words we studied in this unit. The first letters are shown in brackets. Write the whole word.

a. fortunately, [luc] _____

b. attractive, [beau] _____

c. less difficult, [eas] _____

d. state of being empty, [emp] _____

e. more lovely, [lov] _____

f. means of supporting oneself, [liv] _____

g. in an angry way, [ang] _____

h. bothersome, [wor] _____

i. changeable, [var] _____

j. dependable, [rel] _____

k. probability, [lik] _____

l. more happy, [hap] _____

12

a. pitiful

b. prettier

c. studious

d. reliability

e. liveliness

14

Follow the instructions for Frame 13.

a. state of being lazy, [laz] ＿＿＿＿＿＿

b. buying and selling, [bus] ＿＿＿＿＿＿

c. in a pretty manner, [pret] ＿＿＿＿＿＿

d. in a hungry way, [hun] ＿＿＿＿＿＿

e. religiousness, [hol] ＿＿＿＿＿＿

f. state of being lovely, [lov] ＿＿＿＿＿＿

g. most lively, [liv] ＿＿＿＿＿＿

h. more pretty, [pret] ＿＿＿＿＿＿

i. fond of study, [stu] ＿＿＿＿＿＿

j. dependability, [rel] ＿＿＿＿＿＿

k. state of being friendly, [fri] ＿＿＿＿＿＿

l. state of being lively, [liv] ＿＿＿＿＿＿

13

a. luckily	g. angrily
b. beautiful	h. worrisome
c. easier	i. variable
d. emptiness	j. reliable
e. lovelier	k. likelihood
f. livelihood	l. happier

15

Study each word that you misspelled in Frames 8–14, and write it correctly three times. Check your answers against the list above Frame 1.

14

a. laziness	g. liveliest
b. business	h. prettier
c. prettily	i. studious
d. hungrily	j. reliability
e. holiness	k. friendliness
f. loveliness	l. liveliness

UNIT 7 · Words like *babies* and *cried*

WORDS TREATED

accompanied	cities	flies	ladies	theories
allies	cried	fraternities	luxuries	tries
babies	enemies	hurried	skies	varies
carried	fantasies	implied	stories	

1

As you know, we may add –s or –ed to many words without making any changes in the words: *book + –s = books; help + –ed = helped.*

But when we add –s to *baby,* the result is ＿＿＿＿＿＿ (What word?). When we add –ed to *cry,* the result is ＿＿＿＿＿＿ (What word?). (Look at the title of this unit if you are not sure.)

2 **baby** **cry** **lady** **try**	**1**
Look at the four words at the top of this frame.	babies
a. The last letter of each word is _____ (What?).	cried
b. The next-to-last letter of each word is a _____ (*vowel* or *consonant*?).	

3	**2**
a. When we change *baby* to *babies* or *cry* to *cried*, or when we make similar changes in several hundred other words that end in a consonant plus *y*, the *y* changes to _____ (What letter?) before *–es* or *–ed*.	a. *y*
b. one *lady*, two l_____	b. consonant
c. I *try*, he t_____	

4 **city** **sky** **fly**	**3**
a. Does each word above end in a consonant plus *y*? _____	a. *i*
b. Write the words that mean more than one city, more than one sky, more than one fly.	b. ladies
_____ , _____ , _____	c. tries (*or* tried)

5	**4**
Write in full the unfinished words, using the clues supplied.	a. yes
a. I carry a canteen. I [c] _____ a canteen yesterday.	b. cities, skies, flies
b. Does a person's voice ever vary? Yes, it [v] _____ a little from day to day.	
c. Are they friends? No, they are [en] _____ .	

6	**5**
Follow the instructions for Frame 5.	a. carried
a. Did he imply that I was mistaken? Yes, that is what he [i] _____ .	b. varies
b. Will you live in a fraternity? No, because my father is opposed to [fr] _____ .	c. enemies
c. I hope that he becomes an ally, because we need more [a] _____ _____ .	

7	**6**
Follow the instructions for Frame 5.	a. implied
a. Most children like bedtime [st] _____ .	b. fraternities
b. You live in a land of fantasy, and your [fa] _____ are completely impossible.	c. allies
c. Will someone accompany her? Yes, she will be [a] _____ _____ by her aunt.	

8

Follow the instructions for Frame 5.

a. What is your theory? I have two [t] _____.

b. The real necessities of life are few, but some of us have come to believe that [lux] _____ are necessities.

c. Why did you hurry? I [h] _____ because I was almost late.

9

Match the definitions below by writing words we studied in this unit. The first letters have been supplied.

a. places where many people live, [ci] _____

b. infants, [ba] _____

c. the heavens, [sk] _____

d. went with, [acc] _____

e. groups of college men living together, [frat] _____

10

Follow the instructions for Frame 9.

a. pleasant but unnecessary things, [lux] _____

b. hastened, [hur] _____

c. tales, [st] _____

d. attempts, [tr] _____

e. soars through the air, [fl] _____

11

Follow the instructions for Frame 9.

a. explanations based on reasoning, [th] _____

b. wild, strange fancies, [fan] _____

c. persons or nations that work together, [al] _____

d. foes, [en] _____

e. hinted or suggested, [im] _____

12

Follow the instructions for Frame 9.

a. women who behave well, [la] _____

b. took from one place to another, [car] _____

c. changes, differs, [var] _____

d. wept or shouted, [cr] _____

7

a. stories
b. fantasies
c. accompanied

8

a. theories
b. luxuries
c. hurried

9

a. cities
b. babies
c. skies
d. accompanied
e. fraternities

10

a. luxuries
b. hurried
c. stories
d. tries
e. flies

11

a. theories
b. fantasies
c. allies
d. enemies
e. implied

13

Study each word that you misspelled in Frames 9–12. Write each missed word correctly three times. Check your answers against the list above Frame 1.

12

a. ladies
b. carried
c. varies
d. cried

UNIT 8 · Words starting with *dis* or *mis*

WORDS TREATED

disagree	disciple	dissent	misbehave	missile	mistake
disappear	discipline	dissimilar	misconduct	mission	misunderstand
disappoint	disease	dissipate	misfortune	misspell	
disapprove	dissatisfied	disturb	mispronounce	misstep	

---

1   disapprove   dissatisfied

Let's see why *disapprove* has only one *s* and *dissatisfied* has two *s*'s together.
a. We add the prefix *dis* to the word *approve,* and the result is _____ (What?).
b. We add the prefix *dis* to the word *satisfied,* and the result is _____ (What?).

---

2   mistake   misspell

Now let's see why *mistake* has only one *s* and *misspell* has two *s*'s.

a. We add the prefix *mis* to the word *take,* and the result is _____ (What?).
b. We add the prefix *mis* to the word *spell,* and the result is _____ (What?).

1

a. disapprove
b. dissatisfied

3

a. *dis + appoint =* _____
b. *dis + appear =* _____

2

a. mistake
b. misspell

4

a. *dis + agree =* _____
b. *dis + ease =* _____
c. *dis + similar =* _____

3

a. disappoint
b. disappear

5

a. *mis + understand* = _____

b. *mis + step* = _____

6

a. *mis + fortune* = _____

b. *mis + behave* = _____

c. *mis + conduct* = _____

d. *mis + pronounce* = _____

7

Dis and *mis* also appear in some other words that are not combinations with whole English words. Except for *dissent, dissipate, missile,* and *mission,* most of these common words have only one *s*.

Copy: The *dissipated* general *dissented,* wanting to use *missiles* for the *mission*.

_____

_____

8

Here are some of the common *dis* and *mis* words with one *s*:

disciple   discipline   disturb

Copy those three words.

_____ , _____ , _____

9

In Frames 9–13, spell correctly in full the incomplete *dis* or *mis* words, using those we have studied. Note that some require *diss* or *miss*.

"I hate to _____ [appoint] you," she said, "but there are two _____ [takes] in your paper. You have _____ [pelled] _____ [ipate] and _____ [fortune]."

10

Follow the instructions for Frame 9.

I _____ [agree] with your statement that _____ [conduct] should not be punished. I believe that _____ [cipline] is important. A student who _____ [turbs] others or _____ [behaves] in a serious way represents a serious problem.

4

a. disagree

b. disease

c. dissimilar

5

a. misunderstand

b. misstep

6

a. misfortune

b. misbehave

c. misconduct

d. mispronounce

7

The *dissipated* general *dissented,* wanting to use *missiles* for the *mission*.

8

disciple

discipline

disturb

9

disappoint

mistakes

misspelled

dissipate

misfortune

11

Follow the instructions for Frame 9.

As a _____ [ciple] of our great leader, you cannot afford a _____ [tep]. I _____ [ent] from the belief that your situation is _____ [similar] to that of other followers.

12

Follow the instructions for Frame 9.

The _____ [ion] of our task force was to examine the _____ile. We were _____ [atisfied] when we heard that one of the technicians had _____ [appeared]. We _____ [approved] of the way the whole operation was handled.

13

Follow the instructions for Frame 9.

I hope that you will not _____ [understand] the doctor's concern about this _____ [ease], even though I _____ [pronounced] the name.

14

Match each of these definitions with one of the words studied in this unit. Some of the last letters are supplied. Write the words in full.

a. error, _____ [take]
b. spell wrongly, _____ [pell]
c. ill luck, _____ [fortune]
d. bad behavior, _____ [conduct]
e. disagree, _____ [ent]
f. find fault with, _____ [approve]
g. vanish, _____ [appear]
h. unlike, _____ [imilar]
i. follower, _____ [ciple]
j. not pleased, _____ [atisfied]
k. illness, _____ [ease]
l. bother, _____ [turb]
m. say wrongly, _____ [pronounce]
n. false step, _____ [tep]
o. control of conduct, _____ [cipline]

10

disagree
misconduct
discipline
disturbs
misbehaves

11

disciple
misstep
dissent
dissimilar

12

mission
missile
dissatisfied
disappeared
disapproved

13

misunderstand
disease
mispronounced

15

Study the correct spellings of any words you misspelled in Frames 9–14. Write each missed word correctly three times. Check your spellings against the list above Frame 1.

14

a. mistake   i. disciple
b. misspell   j. dissatisfied
c. misfortune   k. disease
d. misconduct   l. disturb
e. dissent   m. mispronounce
f. disapprove   n. misstep
g. disappear   o. discipline
h. dissimilar

UNIT 9 · Is it *ei* or *ie*?

WORDS TREATED

achieve	conceited	grieve	receipt	siege	Exceptions:	
belief	conceive	hygiene	receive	thief	either	species
believe	deceit	niece	relieve	wield	financier	weird
ceiling	field	perceive	retriever	yield	leisure	
chief	fiend	piece	shield		neither	
conceit	grief	priest	shriek		seize	

1

Read the words listed below, and decide whether the *ei* or *ie* in each is pronounced like *ee* or like some other sound.

    receive   fiend   grieve   conceit
    belief   deceit   wield   receipt
    chief   ceiling   yield   priest

    In each of the words in the list, *ie* or *ei* is pronounced like _____ (*ee* or *some other sound?*).

2

All the words in the list in Frame 1, we have seen, have either *ei* or *ie* pronounced like *ee*.
Copy below the words from Frame 1 with *ei*.

_____, _____,

_____, _____, _____

Copy below the words from Frame 1 with *ie*.

_____, _____, _____,

_____, _____, _____, _____

1

ee

3

a. Look at the words you wrote in the first part of your answer to Frame 2. Do all of them contain *ei* pronounced as *ee*? _____

b. What letter comes just before each *ei*? _____.

2

receive	belief
deceit	chief
ceiling	fiend
conceit	grieve
receipt	wield
	yield
	priest

4

The first three frames have shown us that when we have a word with an *ee* sound, and we do not know whether to spell it with an *ei* or an *ie*, we choose the *ei* if the letter just ahead is _____ (What letter?).

3

a. yes (They should.)
b. *c*

5

a. Now look at the words you wrote in the second column of your answer to Frame 2. Do all of them contain *ie* pronounced as *ee*? _____

b. In that column, does the letter *c* ever come just before the *ie*? _____

4

c

6

Frame 5 showed us that when we have a word with an *ee* sound, and we do not know whether to spell it with an *ei* or an *ie*, we choose the *ie* if the letter just ahead is anything except _____ (What letter?).

5

a. yes (They should.)
b. no

7

a. Let us say that you do not know the letters representing the *ee* sound in perc_____ve. You notice that the letter just ahead of the missing letters is *c*. Write the complete word correctly. _____

b. Now let us say that you do not know the letters representing the *ee* sound in th_____f. You notice that the letter just ahead of the missing letters is not a *c*. Write the complete word correctly. _____

6

c

8

a. When you are in doubt about whether to write *ei* or *ie* in a word with an *ee* sound, you will use *ei* if the letter just ahead is a _____ (What letter?).

b. If the letter just ahead is any other letter, you will write _____ (What two letters?).

7

a. perceive
b. thief

9

Complete the unfinished words. Add only the missing letters. (Some of the words have not been used previously in this unit.)

a. A fly was crawling along the c_____ling.
b. A shr_____k is a loud yell.
c. May I have a p_____ce of pie, please?
d. A person who lies is guilty of dec _____ t.
e. Farmers were plowing their f _____ lds.

10

Follow the instructions for Frame 9.

a. The knights buckled on their armor and picked up their sh_____lds.
b. The s_____ge of the city lasted for a month.
c. I paid the money and got a rec_____pt.
d. She bowed her head in gr_____f and began to sob.

11

Follow the instructions for Frame 9.

a. That dog is an excellent retr_____ver.
b. Back home, if a person is conc_____ted, we say that he has a big head.
c. An ice pack helped to rel_____ve the pain.
d. A critic should perc _____ ve good as well as bad qualities.
e. Her nephew and her n _____ ce came for lunch.

12

Follow the instructions for Frame 9.

a. A soldier likes to rec_____ve mail.
b. I bel_____ve that those are violets.
c. This corn may y_____ld over a hundred bushels.
d. The study of health is sometimes called hyg_____ne.

13

Follow the instructions for Frame 9.

a. What a remarkable ach_____vement!
b. A minister, a rabbi, and a pr_____st were present.
c. Sitting Bull was an Indian ch_____f.
d. I can't conc_____ve of Mary's saying that!

8

a. *c*
b. *ie*

9

a. ceiling
b. shriek
c. piece
d. deceit
e. fields

10

a. shields
b. siege
c. receipt
d. grief

11

a. retriever
b. conceited
c. relieve
d. perceive
e. niece

12

a. receive
b. believe
c. yield
d. hygiene

14

The only important exceptions to the rule we have just been using are contained in the following sentence, which you should memorize:

Neither financier seized either species of weird leisure.

When you know that sentence by heart, write it.

_____

_____

15

Look carefully at the correct spelling of each word you missed in Frames 9–14. Notice why an *ei* or an *ie* is needed. Write the word three times, and check above Frame 1 to make sure that you spelled it correctly.

13

a. achievement
b. priest
c. chief
d. conceive

14

Neither financier seized either species of weird leisure.

UNIT 10 · Words that end in *–ally*

WORDS TREATED

accidentally	beneficially	fundamentally	naturally	usually
adverbially	chemically	generally	principally	
artistically	controversially	grammatically	specifically	
basically	frantically	incidentally	systematically	

1   accidental + –ly = accidentally

When an adjective that ends in *al*, like *accidental*, is changed to an adverb by the addition of *–ly*, there are, of course, two *l*'s: *–ally*.

Write *accidentally* twice.

_____ , _____

2   specific + –ally = specifically

When an adjective that ends in *ic*, like *specific*, is changed to an adverb, it is customary to add *–ally*.

Write *specifically* twice.

_____ , _____

3

The words *accidentally* and *specifically* illustrate the two chief kinds of words that end in *–ally*. It is necessary to remember that when *–ly* is added to a word ending in *–al*, the result is _____ (What four letters?). Also, when an adjective ends in *–ic*, it is customary to add _____ (What four letters?) in changing the word to an adverb.

1

accidentally
accidentally

2

specifically
specifically

4

a. Add *–ly* to *beneficial.* _____

b. Add *–ly* to *principal.* _____

c. Add *–ly* to *controversial.* _____

d. Add *–ly* to *grammatical.* _____

3

ally

ally

5

a. Spell the adverbial form of *incidental.* _____

b. Spell the adverbial form of *fundamental.* _____

c. Spell the adverbial form of *usual.* _____

d. Spell the adverbial form of *general.* _____

4

a. beneficially

b. principally

c. controversially

d. grammatically

6

a. Spell the adverbial form of *natural.* _____

b. Spell the adverbial form of *chemical.* _____

c. Spell the adverbial form of *adverbial.* _____

5

a. incidentally

b. fundamentally

c. usually

d. generally

7

a. Spell the adverbial form of *basic.* _____

b. Spell the adverbial form of *artistic.* _____

c. Spell the adverbial form of *frantic.* _____

d. Spell the adverbial form of *systematic.* _____

6

a. naturally

b. chemically

c. adverbially

8

Match each definition with the appropriate adverb from this unit. The first letters are supplied. Write each word in full.

a. by chance or by accident, [acc] _____

b. in an artistic manner, [art] _____

c. in a manner related to chemistry, [chem] _____

7

a. basically

b. artistically

c. frantically

d. systematically

9

Follow the instructions for Frame 8.

a. like an adverb, [adv] _____

b. in a frantic manner, [fran] _____

c. in a helpful way, [ben] _____

8

a. accidentally

b. artistically

c. chemically

10

Follow the instructions for Frame 8.

a. mainly, [prin] _____

b. in an argumentative manner, [contro] _____

c. fundamentally, [bas] _____

9

a. adverbially

b. frantically

c. beneficially

11

Follow the instructions for Frame 8.

a. basically, [fun] _____

b. in a natural way, [nat] _____

c. in accordance with grammar, [gram] _____

10

a. principally
b. controversially
c. basically

12

Follow the instructions for Frame 8.

a. as a rule, [usu] _____

b. ordinarily, [gen] _____

c. as an incident along with something else, [inc] _____

d. in a systematic way, [sys] _____

e. in a definite way, [spec] _____

11

a. fundamentally
b. naturally
c. grammatically

13

Name the two kinds of words that are most likely to end in –ally.

a._____

b._____

12

a. usually
b. generally
c. incidentally
d. systematically
e. specifically

14

Study each word that you misspelled in Frames 8–12. Write each missed word correctly three times. Check your spellings against the list above Frame 1.

13   Models:

a. Adjectives ending in –al, to which –ly is added to form adverbs

b. Adjectives ending in –ic, to which –ally is added to form adverbs

UNIT 11 · Dropping final *e* (I)

WORDS TREATED

arguing	becoming	excitable	guiding	simply	Exceptions:	outrageous
arousing	coming	excusable	hoping	using	courageous	shoeing
arranging	continual	famous	noticing	writer	dyeing	singeing
arriving	desirability	guidance	shining	writing	noticeable	toeing
				written		

1   use   excite   fame   continue

a. Each of the four words above ends in _____ (What letter?).

b. In the four words above, the final *e* is _____ (*pronounced* or *silent*?).

2   –ing   –able   –ous   –al

Each of the four suffixes above may be added to hundreds of English words. Each begins with a _____ (*consonant* or *vowel*?).

---

3   use + –ing = using
excite + –able = excitable
fame + –ous = famous
continue + –al = continual

The examples above show that when we add a suffix beginning with a vowel (like *–ing*) to a word ending with a silent *e* (like *use*), we _____ (Do what to?) the *e*.

4

Write *using, excitable, famous,* and *continual* twice each.

_____, _____ _____, _____
_____, _____ _____, _____

5

The principle that you are studying applies to thousands of English words. We shall consider a few more of them and then notice a few exceptions.

a. Write the combination of *argue* + *–ing.* _____
b. Write the combination of *notice* + *–ing.* _____
c. Write the combination of *shine* + *–ing.* _____
d. Write the combination of *come* + *–ing.* _____
e. Write the combination of *write* + *–ing.* _____

(*Writer* also drops an *e*, but regains it from the suffix *–er*. *Written* has two *t*'s because of the "short" sound of *i*; it rhymes with *bitten* and *kitten*.)

6

Write the following combinations:

a. *hope* + *–ing* = _____
b. *become* + *–ing* = _____
c. *arrive* + *–ing* = _____
d. *arrange* + *–ing* = _____
e. *guide* + *–ing* = _____
f. *arouse* + *–ing* = _____

1

a. *e*
b. silent

2

vowel

3

drop

4

using, using
excitable, excitable
famous, famous
continual, continual

5

a. arguing
b. noticing
c. shining
d. coming
e. writing

7

a. *guide* + *–ance* = _____
b. *excuse* + *–able* = _____
c. *desire* + *–ability* = _____
d. *simple* + *–y* = _____

6

a. hoping
b. becoming
c. arriving
d. arranging
e. guiding
f. arousing

8

A few words, of two kinds, are exceptions and do not drop the final *e*.

The first are words like *dye* (to change color) + *–ing*, *singe* (to burn) + *–ing*, or *shoe* + *–ing*. The reason that these words keep the *e* is that otherwise they might be confused with other words or look hard to pronounce.

Copy: I'm *toeing* the mark.
No more *dyeing* my hair,
Or *singeing* my whiskers,
Or *shoeing* Joe's mare.

_____
_____
_____
_____

7

a. guidance
b. excusable
c. desirability
d. simply

9

The other exceptions are a few words like *noticeable*, *courageous*, and *outrageous*. Keeping the *e* helps to show that the *c* in these words is pronounced like *s*, or the *g* like *j*.

Copy: It was *noticeable* that his manner was both *courageous* and *outrageous*.

_____
_____

8

I'm *toeing* the mark.
No more *dyeing* my hair,
Or *singeing* my whiskers,
Or *shoeing* Joe's mare.

10

Write in full each incomplete word, choosing the most suitable one from those studied in this unit.

My brother and I were [arg] _____ about the quality of his [writ] _____. He is [hop] _____ to become a [fam] _____ [wr] _____. I said that most good modern authors write [simp] _____, but he believes in [us] _____ flowery language. His [contin] _____ use of [shin] _____ figures of speech is almost [outrag] _____.

9

It was *noticeable* that his manner was both *courageous* and *outrageous*.

11

Follow the instructions for Frame 10.

a. They spent their time in [sh] _____ horses and [dy] _____ wool.
b. We had been [notic] _____ his [cour] _____ behavior.
c. [To] _____ the line is [arous] _____ his anger.
d. I was [guid] _____ the [excit] _____ horse as well as I could.

10

arguing	using
writing	continual
hoping	shining
famous	outrageous
writer	
simply	

12

Follow the instructions for Frame 10.

a. Several students are [com] _____ to their counselor for [guid] _____. They are [arriv] _____ in a few minutes.
b. She was [arrang] _____ for [sing] _____ her hair.
c. The increasing shortness of the days was [becom] _____ [notic] _____.
d. Your conduct is [excus] _____, but I question its [desir] _____.

11

a. shoeing, dyeing
b. noticing, courageous
c. Toeing, arousing
d. guiding, excitable

13

Match each synonym with a word we studied in this unit. The first letters are supplied.

a. can be seen, [not] _____
b. pardonable, [exc] _____
c. very offensive, [out] _____
d. burning lightly, [sin] _____
e. debating, [arg] _____
f. one who writes, [wri] _____
g. quality of being wanted, [des] _____
h. gleaming, [shi] _____
i. able to be excited, [exci] _____
j. arriving, [com] _____
k. employing, [us] _____
l. putting in order, [arr] _____

12

a. coming, guidance, arriving
b. arranging, singeing
c. becoming, noticeable
d. excusable, desirability

14

Follow the instructions for Frame 13.

a. putting shoes on, [sho] _____
b. touching with toes, [to] _____
c. showing the way, [gui] _____
d. waking, [aro] _____
e. well known, [fam] _____
f. coming, [arr] _____
g. coming to be, [bec] _____
h. forgivable, [excu] _____
i. wishing, [hop] _____
j. in a simple manner, [sim] _____
k. steady, regular, [con] _____
l. changing color, [dy] _____
m. not oral, [wr] _____

13

a. noticeable
b. excusable
c. outrageous
d. singeing
e. arguing
f. writer
g. desirability
h. shining
i. excitable
j. coming
k. using
l. arranging

15

Study each word that you misspelled in Frames 10–14. Notice the trouble spots, especially whether or not the *e* is dropped. Write correctly three times each word that you missed. Check your spellings against the list above Frame 1.

14

a. shoeing
b. toeing
c. guiding
d. arousing
e. famous
f. arriving
g. becoming
h. excusable
i. hoping
j. simply
k. continual
l. dyeing
m. written

UNIT 12 · Dropping final *e* (II)

WORDS TREATED

admirable	definition	indefinable	slimy	vegetation	Exceptions:
bridal	dining	invitation	spicy	wholly	canoeing
collegiate	encouraging	practical	usage		changeable
considerably	gambling	scraping	valuable		

---

1   admire   gamble   bride   college

a. Each of the four words above ends in _____ (What letter?).
b. In the four words above, the final *e* is _____ (*pronounced* or *silent*?).

---

2   –able   –ing   –al   –iate

The four suffixes above may be added to hundreds of English words. Each begins with a _____ (*consonant* or *vowel*?).

1

a. *e*
b. silent

3

      admire + –able = admirable
      gamble + –ing = gambling
      bride + –al = bridal
      college + –iate = collegiate

The examples above show that when we add a suffix beginning with a vowel (like *–able*) to a word ending with a silent *e* (like *admire*), we _____ (Do what to?) the *e*.

4

Copy: Her *collegiate* friends thought that *gambling* on *bridal* bliss was *admirable*.

    _____

    _____

5

The principle that you are studying applies to thousands of English words. We shall consider a few more of them and then notice a few exceptions.

Write the following combinations:

a. *define + –ition* = _____
b. *dine + –ing* = _____
c. *encourage + –ing* = _____
d. *in + define + –able* = _____
e. *practice + –al* = _____
f. *value + –able* = _____

6

Write the following combinations:

a. *invite + –ation* = _____
b. *scrape + –ing* = _____
c. *use + –age* = _____
d. *vegetate + –ion* = _____

7

The letter *y* is pronounced as a vowel at the end of a word, so our principle applies to it, also.

Write the following combinations:

a. *slime + –y* = _____
b. *spice + –y* = _____
c. *considerable + –y* = _____
d. *whole + –ly* = _____ (Note: This word drops the *e* even though the suffix does not start with a vowel.)

2

vowel

3

drop

4

Her *collegiate* friends thought that *gambling* on *bridal* bliss was *admirable*.

5

a. definition   d. indefinable
b. dining   e. practical
c. encouraging f. valuable

6

a. invitation
b. scraping
c. usage
d. vegetation

8

The few exceptions to our principle about dropping silent *e* before adding a suffix starting with a vowel are of two kinds, illustrated by *canoeing* and *changeable*.

a. *Canoeing* keeps the *e* because the word would look strange and hard to pronounce without it. Write *canoeing*. _____

b. *Changeable* keeps the *e* because otherwise *chang* might be mispronounced to rhyme with *rang*. Write *changeable*. _____

9

Match each synonym with a word we studied in this unit. The first letters are supplied. Write the word in full.

a. wonderful; praiseworthy, [adm] _____
b. spice-flavored, [sp] _____
c. request for your presence, [inv] _____
d. eating, [din] _____
e. wagering, [gam] _____
f. of a wedding, [bri] _____
g. a meaning, [def] _____

10

Follow the instructions for Frame 9.

a. riding in a canoe, [can] _____
b. coated with slime, [sl] _____
c. entirely, [who] _____
d. plant life, [veg] _____
e. not able to be defined, [inde] _____
f. pertaining to college, [col] _____

11

Follow the instructions for Frame 9.

a. helping or supporting, [enc] _____
b. rubbing with something sharp, [scra] _____
c. fickle or variable, [chan] _____
d. customary practice, [us] _____
e. to a considerable extent, [cons] _____
f. having value, [val] _____
g. useful, [prac] _____

7

a. slimy
b. spicy
c. considerably
d. wholly

8

a. canoeing
b. changeable

9

a. admirable   e. gambling
b. spicy   f. bridal
c. invitation   g. definition
d. dining

10

a. canoeing   e. indefinable
b. slimy   f. collegiate
c. wholly
d. vegetation

12

Write in full each incomplete word, choosing the most suitable one from those studied in this unit.

We were [can] _____ on the lake. Suddenly our canoe began [scra] _____ along the edge of a [sli] _____ log floating in the water. The log had been [who] _____ hidden by the [veg] _____, mainly water lilies, growing in the lake. We were [cons] _____ frightened because our canoe might easily have upset.

13

Follow the instructions for Frame 12.

a. My parents are [enc] _____ me to take more mathematics, telling me it is a [prac] _____ thing to study and that it will be [val] _____ in my future work.
b. I don't know a satisfactory [def] _____ of *love*. Maybe it is [inde] _____.
c. A [spi] _____ aroma was coming from the [din] _____ room.

14

Follow the instructions for Frame 12.

a. The [us] _____ of the English language is not constant. Over several centuries it may be seen to be highly [chan] _____ _____.
b. [Coll] _____ [din] _____ rooms are generally informal places.
c. I received an [inv] _____ to a [bri] _____ shower.
d. Few persons consider [gamb] _____ [admi] _____ _____.

15

Study each word that you misspelled in Frames 9–14. Note particularly whether an *e* should be dropped and the reason it is not dropped in *canoeing* and *changeable*. Write each missed word correctly three times. Check your spellings against the list above Frame 1.

11

a. encouraging   e. considerably
b. scraping   f. valuable
c. changeable   g. practical
d. usage

12

canoeing
scraping
slimy
wholly
vegetation
considerably

13

a. encouraging, practical, valuable
b. definition, indefinable
c. spicy, dining

14

a. usage, changeable
b. collegiate, dining
c. invitation, bridal
d. gambling, admirable

UNIT 13 · When *c* changes to *ck*

WORDS TREATED

				Exceptions:
bivouacked	mimicked	picnicked	shellacking	arced
bivouacking	mimicking	picnicking	trafficked	disced (*or* disked)
colicky	panicked	politicked	trafficking	frolicsome
frolicked	panicking	politicking		mimicry
frolicking	panicky	shellacked		

1

a. Pronounce *iced* and *icing* (like the *icing* on a cake).

b. If we took the word *picnic* and added *–ed* or *–ing* to it without any change, the resulting word *picniced* or *picnicing* would look as if it should rhyme with *iced* or *icing*. A reader might then mispronounce it. To prevent confusion of the "soft" *c* as in *icing* with the "hard" *c* of *picnic*, we correctly spell the words *picnicked* and *picknicking*.

Copy: They enjoy *picnicking* so much that they *picnicked* all summer.

_____

_____

2

The same principle applies to a small number of other fairly common words that have a hard *c* sound.

a. Spell the *–ed* and *–ing* forms of *frolic*. _____ ,

_____

b. Spell the *–ed* and *–ing* forms of *mimic*. _____ , _____

_____

1

They enjoy *picnicking* so much that they *picnicked* all summer.

3

a. Spell the *–ed* and *–ing* forms of *shellac*. _____ ,

_____

b. Spell the *–ed* and *–ing* forms of *bivouac*. _____ ,

_____

2

a. frolicked, frolicking
b. mimicked, mimicking

4

a. Spell the *–ed* and *–ing* forms of *traffic*. _____ ,

_____

b. Spell the *–ed* and *–ing* forms of *politic*. _____ ,

_____

3

a. shellacked, shellacking
b. bivouacked, bivouacking

5

a. *Colic* plus *–y* gives *colicky*. Write *colicky*. _____
b. Spell the *–y, –ed,* and *–ing* forms of *panic*. _____,
_____, _____

6

Two exceptions to the principle we have been learning are *arced* and *disced* (or *disked*), for which the spellings *arcked* and *discked* are rare.

Words like *frolicsome* and *mimicry* do not need a *k* because there is no tendency to mispronounce them without it.

Copy: The *frolicsome* clown, adept at *mimicry, arced* through the air like an acrobat.

_____

_____

7

To summarize: *c* in a few words is changed to *ck* before a few suffixes to remind the reader that in these words the *c* has a _____ (*soft* or *hard*?) sound.

8

Choose suitable words from this unit to complete each sentence. Use a different form in each blank, and write the words in full.

a. We were [pic] _____ near a stream. We had [pic] _____ there before.
b. A decisive defeat is sometimes called in slang a "[shel] _____." We [shel] _____ the Viking football team yesterday.
c. The little boys began [mim] _____ the old man. They had never [mim] _____ him before.

9

Follow the instructions for Frame 8.

a. The soldiers were [biv] _____ in a small grove. They had [biv] _____ there for forty-eight hours.
b. The kittens are [frol] _____ as kittens have always [frol] _____.
c. I'm afraid that the baby is becoming [col] _____.

4

a. trafficked, trafficking
b. politicked, politicking

5

a. colicky
b. panicky, panicked, panicking

6

The *frolicsome* clown, adept at *mimicry, arced* through the air like an acrobat.

7

hard

8

a. picnicking, picnicked
b. shellacking, shellacked
c. mimicking, mimicked

10

Follow the instructions for Frame 8.

a. Don't get [pan] _____. I remember that I [pan] _____ _____ once, and I decided then that [pan] _____ doesn't do any good.

b. As usual, the governor is [pol] _____. He has [pol] _____ every day since his inauguration.

c. They are accused of [traf] _____ in opium. They may have [traf] _____ for a long time.

11

a. Add *–ed* to *arc*. _____
b. Add *–some* to *frolic*. _____
c. Add *–ry* to *mimic*. _____

12

Study each word that you misspelled in Frames 8–11. Write it correctly three times. Check your spellings against the list above Frame 1.

9

a. bivouacking, bivouacked
b. frolicking, frolicked
c. colicky

10

a. panicky, panicked, panicking
b. politicking, politicked
c. trafficking, trafficked

11

a. arced
b. frolicsome
c. mimicry

UNIT 14 · Faulty pronunciation: too many sounds

WORDS TREATED

athlete	drowned	laundry	suffrage
athletic	film	mischievous	umbrella
attacked	grievous	reforestation	
barbarous	height	statue	

1

Some words are misspelled because people incorrectly put in an extra sound in pronouncing. This unit concerns fourteen such words.

For example, some people pronounce *ath lete* as if it were three syllables. You can tell, from the way we have divided it, that *ath lete* contains only _____ (How many?) syllables.

2　　athlete　　athletic

Ath lete has only two syllables, and *ath let ic* has only three.

a. Say *ath lete* to yourself. Be sure to say only two syllables.
b. Say *ath let ic* to yourself. Be sure to say only three syllables.
c. Say *ath lete, ath let ic, athlete, athletic.*
d. Copy: An *ath lete* is *ath let ic.*
　　　An *athlete* is *athletic.*

_____

_____

3　　attacked

a. Say *hacked, packed, tacked* to yourself.
b. Now say *attacked.* Be sure that it has only two syllables and that it rhymes with *hacked.*
c. Copy: The ship *tacked* and then *attacked.*

_____

4　　drowned

a. Say *frowned, crowned* to yourself.
b. Now say *drowned* to yourself. Be sure that it rhymes with *frowned* and *crowned* and that it has only one syllable.
c. Copy: Her lover *frowned*
　　　When he heard she'd *drowned.*

_____

_____

5　　mischievous　　barbarous

a. *Mis chie vous* and *bar ba rous* each have only _____ (How many?) syllables.
b. Pronounce *mischievous* and *barbarous* to yourself. Be sure to pronounce only three syllables in each. Accent the first syllable in each.
c. The last four letters in *mischievous* are _____ (What?), and the last four letters of *barbarous* are _____ (What?).
d. Copy: He's a *mis chie vous, bar ba rous* child.
　　　He's a *mischievous, barbarous* child.

_____

_____

6　　grievous

a. *Griev ous* has only _____ (How many?) syllables.
b. Pronounce *griev ous.* Be sure to pronounce only two syllables.
c. The last four letters of *grievous* are _____ (What?).
d. Copy: If you'd leave us,
　　　'Twould be *grievous.*

_____

_____

1

two

2

d. An *ath lete* is *ath let ic.*
　　An *athlete* is *athletic.*

3

c. The ship *tacked* and then
　　attacked.

4

c. Her lover *frowned*
　　When he heard she'd *drowned.*

5

a. three
c. *vous, rous*
d. He's a *mis chie vous, bar ba rous* child.
　　He's a *mischievous, barbarous* child.

7 film

a. Some people mispronounce *film*. They make it sound like *fill 'em* in *fill 'em up*. Like *silk* or *tilt*, *film* is really a _____ (How many?) syllable word.

b. Say *film* three times to yourself. Be sure to pronounce only one syllable.

c. Copy: I took the helm while she used up our *film*.

_____

6

a. two

c. *vous*

d. If you'd leave us,
   'Twould be *grievous*.

---

8 umbrella

a. *Um brel la* has only _____ (How many?) syllables.

b. Say *brel, brel, brella, brella.*

c. Now say *um brel la* three times. Be sure to pronounce only three syllables.

d. Copy: A girl named *Glum Ella*
   Forgot her *umbrella*.

_____

_____

7

a. one

c. I took the helm while she used up our *film*.

---

9 statue   reforestation

Careless speakers insert in *statue* and *reforestation* an *r* that does not belong. (*Stature*, meaning height, is a different word.)

a. Say *stat ue, statue*.

b. Say *re for est a tion, reforestation*.

c. Copy: This *statue* honors a pioneer in *reforestation*.

_____

8

a. three

d. A girl named *Glum Ella*
   Forgot her *umbrella*.

---

10 height

a. The last letter of *height* is _____ (What?).

b. Pronounce *height* to rhyme with *kite*. Say to yourself *kite, height, kite, height*. Be sure not to have a *th* sound at the end.

c. Copy: He stood upon a *height* of land
   Practicing his *sleight* of hand.

_____

_____

9

c. This *statue* honors a pioneer in *reforestation*.

---

11 laundry   suffrage

a. *Laun dry* and *suf frage* each have only _____ (How many?) syllables.

b. Say *laun dry, laundry, suf frage, suffrage*. Be sure to have only two syllables in each. Do not insert a vowel sound before the *r*.

c. Write: *laun dry, laundry*
   suf frage, suffrage.

_____ , _____

_____ , _____

10

a. *t*

c. He stood upon a *height* of land
   Practicing his *sleight* of hand.

12

Choose from this unit the words necessary to complete the following passage. The first letters have been supplied. Write the words in full.

The [ath] _____, whose [h] _____ was more than six feet, was a [mis] _____ chap who once took his camera and made a [f] _____ of my troubles with an [um] _____ in a strong wind. Another time he painted a mustache on a [stat] _____, and once he put a dead mouse in my [laun] _____ .

13

Follow the instructions for Frame 12.

Perhaps [suf] _____ is a civilizing influence. Our enemies, who knew nothing about voting, were [bar] _____. Their [ath] _____ soldiers [at] _____ us by scrambling over the wall. They inflicted [gr] _____ injuries and [dr] _____ several of our men by tossing them into the moat. They burned so much woodland that [refor] _____ _____ would take many years.

14

For each definition, write in full a synonym that we have studied. The first letter has been supplied.

a. savage, [b] _____
b. strong, active, [a] _____
c. assaulted, [a] _____
d. died in water, [d] _____
e. saddening, [g] _____

15

Follow the instructions for Frame 14.

a. material for photographs, [f] _____
b. a strong, active person, [a] _____
c. parasol, [u] _____
d. degree of tallness, [h] _____
e. impish, bothersome, [m] _____
f. right to vote, [s] _____
g. replanting trees, [r] _____
h. items washed, [l] _____
i. carved or hewn image, [s] _____

11

a. two
c. *laun dry, laundry*
   suf frage, suffrage

12

athlete
height
mischievous
film
umbrella
statue
laundry

13

suffrage
barbarous
athletic
attacked
grievous
drowned
reforestation

14

a. barbarous
b. athletic
c. attacked
d. drowned
e. grievous

16

Look carefully at the correct spelling of each word you missed in Frames 12–15. Go back to earlier frames to make sure that you can pronounce the word correctly. Write each missed word correctly three times, and check above Frame 1 to be sure that you have now spelled it correctly.

15

a. film
b. athlete
c. umbrella
d. height
e. mischievous
f. suffrage
g. reforestation
h. laundry
i. statue

UNIT 15 · Faulty pronunciation: leaving sounds out (I)

WORDS TREATED

antarctic	candidate	government	mathematics
arctic	environment	grandfather	quarter
bachelor	February	history	
boundary	further	library	

1

A number of words are misspelled because people leave out certain sounds when they say the words. Then they make spelling conform to the faulty pronunciation.

For example, the words *arctic* and *antarctic* come from a Greek word, *arktos,* meaning a bear. (Arctic regions are beneath the constellation called the Great Bear or the Big Dipper.)

Just as the *k* was pronounced in the Greek word, so the first _____ (What letter?) in *arctic* is pronounced by most careful speakers.

2   arctic   antarctic

a. Say the words *arctic* and *antarctic* to yourself. Be sure to pronounce the first *c* in each.
b. Copy: It's no lark, Dick,
         To live in the *arctic*
         (Or the *antarctic*).

_____

_____

_____

1

c

3   bachelor   mathematics

Bachelor and *mathematics* are alike in that careless speakers often leave out the *e* in pronouncing these words.

a. Say *bach e lor,* being sure to say three syllables.
b. Say *math e mat ics,* being sure to say four syllables.
c. Write *bachelor* and *mathematics,* emphasizing the fifth letter by making it a capital.

_____, _____

2

b. It's no lark, Dick,
   To live in the *arctic*
   (Or the *antarctic*).

4   February

The word *February* comes from Latin *februa*, meaning a feast held in *Februarius*, the second month of the year. Because *februa* was spelled with an *r* after the *b*, we keep the *r* in English. Careless or informal speakers, though, often leave it out.

a. Say *Feb ru ar y*. Do not leave out an *r*.
b. Write *February* three times.

_____ , _____ , _____

---

5   library

In Latin a book was called *liber*, and a place where books were kept was called *librarius*. Our word *library* comes from *librarius*. Note the two *r*'s. Careless speakers leave out the first.

a. Say *li brar y*. Do not leave out an *r*.
b. Write *library* twice, capitalizing both *r*'s for emphasis.

_____ , _____

---

6   grandfather   candidate

Grandfather and *candidate* are alike in that careless speakers often leave out the *d* in the first syllable.

a. Say *grand fa ther*. Do not leave out the *d*.
b. Say *can di date*. Do not leave out a *d*.
c. Copy: My *grandfather* was often a *candidate*.

_____

---

7   further   quarter

Further and *quarter* are alike in that some persons leave out the first *r* sound.

a. Say *fur ther*. Make the *r*'s distinct.
b. Say *quar ter*. Make the *r*'s distinct.
c. Write *further* and *quarter*, capitalizing the *r*'s for emphasis.

_____ , _____

---

8   boundary

a. *Bound a ry* has _____ (How many?) syllables, as our division shows.
b. Say *bound a ry*. Do not leave out the second syllable.
c. Write: *bound a ry, boundary*.

_____ , _____

3

c. bachElor, mathEmatics

4

b. February, February, February

5

b. libRaRy, libRaRy

6

c. My *grandfather* was often a
   candidate.

7

c. fuRtheR, quaRteR

---

9   history

History comes from Latin *historia*, which goes back to an earlier Greek *histor*, which meant knowing. The sound of the *o* is much less distinct in English than it was in Latin and is missing in some persons' speech.

a. Say *his to ry*. Say the second syllable more distinctly than is normal, to help you remember the *o*.
b. Copy: *History* is derived from *historia*.

_____

10   environment

Notice that *environment* has *iron* in the middle.

a. Say *i ron*. As a help in spelling, be sure to pronounce the *r* sound before the *o* sound.
b. Say *en vi ron ment*. Be sure that the four sounds in *iron* are in the right order.
c. Copy: Listen for the *iron* in *environment*.

_____

11   government

Notice that *government* consists of the word *govern* and the suffix *–ment*. *Government* is hard to pronounce because of the *n* and the *m* together.

a. Say *gov ern ment*. Make the first *n* unnaturally distinct.
b. Copy: It has been said that the best *government governs* least.

_____

_____

12

Use words we studied in this unit to complete the following paragraph. Write each incomplete word in full.

That [Feb] _____ day my [gran] _____ first entered the [Ar] _____ Ocean. It was bitterly cold. "Would the [Ant] _____ be warmer?" he wondered. That frigid [env] _____ made him long for the warmth and comfort of his [lib] _____ at home, with his books on science and [math] _____ .

8

a. three
c. *bound a ry, boundary*

9

b. *History* is derived from *historia*.

10

c. Listen for the *iron* in *environment*.

11

b. It has been said that the best *government governs* least.

13

Follow the instructions for Frame 12.

[His] _____ books show that a [bach]_____ is seldom as effective a political [can] _____ as a married man. Numerous voters seem to think that an official in the [gov] _____ should have a family. [Fu] _____, an attractive wife and children are good vote-getters. Frequently the [boun] _____ between victory and defeat in an election is narrow, and a pleasant family may influence an eighth or even a [qua] _____ of the voters.

14

For each term, write a synonym that we have studied. The first letter has been supplied.

a. cold southern region, [a] _____
b. cold northern region, [a] _____
c. unmarried man, [b] _____
d. science of numbers, [m] _____
e. second month, [F] _____
f. place for books, [l] _____
g. father's father, [g] _____
h. office seeker, [c] _____
i. ruling power, [g] _____
j. in addition; also, [f] _____
k. one-fourth, [q] _____
l. study of the past, [h] _____
m. edge of a state, etc., [b] _____
n. surroundings, [e] _____

15

Look carefully at the correct spelling of each word you missed in Frames 12–14. Go back to earlier frames to be sure that you are pronouncing the word correctly. Write each missed word three times, and check above Frame 1 to make sure that you spelled it correctly.

12

February
grandfather
Arctic
Antarctic
environment
library
mathematics

13

History
bachelor
candidate
government
Further
boundary
quarter

14

a. antarctic
b. arctic
c. bachelor
d. mathematics
e. February
f. library
g. grandfather
h. candidate
i. government
j. further
k. quarter
l. history
m. boundary
n. environment

UNIT 16 · Faulty pronunciation: leaving sounds out (II)

WORDS TREATED

bankruptcy	literature	recognize	surprise	vacuum
identical	miniature	sophomore	temperament	
laboratory	probably	strength	temperature	
length	quantity	strict	tentative	

---

1   laboratory

In this unit we shall look at some words in which many persons leave out letters, usually because of mispronouncing.

a. For instance, some persons pronounce *lab o ra to ry* as only four syllables. As you can see from the division, it has _____ (How many?) syllables.

b. Pronounce *lab o ra to ry* to yourself, being careful not to omit any syllables.

c. Copy: Chemists *labor* in the *laboratory*.

    _____

---

2   literature   miniature

a. *Lit er a ture* and *min i a ture* each have _____ (How many?) syllables.

b. Pronounce *lit er a ture* and *min i a ture*, being careful not to omit any syllables.

c. Write: *lit er a ture, literature*
            min i a ture, miniature.

     _____, _____

     _____, _____

---

3   temperature   temperament

a. *Tem per a ture* and *tem per a ment* each have _____ (How many?) syllables.

b. Pronounce *tem per a ture* and *tem per a ment*, being careful not to omit the *a*.

c. Copy: Does *temperature* affect *temperament?*

    _____

1

a. five

c. Chemists *labor* in the *laboratory*.

2

a. four

c. *lit er a ture, literature*
     min i a ture, miniature

---

4   length   strength

Length and *strength* sometimes cause trouble because people mis-takenly omit the *g* in pronouncing them. Remember that these words are related to *long* and *strong*.

a. Say *length* and *strength*. Be sure that you can hear the *g*.
b. Write *length* and *strength* twice each, capitalizing each *g* for emphasis.

_____ , _____

_____ , _____

5

Here are four words in which a *t* sometimes gets lost in the pro-nunciation:

bankrupTcy idenTical quanTity tenTative

a. Pronounce the four words, being sure not to leave out any *t* sound.
b. Write *bankruptcy*, *identical*, *quantity*, and *tentative*, capitalizing the troublesome *t*'s.

_____ , _____ , _____ , _____

6   probably

In *prob a bly*, careless speakers leave out the second *b*. The word comes from Latin *probabilis*, which accounts for the two *b*'s.

a. Say *prob a bly*. Do not leave out a *b*.
b. Copy: *Comfortably* and *probably* both end in *–ably*.

_____

_____

7   recognize

The Latin ancestor of *recognize* contains a *g*. That is why it is in the English word.

a. Say *rec og nize*. Do not forget the *g*.
b. Copy: To be *cognizant* of something is to *recognize* it.

_____

_____

8   sophomore

Sophomore comes from Greek *sophos*, meaning wise, and *moros*, meaning foolish. Supposedly, then, a sophomore is wise and foolish at the same time. The second *o* in *sophos* explains the second *o* in *sophomore*.

a. Say *soph o more* (three syllables).
b. Write: *soph o more, sophomore.*

_____ , _____

3

a. four
c. Does *temperature* affect *temperament?*

4

b. lenGth, lenGth
   strenGth, strenGth

5

b. bankrupTcy, quanTity, idenTical, tenTative

6

b. *Comfortably* and *probably* both end in *–ably.*

7

b. To be *cognizant* of something is to *recognize* it.

9   **strict**

Strict rhymes with *predict*. The final *t* should be pronounced.

a. Say *strict, strict, strict*. Be sure to hear the final *t*.
b. Copy: I don't like to *restrict* you, but I must be *strict*.

_____

_____

---

10   **surprise**

In *sur prise*, the sound often incorrectly omitted is that of the first *r*.

a. Say *sur prise*. Pronounce both *r*'s.
b. Copy: Her eyes
     surprise.

_____

_____

---

11   **vacuum**

a. *Vac u um,* as the division shows, has _____ (How many?) syllables.
b. Say *vac u um,* as if it were spelled *vack you um.*
c. Write *vacuum* three times. (This is the only common English word with two *u*'s together.)

_____, _____, _____

12

Use words studied in this unit to complete the following paragraph. Write each word in full.

     Although the [temp] _____ in the [lab] _____ _____ was low, the [soph] _____ went in to complete his study of a [vac] _____ pump. To his [su] _____, a person whom he did not [reco] _____ was already there. A [stri] _____ rule against admitting strangers was in effect, because a [quan] _____ of materials had been stolen in a short [len] _____ of time.

13

Follow the instructions for Frame 12.

     The [lit] _____ assignment was a very short story about the [bankrup] _____ of a merchant who sold [min] _____ paintings and had a peculiar [temp] _____. The [stren] _____ of the story [prob] _____ lay in the fact that almost no two persons would have reacted to the circumstances in [iden] _____ ways. At least that was the [ten] _____ decision of the class.

8

b. *soph o more, sophomore*

9

b. I don't like to *restrict* you, but I must be *strict*.

10

b. Her eyes
     surprise.

11

a. three
c. *vacuum, vacuum, vacuum*

12

temperature
laboratory
sophomore
vacuum
surprise
recognize
strict
quantity
length

14

For each term, write a synonym that we have studied. The first letter has been supplied.

a. amount, [q] _____
b. more than likely, [p] _____
c. power, [s] _____
d. literary works, [l] _____
e. astonishment, [s] _____
f. heat and cold, [t] _____
g. second-year student, [s] _____
h. empty space, [v] _____
i. identify, [r] _____
j. small, [m] _____
k. science workroom, [l] _____
l. rigorous; exact, [s] _____
m. business failure, [b] _____
n. exactly the same, [i] _____

13

literature
bankruptcy
miniature
temperament
strength
probably
identical
tentative

15

Look carefully at the correct spelling of each word you missed in Frames 12–14. Go back to earlier frames to be sure that you are pronouncing the word correctly. Write each missed word three times, and check above Frame 1 to make sure that you spelled it correctly.

14

a. quantity   h. vacuum
b. probably   i. recognize
c. strength   j. miniature
d. literature   k. laboratory
e. surprise   l. strict
f. temperature   m. bankruptcy
g. sophomore   n. identical

UNIT 17 · Faulty pronunciation: leaving sounds out (III)

WORDS TREATED

amount	finally	studying	worrying
asked	poem	ventilate	
auxiliary	practically	where	
chocolate	pumpkin	which	

1   amount

A number of words are misspelled because people leave out certain sounds when they say the words. Then they make spellings conform to the faulty pronunciation.

For example, careless speakers do not pronounce the *n* in *amount*. The word should rhyme with *count*.

a. Say to yourself *count, mount, amount.*
b. Write: *count, mount, amount.*

_____, _____, _____

2   finally   practically

To pronounce *finally* correctly, say *final* and add the suffix *–ly*. *Finally* has three syllables.

To pronounce *practically* correctly, say *practical* and add the suffix *–ly*. *Practically* has four syllables.

a. Say to yourself *final, final ly, finally.*
b. Say to yourself *practical, practical ly, practically.*
c. Write the words as you pronounced them for *a* and *b*.

_____, _____, _____

_____, _____, _____

---

3   worrying   studying

To pronounce *worrying* correctly, say *worry* and add the suffix *–ing*. *Worrying* has three syllables.

To pronounce *studying* correctly, say *study* and add the suffix *–ing*. *Studying* has three syllables.

a. Say to yourself *worry, worry ing, worrying.*
b. Say to yourself *study, study ing, studying.*
c. Write *worrying* and *studying* twice each.

_____, _____

_____, _____

---

4   chocolate   ventilate

Although *chocolate* may be pronounced as two syllables, it will help you to remember the second *o* if you make it three: *choc o late.*

In *ventilate*, do not forget the first *t*.

a. Say *chocolate* to yourself, as three syllables.
b. Say to yourself *vent, ventilate.*
c. Write *chocolate* and *ventilate* twice each. Capitalize the troublesome letter in each.

_____, _____

_____, _____

---

5   which   where

Words like *which, when,* and *where* are often pronounced rapidly without a beginning *h* sound. You are less likely to forget the *h* in writing if you pronounce it. (These words were once spelled more logically, with the *h* first.)

a. Say *which* and *where* to yourself, exaggerating an *h* sound before the *w* sound.
b. Copy: *Where* is Mount Etna, *which* you were telling us about?

_____

_____

1

b. count, mount, amount

2

c. final, final ly, finally
   practical, practical ly, practically

3

c. worrying, worrying
   studying, studying

4

c. chocOlate, chocOlate
   venTilate, venTilate

---

6   pumpkin   auxiliary

Pumpkin consists of *pump* plus *kin.*

Auxiliary sometimes loses the sound of *i* in pronunciation, and misspelling may result. Pronounce the last four letters like *yuh ree.*

a. Say to yourself *pump kin, pumpkin.*

b. Say to yourself *ogg zil yuh ree, auxiliary.*

c. Copy: The Ladies' *Auxiliary* served *pumpkin* pie.

_____

_____

7   asked   poem

In using the past tense of *ask,* as in *I asked you a question ten minutes ago,* some speakers carelessly omit the *t* sound that *–ed* has in this word.

    Poem is a two-syllable word, as this rhyme reveals:

I'm going to show 'em

I can write a *poem.*

a. Say to yourself *I ask you now. I asked you yesterday.* Note the difference in sound between *ask* and *asked.*

b. Say to yourself *po em, poem.*

c. Write a short sentence using *asked* and *poem.*

_____

_____

8

To match each synonym given below, write in full a word studied in this unit. The beginning letter or letters have been supplied. Before writing, say the word to yourself.

a. large, orange-yellow fruit, [pu] _____

b. kind of candy, [choc] _____

c. helping or helper, [aux] _____

d. at last, [fin] _____

e. change the air in, [ven] _____

f. in what place, [w] _____

9

Follow the instructions for Frame 8.

a. sum or total, [am] _____

b. inquired, [a] _____

c. feeling anxious, [wor] _____

d. learning by reading, etc., [stud] _____

e. that; the one that, [w] _____

f. in a practical way, [pr] _____

5

b. *Where* is Mount Etna, *which* you were telling us about?

6

c. The Ladies' *Auxiliary* served *pumpkin* pie.

7   Model:

c. We *asked* him to recite a *poem* yesterday.

8

a. pumpkin   d. finally

b. chocolate   e. ventilate

c. auxiliary   f. where

10

Write in full each unfinished word, choosing the most suitable one from the words studied in this unit.

I was [stud] _____ my mathematics and [wor] _____ _____ about the examination. I got up to open the window and [ven] _____ the room, [w] _____ was becoming stuffy. [Fin] _____ I decided that I needed a piece of [pu] _____ pie.

11

Follow the instructions for Frame 10.

a. I went to the teacher and [a] _____ her [w] _____ I should start reading.
b. The [choc] _____ candy was [prac] _____ gone.
c. [Aux] _____ verbs are used a large [am] _____ of the time in modern English.

12

Study each word that you misspelled in Frames 8–11. Look back as necessary to Frames 1–7 to check your pronunciation. Say each missed word several times to yourself. Write each missed word correctly three times. Check your answers against the list above Frame 1.

9

a. amount   d. studying
b. asked   e. which
c. worrying   f. practically

10

studying
worrying
ventilate
which
Finally
pumpkin

11

a. asked, where
b. chocolate, practically
c. Auxiliary, amount

UNIT 18 · Faulty pronunciation: transposed sounds

WORDS TREATED

brethren	hundred	performance	pervade
cavalry	interpret	perhaps	prefer
children	irrelevant	permit	prepare
enmity	perform	perspiration	tragedy

---

1   hundred

We misspell some words because our pronunciation misleads us. We sometimes reverse the order of letters because we pronounce the sounds of those letters in reverse order. (Some of the words in this unit have more than one pronunciation, but we shall use the one listed first in most dictionaries.)

For instance, *hundred* ends in *red*, pronounced almost like *red* in *red coat.*

a. Say to yourself *red, red, hund red, hundred.*
b. Copy: a *hundred* red foxes.

2   children   brethren

Both *children* and *brethren* (a plural of *brother*) end in *–ren*.

a. Say to yourself *–ren, –ren, children, children, brethren, brethren.*
b. Copy: The *brethren* have twelve *children.*

---

3   perhaps   perform   performance

Note that the three words above start with *per*, pronounced about like the word for the sound that a cat makes.

a. Say to yourself *purr, per, per, perhaps, perform, performance.*
b. Copy: *Perhaps* you may *perform* in the next *performance.*

---

4   permit   pervade   perspiration

a. Three more *per* words are printed above. Say to yourself *purr, per, permit, pervade, perspiration.*
b. Copy: We must not *permit* the odor of *perspiration* to *pervade* the air.

---

5   enmity   cavalry

Notice that *enmity* starts with *en*, just as the related word *enemy* does.

    Notice that *cavalry*, meaning soldiers on horseback, starts with *cav*. It may help you to remember the place of the *v* if you associate *cavalry* with *chivalry.*

a. Say to yourself *en, en, enmity, enmity.*
b. Say to yourself *cav, cav, cavalry, cavalry.*
c. Copy: The *enmity* of the *cavalry* and infantry was well known.

---

6   tragedy   irrelevant

Notice that *tragedy* starts with *trag*. The word goes back to Greek *tragos*, meaning goat, as some early actors wore goat skins. Like *comedy*, it ends with *–edy*.

    Observe that the second syllable of *irrelevant* is *rel*. A remark is irrelevant if it is not *rel*ated to the conversation. *Irrelevant* is the antonym of *relevant.*

a. Pronounce *tragedy* and *irrelevant.*
b. Write the antonym of *relevant.* _____
c. A play that is not a comedy is perhaps a _____ (What sort of play?).

1

b. a *hundred* red foxes

2

b. The *brethren* have twelve *children.*

3

b. *Perhaps* you may *perform* in the next *performance.*

4

b. We must not *permit* the odor of *perspiration* to *pervade* the air.

5

c. The *enmity* of the *cavalry* and infantry was well known.

58

7   **prefer   prepare   interpret**

Careless speakers transpose sounds in the *pre* part of each of the words above, and careless spellers transpose the letters that represent those sounds.

a. Say to yourself, *pre, pre, prefer, prepare.*

b. Say to yourself *pret, interpret.*

c. Copy: The teacher *prefers* that you *prepare* to *interpret* the poem for yourself.

_____

_____

8

Choose and write in full the word we studied in this unit that matches the synonym below. The first letter or letters have been supplied.

a. brothers, [br] _____

b. mounted soldiers, [ca] _____

c. more than one child, [ch] _____

d. feeling that enemies share, [e] _____

e. ninety-nine plus one, [hun] _____

f. explain or translate, [inter] _____

g. not related, [ir] _____

h. do, [p] _____

9

Follow the instructions for Frame 8.

a. the giving of a play, etc., [p] _____

b. maybe, [p] _____

c. to allow, [p] _____

d. sweat, [p] _____

e. to spread throughout, [p] _____

f. to like better than, [p] _____

g. to make ready, [p] _____

h. a serious play, [tr] _____

10

Complete each incomplete word, choosing the most suitable one from those studied in this unit. Add only the missing letters.

a. I wish I could have seen John Barrymore p_____form.

b. P_____haps it will rain tonight.

c. P_____ation dripped from his forehead.

d. The orchestra gave a splendid p_____ance.

e. Did the teacher p_____mit you to go to the library?

6

b. irrelevant

c. tragedy

7

c. The teacher *prefers* that you *prepare* to *interpret* the poem for yourself.

8

a. brethren   e. hundred

b. cavalry   f. interpret

c. children   g. irrelevant

d. enmity   h. perform

9

a. performance   e. pervade

b. perhaps   f. prefer

c. permit   g. prepare

d. perspiration   h. tragedy

11

Follow the instructions for Frame 10.

a. The odor of stale cigar smoke p_____ded the house.
b. The loss of such a great man is a national tra_____.
c. Your comments don't fit; they are ir_____ant.
d. Since I cannot speak Swedish, will you inter_____ for me?
e. Your paper is perfect—one hun_____ per cent.

12

Follow the instructions for Frame 10.

a. You like the green scarf, but I p_____r the blue one.
b. Did you p_____re all your lessons?
c. Joseph was disliked by his bre_____.
d. Both the infantry and the ca_____ took part in the assault.
e. How many chil_____ did Lady Macbeth have?
f. The first quarrel was over a trivial matter, but soon a bitter e_____ty developed.

13

Look carefully at each word that you misspelled in Frames 8–12. Refer to Frames 1–7 for a clue to its pronunciation, and say it several times to yourself. Write each missed word correctly three times. Check your spellings against the list above Frame 1.

10

a. perform
b. Perhaps
c. Perspiration
d. performance
e. permit

11

a. pervaded
b. tragedy
c. irrelevant
d. interpret
e. hundred

12

a. prefer
b. prepare
c. brethren
d. cavalry
e. children
f. enmity

UNIT 19 · Faulty pronunciation: using the wrong sounds (I)

WORDS TREATED

affect	dilapidated	divine	prospective	then
appreciate	discretion	effect	sense	undoubtedly
appreciation	disgusted	geography	since	
caterpillar	divide	introduce	than	

1   divide   divine

Some persons pronounce *divide* and *divine* as if they started with *de*. As a result, they tend to misspell the words.

a. Say *divide* and *divine* to yourself. Make the first *i* sound like the *i* of *did*.
b. Write *divide* and *divine* twice each. Make the first *i* a capital for emphasis.

_____, _____

_____, _____

2   dilapidated   discretion   disgusted

Note that the three words above also start with *di*.

a. Say *dilapidated, discretion,* and *disgusted* to yourself. Make the first *i* sound like the *i* of *did*. Note the g in *disgusted*.
b. Write *dilapidated, discretion,* and *disgusted* twice each.

_____ , _____

_____ , _____

_____ , _____

---

3   sense   since

Sense, as in *common sense,* rhymes with *dense* and *tense. Since,* as in *since you left,* rhymes with *mince* and *quince.*

a. Say *sense* and *since* to yourself. Be sure that they do not sound alike.
b. Make up a short sentence using *sense,* and another short sentence using *since.*

_____

_____

---

4   than   then

Than and *then* are sometimes confused in sound and in spelling. *Than* is used in an expression like *more than I expected. Then* refers to time, as in *Then John came home.*

a. Say to yourself *more than I expected,* exaggerating the *a* as in the word *man.* Say to yourself *Then John came home,* exaggerating the *e* sound as in the word *ten.*
b. Make up a short sentence with *than,* and another with *then.*

_____

_____

---

5   caterpillar   undoubtedly

Note the *er* in the first part of *caterpillar,* and the *ar* at the end. Note the *ed* in *undoubtedly.*

a. Pronounce *cat er pil lar* to yourself, exaggerating both the *er* and the *ar.*
b. In *undoubtedly,* note the silent *b.* Note also that the next-to-last syllable is *ed.* Pronounce the word three times, exaggerating the *ed.*
c. Write a short sentence about what will *undoubtedly* happen to a fuzzy *caterpillar.*

_____

_____

1

b. dIvide, dIvide
   dIvine, dIvine

2

b. dilapidated, dilapidated
   discretion, discretion
   disgusted, disgusted

---

3   Models:

b. You have very good *sense.*
   I have not seen him *since* yesterday.

---

4   Models:

b. He earned more money *than* before.
   Then he found that he was spending more.

6 affect effect

It will help you to spell *affect* and *effect* if you do not pronounce them quite the same. Say *uh* for the first sound of *affect*, and *eh* for the first sound of *effect*.

a. Pronounce *affect* and *effect* to yourself as suggested.
b. Copy: The bad news *affected* the stock market.
     The *effect* of the medicine did not last long.
     The new ruler *effected* many changes of policy.

_____

_____

_____

7 introduce prospective geography

a. Say to yourself *in tro duce*. Exaggerate the *tro*.
b. Say to yourself *pro spec tive*. Exaggerate the *pro*. (*Prospective* refers to something expected to happen in the near future, as *a prospective trip*.)
c. Say to yourself *ge og ra phy*. Exaggerate the pause between *ge* and *og*, and exaggerate the *ra*.
d. Copy: I *introduced* my *prospective* wife to the *geography* of the area.

_____

_____

8 appreciate appreciation

a. Although there are several accepted pronunciations for each of these words, you will be more likely to remember the spelling if you use an ē sound in the second syllable. Also note the double *p*. Say the word several times, exaggerating the *e*.
b. Write a short sentence for each of the words.

_____

_____

9

Match each of the following definitions with one of the words studied in this unit. Either the first or the last letters have been supplied. Write the word in full.

a. from the past time to now, [s] _____
b. filled with dislike, _____ [usted]
c. the result, _____ [fect]
d. certainly, very probably, [und] _____
e. show gratitude for, [ap] _____

5 Model:

c. *Undoubtedly* a fuzzy *caterpillar* will someday turn into a moth.

6

b. The bad news *affected* the stock market.
    The *effect* of the medicine did not last long.
    The new ruler *effected* many changes of policy.

7

d. I *introduced* my *prospective* wife to the *geography* of the area.

8 Models:

b. We *appreciate* your gift.
    Our *appreciation* is genuine.

10

Follow the instructions for Frame 9.

a. in comparison with, [th] _____
b. study of the surface of the earth, _____ [phy]
c. expected to happen in the near future, _____ [spective]
d. to separate, _____ [vide]
e. gratitude, [ap] _____

11

Follow the instructions for Frame 9.

a. a future moth or butterfly, [cat] _____
b. worn and rickety, _____ [dated]
c. next; at that time, [th] _____
d. bring into use; present formally, _____ [duce]

12

Follow the instructions for Frame 9.

a. to have influence upon, _____ [fect]
b. holy, _____ [vine]
c. judgment, _____ [cretion]
d. power of the mind, _____ [nse]

13

Choose from the words we studied in this unit the one that best fits each blank, and write it in full. Either the first or the last letters have been supplied.

A [cat] _____ was crawling up the wall of the _____ [dated] garage. Timmy wondered what the _____ [fect] would be if he poked the wee beastie. _____ [nce] Timmy was not very brave, he used _____ [cretion] and picked up a twig to poke with. [Th] _____ he approached the furry creature slowly.

14

Follow the instructions for Frame 13.

a. Missing short putts always makes my father _____ [usted].
b. Grades _____ [fect] one's chances of getting into college.
c. _____ [vide] 343 by 7.
d. Let me _____ [duce] you to my sister.
e. In _____ [phy] we learned about the rivers of Europe.

9

a. since
b. disgusted
c. effect
d. undoubtedly
e. appreciate

10

a. than
b. geography
c. prospective
d. divide
e. appreciation

11

a. caterpillar
b. dilapidated
c. then
d. introduce

12

a. affect
b. divine
c. discretion
d. sense

13

caterpillar
dilapidated
effect
Since
discretion
Then

15

Follow the instructions for Frame 13.

a. You will need more [th] _____ six dollars.
b. In a blind person the _____ [nse] of touch may be strongly developed.
c. He asked the blessing of the _____ [vine] Power.
d. The _____ [spective] bridegroom was already panicky.
e. I [ap] _____ all the work you have done.

14

a. disgusted
b. affect
c. Divide
d. introduce
e. geography

16

Study each word that you misspelled in Frames 9–15. Pronounce it to yourself slowly and carefully, exaggerating the part that is a trouble spot for you. Write the correct spelling of each missed word three times. Check your spellings against the list above Frame 1.

15

a. than
b. sense
c. divine
d. prospective
e. appreciate

UNIT 20 · Faulty pronunciation: using the wrong sounds (II)

WORDS TREATED

accept	despair	especially	religion	vicinity
advice	destroy	except	response	
describe	destruction	inaugurate	series	
description	device	partner	trustee	

1   partner   inaugurate

Partner and *inaugurate* are two of the words often misspelled because a wrong sound creeps into the pronunciation.

a. Say to yourself *part ner*. Say the *t* clearly.
b. Say to yourself *in au gu rate*. Exaggerate the *u* in *gu*.
c. Copy: His *partner* decided to *inaugurate* a new scheme.

_____

_____

2   describe   description   destroy   destruction

Careless pronunciation of the first syllable in each of the four words above also may lead to misspelling.

a. Say to yourself *de scribe, de scrip tion, de stroy, de struc tion*. Say the *de* very strongly.
b. Copy: To *describe* is to give a *description*.
  To *destroy* is to engage in *destruction*.

_____

_____

1

c. His *partner* decided to *inaugurate* a new scheme.

3   especially   response   despair

Notice the *esp* in each of the words above.

a. Say *especially* to yourself, exaggerating the *es*.
b. Say *response* and *despair* to yourself, exaggerating the *re* and *de*.
c. Copy: *Especially,* your *response* must not be one of *despair.*

_____

_____

4   accept   except

Accept should be pronounced as if the first two letters were *ak*. *Except* has the sound of *eks* at the beginning, as the letter *x* stands for two sounds, *k* and *s*. You *accept* a gift. If you make an exception of something, you *except* it.

a. Pronounce to yourself *ac cept the gift.* Exaggerate the *ac*.
b. Pronounce to yourself *all ex cept Mabel.* Exaggerate the *ex*.
c. Copy: *accept* the gift
        all *except* Mabel

_____

_____

5   religion   trustee

Note the *e* in *religion*. In *trustee* (like a trustee of a bank) note the *ee*. (A trusted prisoner is called a *trusty*, not a *trustee*; a banker would not like to be called a *trusty*.)

a. Say *re li gion* to yourself. Exaggerate the *re*.
b. Say *trus tee* to yourself. Say the *tee* very strongly.
c. Copy: Each *trustee* of the bank believes in a different *religion*.

_____

_____

6   device   advice

If you wonder whether to write *device* or *devise*, *advice* or *advise*, notice the pronunciation. If it is pronounced like *ice*, use *ice*. *Device* and *advice* are both nouns.

a. Say *advice, device.* Be sure to end with *ice*.
b. Copy: He took my *advice*
        About a *device*
        To catch mice
        On the ice.

_____

_____

_____

2

b. To *describe* is to give a *description*.
   To *destroy* is to engage in *destruction*.

3

c. *Especially,* your *response* must not be one of *despair.*

4

c. *accept* the gift
   all *except* Mabel

5

c. Each *trustee* of the bank believes in a different *religion.*

7 series vicinity

Vicinity comes from Latin *vicinus*, meaning neighboring or nearby. That is why the second letter is an *i*, although it is sometimes misspelled since the sound of that letter is not distinctly pronounced.

a. Say *vi cin i ty* to yourself. Exaggerate the sound of the first *i*, pronouncing it like the *i* in *did*.

b. Some people make *series* sound like *serious* (maybe because they take the World Series so seriously!). The normal pronunciation, though, is *seer'ēz*. Say *series* aloud twice.

c. Copy: A *series* of burglaries occurred in the *vicinity*.

_____

_____

8

Match each of the following definitions with a word studied in this unit. Either the first or the last letters have been supplied.

a. one who shares work or a business, [pa] _____
b. suggestion, [ad] _____
c. neighborhood, _____ [inity]
d. one thing after another, [se] _____

9

Follow the instructions for Frame 8.

a. install; begin, [inaug] _____
b. gadget; mechanism, [de] _____
c. person responsible for belongings or affairs of another, [trus] _____
d. tell about the appearance of, _____ [scribe]

10

Follow the instructions for Frame 8.

a. do away with, _____ [stroy]
b. particularly, _____ [pecially]
c. hopelessness, _____ [spair]
d. to receive; take willingly, _____ [cept]

11

Follow the instructions for Frame 8.

a. an account of the appearance of, _____ [scription]
b. a breaking up or getting rid of, _____ [uction]
c. deep belief, _____ [ligion]
d. other than; to leave out, _____ [cept]
e. an answer, _____ [sponse]

6

b. He took my *advice*
   About a *device*
   To catch mice
   On the ice.

7

c. A *series* of burglaries occurred in the *vicinity*.

8

a. partner
b. advice
c. vicinity
d. series

9

a. inaugurate
b. device
c. trustee
d. describe

10

a. destroy
b. especially
c. despair
d. accept

12

Choose from the words we studied in this unit the one that best fits each blank. Either the first or the last letters have been supplied. Write each word in full.

The [ad] _____ of his [par] _____, who was a [trus] _____ of the bank, was that he should make no _____ [sponse] to the letter. But George was so deep in _____ [spair] that he could think of nothing _____ [cept] seeing a lawyer at once.

13

Follow the instructions for Frame 12.

a. The _____ [struction] caused by the tornado was great.
b. Many a war has been fought over _____ [ligion].
c. Dotty wrote a vivid _____ [scription] of the scene.
d. Will you _____ [cept] the offer?
e. The sunburn was _____ [pecially] painful.

14

Follow the instructions for Frame 12.

a. In January every four years we [inaug] _____ a President.
b. Are there any lakes in the _____ [nity]?
c. I can't _____ [scribe] the bandit accurately.
d. An anemometer is a _____ [vice] to measure wind velocity.
e. When you have read the letters, _____ [stroy] them.
f. The Yankees were in the World [Se] _____ that year.

15

Study each word that you misspelled in Frames 8–14. Pronounce it to yourself slowly and carefully, exaggerating the part that is a trouble spot for you. Write the correct spelling of each missed word three times. Check your spellings against the list above Frame 1.

11

a. description
b. destruction
c. religion
d. except
e. response

12

advice
partner
trustee
response
despair
except

13

a. destruction
b. religion
c. description
d. accept
e. especially

14

a. inaugurate
b. vicinity
c. describe
d. device
e. destroy
f. Series

UNIT 21 · Words like *planned* and *stopping*

WORDS TREATED

batter	dipper	planned	shipping	slimmest	sunning	whipping
biggest	dropped	quizzed	sinner	slipper	swimming	
clannish	fatter	rubbing	sipped	sloppy	tinny	
dimmer	hotter	runner	sitting	stopping	wagged	

---

1   plan   stop   dim

Let's see in what three ways the three words above are alike.
First, how many syllables are in each word? _____

2

Look again at *plan, stop,* and *dim.*
Does each word end in a single consonant or a single vowel? __
_____

1
one

3

Look once more at *plan, stop,* and *dim.*
Just before the final consonant, does each word have (A) a single consonant, (B) a single vowel, or (C) two vowels? _____

2
consonant

4

One syllable	*Single vowel*	*One final consonant*
plan	pl a n	pla n
stop	st__p	sto__
dim	d__m	di__

What letters belong in the empty boxes?

3
B

---

5   planned   stopped   dimmed

When we add *-ed* to these one-syllable words that end in a single vowel and a single consonant, the last letter is _____ (Tell what happens to it).

4
o, p
i, m

---

6   planning   stopping   dimming
         planner   stopper   dimmer

When we add *–ing* or *–er* to these one-syllable words that end in a single vowel and a single consonant, the last letter is _____
(Tell what happens to it).

5
doubled

7

We have added –ed, –ing, and –er to our three words. Is the first letter of –ed, –ing, and –er a consonant or a vowel? _____

8

We have seen that when we add a suffix beginning with a vowel to a one-syllable word that ends with a single vowel and a single consonant, we double the _____ (What?).

9

The rule you have just learned applies to hundreds of words in English. Let's see how it works with a few. Write the words called for in Frames 9–12.

a. Add –est to big. _____

b. Add –ing to swim. _____

c. Add –ed to drop. _____

d. Add –er to dip. _____

10

Now write these words:

a. Add –ish to clan. _____

b. Add –ed to quiz. _____

c. Add –ing to ship. _____

d. Add –er to run. _____

e. Add –ing to sun. _____

f. Add –y to tin, as in John's trumpet sounds _____

11

Write these words:

a. Add –ing to whip. _____

b. Add –ed to sip. _____

c. Add –er to bat. _____

d. Add –er to slip. _____

e. Add –y to slop. _____

f. Add –ing to sit. _____

12

Write these words:

a. Add –er to fat. _____

b. Add –est to slim. _____

c. Add –er to hot. _____

d. Add –ed to wag. _____

e. Add –er to sin. _____

f. Add –ing to rub. _____

6

doubled

7

vowel

8

last letter

9

a. biggest

b. swimming

c. dropped

d. dipper

10

a. clannish

b. quizzed

c. shipping

d. runner

e. sunning

f. tinny

11

a. whipping

b. sipped

c. batter

d. slipper

e. sloppy

f. sitting

13

Let's refresh our minds about what we have been doing.
We take a one-syllable word like *fat*.

We see that it ends in $\boxed{a}$ $\boxed{t}$ and (one vowel / one consonant.)

We add to it $-\boxed{e}$ r, which starts with a vowel.
We double the last letter. Our word is _____ (What?).

12

a. fatter
b. slimmest
c. hotter
d. wagged
e. sinner
f. rubbing

14

a. Our rule does not apply to words like *cheap* → *cheaper* because *cheap* has _____ (How many?) vowels before the *p*.
b. Our rule does not apply to words like *jump* → *jumped* because *jump* has _____ (How many?) consonants at the end.
c. Our rule does not apply to words like *man* → *manly* because *–ly* doesn't start with a _____ (What?).
d. Our rule does not apply to words ending in *x: box* + *–ed* = *boxed; box* + *–er* = _____ (What?).

13

fatter

15

Look carefully at the correct spelling of each word you missed in Frames 9–12. Notice the right way to spell those that you had wrong. Say the words slowly to yourself. Write the words three times each, and check above Frame 1 to make sure that you spelled them correctly.

14

a. two
b. two
c. vowel
d. boxer

UNIT 22 · Words like *beginning* and *occurred*

WORDS TREATED

allotted	controlled	excelled	preferred	transferred
beginner	controlling	forgotten	propeller	unforgettable
beginning	deferred	occurred	referred	
committed	deterred	occurrence	referring	
conferred	equipped	omitted	repellent	

1   begin   occur

Let's see what the words *begin* and *occur* have in common.

a. The accent in both *begin* and *occur* is on the _____ (*first* or *last*?) syllable.
b. Both *begin* and *occur* end with a single _____ (*consonant* or *vowel*?).
c. Just before the last letter of *begin* and *occur* there is a single _____ (*consonant* or *vowel*?).

2

		One vowel	*One consonant*
be	G	I	N
oc	C	U	R

last syllable accented

Which three of the following words follow the same pattern as that shown above for *begin* and *occur*?

predict   control   exceed   suffer   refer   commit

_____ , _____ , _____

3

begin + –ing = beginning
occur + –ed = occurred

When a suffix like *–ing* or *–ed* (starting with a vowel) is added to a word like *begin* or *occur*, what happens to the last letter of the word?

_____

4

A hundred or more common English words are like *begin* and *occur*. That is, they are accented on the last syllable and end in a single vowel and a single consonant. If you understand the principle of doubling the final letter, you can correctly add a suffix starting with a vowel. Try it on these words.

a. Add *–ed* to *control.* _____
b. Add *–ing* to *control.* _____

5

Now apply our principle to these words:

a. Add *–ed* to *refer.* _____
b. Add *–ing* to *refer.* _____
c. Add *–ed* to *commit.* _____
d. Add *–er* to *begin.* _____
e. Add *–ence* to *occur.* _____
f. Add *–ed* to *transfer.* _____

6

a. Add *–ent* to *repel.* _____
b. Add *–ed* to *prefer.* _____
c. Add *–ed* to *equip.* _____
d. Add *–ed* to *deter.* _____
e. Add *–ed* to *allot.* _____
f. Add *–ed* to *confer.* _____

1

a. last
b. consonant
c. vowel

2

control
refer
commit

3

It is doubled.

4

a. controlled
b. controlling

5

a. referred
b. referring
c. committed
d. beginner
e. occurrence
f. transferred

7

a. Add *-ed* to *defer.* _____
b. Add *-ed* to *excel.* _____
c. Add *-en* to *forgot.* _____
d. Add *-er* to *propel.* _____
e. Add *-ed* to *omit.* _____
f. Add *un* + *forget* + *-able.* _____

6

a. repellent
b. preferred
c. equipped
d. deterred
e. allotted
f. conferred

8

Words like *preference* and *reference* are exceptions to our principle because in these words the accent shifts away from the *fer* syllable.

   In *preferred* and *referring* the doubling takes place because in these words the accent _____ (*is* or *is not*) on the part of the word with *fer*.

7

a. deferred
b. excelled
c. forgotten
d. propeller
e. omitted
f. unforgettable

9

Choose the word studied in this unit that best fits each definition. The first letters have been supplied. Write the complete word.

a. an event, [oc] _____
b. fitted out, [eq] _____
c. unpleasant; disagreeable, [rep] _____
d. managing, [con] _____
e. not remembered, [for] _____

8

is

10

Follow the instructions for Frame 9.

a. happened, [oc] _____
b. one who starts, [beg] _____
c. liked better, [pre] _____
d. prevented, [de] _____
e. divided as shares, [al] _____
f. changed from a place, [trans] _____

9

a. occurrence
b. equipped
c. repellent
d. controlling
e. forgotten

11

Follow the instructions for Frame 9.

a. turned for information, [ref] _____
b. memorable, [unfor] _____
c. a device for moving a boat, [pro] _____
d. starting, [beg] _____
e. managed; had charge of, [con] _____
f. left out, [om] _____

10

a. occurred
b. beginner
c. preferred
d. deterred
e. allotted
f. transferred

12

Follow the instructions for Frame 9.

a. mentioning; calling attention to, [ref] _____

b. was better than, [exc] _____

c. postponed, [def] _____

d. consulted, [con] _____

e. pledged; confined, [com] _____

11

a. referred
b. unforgettable
c. propeller
d. beginning
e. controlled
f. omitted

13

In this unit we have learned that the final letter is doubled when a suffix starting with a vowel is added to a word like *begin*, which ends in a single vowel and a single consonant and is accented on the last syllable.

To which of the following additional words would this rule apply?

defeat   deny   forget   permit   impel   offer

_____ (Which words?)

12

a. referring
b. excelled
c. deferred
d. conferred
e. committed

14

Study each word that you misspelled in Frames 9–12. Write each missed word correctly three times. Check your spellings against the list above Frame 1.

13

forget
permit
impel

UNIT 23 · Words ending in –*ise*

WORDS TREATED

advertise	despise	exercise	supervise
advise	devise	improvise	surprise
comprise	disguise	merchandise	
compromise	enterprise	revise	

---

1   exercise

Only some thirty-five fairly common words end with –*ise* in American spelling. (The British use –*ise* for some words that Americans spell with –*ize*.) Since words like *wise* and *rise* cause little difficulty, we need to concentrate on only a dozen or so troublemakers.

One of these is *exercise*. Note the *er* and the *c*, as well as the –*ise* ending.

Write: *ex er cise, exercise* _____ , _____

---

2   disguise

Disguise causes trouble because of the silent *u*, as well as the *–ise*.

Copy: *Guise* and *disguise* are common English words ending in *–uise*.

_____

_____

3   comprise   enterprise   surprise

Note that the three words above all end in *–prise*.

Copy: This *enterprise comprises surprises*.

_____

4   advise   devise

The two words above are used as verbs: I *advise* you to accept; otherwise he will *devise* some solution.

Make up a short sentence of your own with each verb.

_____

_____

5   improvise   revise   supervise

Three more *–vise* words are listed above.

Try to make up a sentence that will include all three.

_____

6   compromise   merchandise

Copy: He would accept no *compromise;* the *merchandise* must be shipped at once.

_____

_____

7   advertise   despise (note the **de**)

Copy: I *despise* companies that *advertise* misleadingly.

_____

_____

8

Match the most appropriate of the words we studied in this unit with each definition. The first letters are supplied. Write each word in full.

a. to examine and improve, [re] _____

b. to give advice, [ad] _____

c. to praise in an attempt to sell, [ad] _____

1

ex er cise,
exercise

2

Guise and *disguise* are common English words ending in *–uise*.

3

This *enterprise comprises surprises*.

4   Models:

Please *advise* me.
Can you *devise* a new test?

5   Model:

Please *supervise* while I *improvise* a way to *revise*.

6

He would accept no *compromise;* the *merchandise* must be shipped at once.

7

I *despise* companies that *advertise* misleadingly.

9

Follow the instructions for Frame 8.

a. active practice, [ex] _____

b. to include or contain, [com] _____

c. to oversee, [super] _____

d. to make up without previous thought, [im] _____

8

a. revise
b. advise
c. advertise

10

Follow the instructions for Frame 8.

a. clothes, etc., used to hide one's identity, [dis] _____

b. settlement of a dispute in which both parties yield something, [com] _____

c. to detest, [de] _____

d. goods, [mer] _____

9

a. exercise
b. comprise
c. supervise
d. improvise

11

Follow the instructions for Frame 8.

a. to think out or create, [de] _____

b. something unexpected, [sur] _____

c. an important undertaking, [ent] _____

10

a. disguise
b. compromise
c. despise
d. merchandise

12

Write in full the unfinished words, choosing from those studied in this unit.

A spelling [ex] _____ must [com] _____ the words studied in a lesson. To [dev] _____ clear sentences or definitions is important. It is often necessary to [re] _____ a single sentence several times. Students sometimes also need to be [ad] _____ [d] about peculiarities of words, some of which may [sur] _____ them. All in all, preparing spelling materials is an interesting [enter] _____ .

11

a. devise
b. surprise
c. enterprise

13

Follow the instructions for Frame 12.

Don't [des] _____ all cheap [mer] _____. Sometimes, without making a [com] _____ with good quality, a store can [ad] _____ really low prices. The goods to be sold may be excellent items that are only a little shopworn. On the other hand, the person who [super] _____ [s] a department may [im] _____ ideas for a sale and [dis] _____ junky items as good ones.

12

exercise
comprise
devise
revise
advised
surprise
enterprise

14

Study each word that you misspelled in Frames 8–13. Write each missed word correctly three times. Check your answers against the list above Frame 1.

13

despise
merchandise
compromise
advertise
supervises
improvise
disguise

UNIT 24 · Words ending in *–eous*

WORDS TREATED

advantageous	erroneous	miscellaneous
beauteous	gorgeous	outrageous
courageous	heterogeneous	righteous
courteous	homogeneous	simultaneous

---

1   erroneous   courageous

If you wonder whether a word ends in *–eous*, *–ious*, *–uous*, or *–ous*, the best guide (though not completely reliable) is careful pronunciation.

   A word that should be spelled with *–eous* generally has fairly distinct ē ŭs sounds at the end, like *erroneous* (e rō nē ŭs). Sometimes it has sounds like *age* (āj) before the end, like *courageous* (kŭ rā jŭs). Say and then write *erroneous* and *courageous*.

_____, _____

---

2   miscellaneous   simultaneous

Say *miscellaneous* and *simultaneous*. Note the *e* sound.

Write *miscellaneous* twice and *simultaneous* three times. Capitalize the *e* before *ous*.

_____, _____

_____, _____,

_____

---

3   homogeneous   heterogeneous

Say *homogeneous* and its opposite, *heterogeneous*. Note the *e* sound.
Copy: Is this class *homogeneous* or *heterogeneous* in ability?

_____

_____

1

erroneous
courageous

2

miscellanEous, miscellanEous
simultanEous, simultanEous,
   simultanEous

---

4 beauteous courteous righteous

Say *beauteous* and *courteous*. The word *righteous* is spelled similarly but lacks the *e* sound that the other words have.

Copy: She's a *beauteous, courteous* damsel, but oh, so *righteous*!

_____

_____

5 advantageous outrageous

Two words that are like *courageous* are *advantageous* and *outrageous*. Note the sound of *age* before the end.

Make up a sentence that includes both *advantageous* and *outrageous*.

_____

6 gorgeous

The word *gorgeous* stands alone in this group, since it has neither an *e* sound nor the sound of *age*. If *gorgeous* troubles you, you may remember that a beautiful ravine might be called a gorgeous gorge.

Write *gorgeous gorge* twice.

_____ , _____

7

Let's try to make up a couple of silly sentences that will contain all twelve of the *–eous* words we have studied. Write each incomplete word in full.

The [court] _____, [beaut] _____, [gorg] _____, and [right] _____ damsel showed that she was [courag] _____ by not bowing to the villain's [outrag] _____ and [heterogen] _____ or [miscellan] _____ demands. It was [erron] _____ of him to persevere and not at all [advantag] _____ to his cause, when a [homogen] _____ group of students made a [simultan] _____ arrival.

3

Is this class *homogeneous* or *heterogeneous* in ability?

4

She's a *beauteous, courteous* damsel, but oh, so *righteous!*

5 Model:

It would not be *advantageous* to accept such *outrageous* demands.

6

gorgeous gorge
gorgeous gorge

8

Match each definition with one of the words we have studied in this unit. The first letters have been supplied. Write the whole word.

a. happening at the same time, [si] _____
b. favorable, or possessing advantages, [ad] _____
c. the opposite of homogeneous, [he] _____
d. the opposite of heterogeneous, [ho] _____
e. brave, [co] _____
f. beautiful, [b] _____

9

Follow the instructions for Frame 8.

a. magnificent, [go] _____
b. showing sincere politeness, [co] _____
c. free of sin, [ri] _____
d. mixed, or of several varieties, [mi] _____
e. in error, [er] _____
f. violent; very offensive, [out] _____

10

Study each word that you misspelled in Frames 7–9. Write each correctly three times. Check your spellings against the list above Frame 1.

7

courteous
beauteous
gorgeous
righteous
courageous
outrageous
heterogeneous
miscellaneous
erroneous
advantageous
homogeneous
simultaneous

8

a. simultaneous
b. advantageous
c. heterogeneous
d. homogeneous
e. courageous
f. beauteous

9

a. gorgeous
b. courteous
c. righteous
d. miscellaneous
e. erroneous
f. outrageous

UNIT 25 · Words with –*sede*, –*ceed*, and –*cede*

WORDS TREATED

accede	exceed	proceed	supersede
antecedent	intercede	recede	
cede	precede	secede	
concede	procedure	succeed	

1

Although only about a dozen English words end in the sound of "seed," they cause considerable trouble because some of them are often used.

The way to learn these spellings is to divide and conquer. Learn that only one word ends in *–sede* and that only three end in *–ceed*.

a. How many English words end in *–sede*? _____
b. How many English words end in *–ceed*? _____

---

2   supersede

General Grant *superseded* him in command.

Supersede is the one English word ending in *–sede*. It comes from Latin *super* (above) and *sedere* (to sit). In the sample sentence, General Grant "sat above" his predecessor when he superseded him.

Copy: *Supersede* is the only English word ending in *–sede*.

_____

_____

---

3   proceed   succeed   exceed

Proceed, succeed, and *exceed* are the only three English words that end in *–ceed*. You will save yourself later trouble if you memorize them now.

Copy: At last we would *succeed*. The guard told us that we might *proceed* if our baggage did not *exceed* one hundred pounds.

_____

_____

_____

4

Make up short sentences of your own using *proceed, succeed,* and *exceed.*

_____

_____

_____

---

5   cede   accede   concede   intercede   precede
**   recede   secede**

All other words that we are considering end in *–cede*.
Copy the seven words above.

_____, _____, _____, _____,

_____, _____, _____

1

a. one
b. three

2

Supersede is the only English word ending in *–sede*.

3

At last we would *succeed*. The guard told us that we might *proceed* if our baggage did not *exceed* one hundred pounds.

4

(Check your spelling:
  proceed
  succeed
  exceed)

6

Procedure and *antecedent* have *ced* in the middle.

Copy: The best *procedure* is to act promptly.

The *antecedent* of this pronoun is *James*.

_____

_____

7

Let's summarize.

a. The only English word ending in *–sede* is _____ (What?).

b. The three English words ending in *–ceed* are _____, _____, _____ (What?).

c. All other words that we are considering end in _____ (What?).

d. Two words with *ced* in the middle are _____, _____ (What?).

8

Using words that we have studied in this unit and that make the best sense, write in full each incomplete word.

a. If at first you don't [s] _____, try, try again.

b. His speed did not [e] _____ thirty miles an hour.

c. You may [p] _____ me; I'll come a little later.

9

Follow the instructions for Frame 8.

a. We watched the flood waters [r] _____ slowly.

b. This [p] _____ will take too long.

c. I regret that I cannot [a] _____ to your wishes.

10

Follow the instructions for Frame 8.

a. When the two boys began fighting, I tried to [i] _____.

b. You must [p] _____ to your destination at once.

c. Some of the states began to [s] _____ from the Union.

d. I [c] _____ the truth of only two of your statements.

11

Follow the instructions for Frame 8.

a. Great Britain agreed to [c] _____ the disputed territory to France.

b. The new regulations [s] _____ those issued last month.

c. A personal pronoun usually refers to an [a] _____.

5

cede	precede
accede	recede
concede	secede
intercede	

6

The best *procedure* is to act promptly

The *antecedent* of this pronoun is *James*.

7

a. supersede

b. proceed, succeed, exceed

c. –cede

d. procedure, antecedent

8

a. succeed

b. exceed

c. precede

9

a. recede

b. procedure

c. accede

10

a. intercede

b. proceed

c. secede

d. concede

12

Match each definition by writing in full a word we studied in this unit. The first letter has been given.

a. go in front of, [p] _____
b. go back, [r] _____
c. agree to, [a] _____
d. gain one's objective, [s] _____
e. that which goes before, [a] _____
f. be greater than, [e] _____
g. admit, as in an argument, [c] _____
h. grant, as territory, [c] _____
i. withdraw, [s] _____
j. go between, [i] _____
k. method of doing, [p] _____
l. replace or supplant, [s] _____
m. move forward, [p] _____

11

a. cede
b. supersede
c. antecedent

13

Study each word that you misspelled in Frames 8–12. Remember that only *supersede* ends in *–sede* and that only *proceed, succeed,* and *exceed* end in *–ceed*. Write each missed word correctly three times. Check your spellings against the list above Frame 1.

12

a. precede
b. recede
c. accede
d. succeed
e. antecedent
f. exceed
g. concede
h. cede
i. secede
j. intercede
k. procedure
l. supersede
m. proceed

UNIT 26 · Words ending in *–ence* or *–ent* (I)

WORDS TREATED

adherence	deference	inherent	recurrence	Exception:
adherent	deterrence	interference	recurrent	perseverance
coherence	deterrent	irreverence	reference	
coherent	inference	irreverent	reverence	
conference	inherence	preference	reverent	

1

People often have trouble in remembering whether some words end in *–ence* or *–ance, –ent* or *–ant*. Although no rules cover all such words, we shall look at some that are generally true.

prefer refer confer

The three words above are alike in that each ends with _____ (What letter?) and each is accented on the _____ (*first* or *last*?) syllable.

2 **preference** **reference** **conference**	**1**
Notice that in the three words above, we start with *prefer*, *refer*, and *confer*, which end in *r* and are accented on the last syllable.	*r* last
a. To make the verb *prefer* into the noun *preference*, we add _____ (What?).	
b. To make the verb *refer* into the noun *reference*, we add _____ (What?).	
c. To make the verb *confer* into the noun *conference*, we add _____ (What?).	
3 **defer** **infer**	**2**
a. Does each of the two verbs above end in *r* and have the accent on the last syllable? _____	a. *ence* b. *ence* c. *ence*
b. Write *–nce* nouns for the two verbs at the top of this frame.	
_____ , _____	
4 **deter** **recur**	**3**
a. Does each of the two verbs above end in *r* and have the accent on the last syllable? _____	a. yes b. deference, inference
b. Write *–nce* nouns for the two verbs at the top of this frame. (Double the final *r* in each word. See also Unit 22.)	
_____ , _____	
c. Write the *–nt* form of *deter* and *recur*.	
_____ , _____	
5	**4**
We have seen that we use an *–ence* or *–ent* spelling when we change a word like *prefer* to a different form. We usually use the same ending if the word ends in *–ere*, like *interfere*.	a. yes b. *deterrence, recurrence* c. *deterrent, recurrent*
Write the *–nce* form of *interfere*. _____	
6	**5**
a. Write the *–nce* and *–nt* forms of *revere*.	interference
_____ , _____	
b. Write the same words again, but this time put *ir* in front of each.	
_____ , _____	
7	**6**
a. Write the *–nce* and *–nt* forms of *cohere*.	a. reverence, reverent b. irreverence, irreverent
_____ , _____	
b. Write the *–nce* and *–nt* forms of *inhere*.	
_____ , _____	
c. Write the *–nce* and *–nt* forms of *adhere*.	
_____ , _____	

8

There is one important exception to the use of *–ence* after words ending in *–ere*. *Perseverance*, because it comes from Latin *perseverantia*, ends in *–ance*.

Copy: *Perseverance* ends in *–ance* because it comes from *perseverantia*.

_____

_____

9

Using words studied in this unit, complete each sentence. Write the words in full.

a. A person in church should be [rev] _____.

b. If all parts of a story fit together well, we say that the story is [coh] _____.

c. In football a huddle is really a [conf] _____ of players.

10

Follow the instructions for Frame 9.

a. You like blue best, but my [pref] _____ is for green.

b. When a person reasons that something is probably true, he is making an [inf] _____.

11

Follow the instructions for Frame 9.

a. One thing that many newlyweds resent is [interf] _____ by in-laws.

b. He bowed his head in [rev] _____.

c. In music a [recu] _____ theme is one that is heard over and over.

12

Follow the instructions for Frame 9.

a. I found a [ref] _____ to Swedish literature somewhere in this magazine.

b. The servant spoke to his aged master with [def] _____ in his voice.

c. He called her for another date. Her coldness was no [de] _____.

7

a. coherence, coherent
b. inherence, inherent
c. adherence, adherent

8

Perseverance ends in *–ance* because it comes from *perseverantia*.

9

a. reverent
b. coherent
c. conference

10

a. preference
b. inference

11

a. interference
b. reverence
c. recurrent

13

Follow the instructions for Frame 9.

a. If something is [inh] _____, it is inborn.
b. Although the minister was standing near him, Joe made an [irrev] _____ remark.
c. Keep trying. [Persev] _____ is a great virtue.
d. One who adheres to a belief is called an [ad] _____.

14

To match the definitions below, write words we studied in this unit. The first letters have been supplied. Write the word in full.

a. act of referring, [r] _____
b. something that deters, [de] _____
c. act of interfering, [i] _____
d. happening over and over, [r] _____
e. respectful, [r] _____
f. a meeting and discussion, [c] _____
g. act of sticking together, [c] _____
h. inborn, [i] _____
i. act of disrespect, [i] _____
j. yielding to the wishes of another, [d] _____
k. persistence, [p] _____
l. the following of a belief or a cause, [ad] _____

15

Study each word that you missed in Frames 9–14. Check to see what its trouble spot is for you. Try to see the words in your mind. Write each missed word three times. Check above Frame 1 to make sure that you are now spelling correctly.

12

a. reference
b. deference
c. deterrent (or deterrence)

13

a. inherent
b. irreverent
c. Perseverance
d. adherent

14

a. reference   g. coherence
b. deterrent   h. inherent
   (or deterrence) i. irreverence
c. interference   j. deference
d. recurrent   k. perseverance
e. reverent   l. adherence
f. conference

UNIT 27 · Words ending in *–ence* or *–ent* (II)

WORDS TREATED

absence	competence	convenience	dependence	evidence	existence
absent	competent	convenient	dependent	evident	existent
adolescence	confidence	correspondence	eminence	excellence	impudence
adolescent	confident	correspondent	eminent	excellent	impudent

1   absEnt—absEnce   correspondEnce—correspondEnt
       competEnt—competEnce   dependEnce—dependEnt

The examples above illustrate the fact that many adjectives ending in
–ent have corresponding nouns ending in *–ence.* If you know how to
spell either one, you should have no trouble with the other.

Copy the eight words at the top of this frame. Capitalize each *e* that
is capitalized above.

_____ , _____

_____ , _____

_____ , _____

_____ , _____

2

Copy the adjectives below, and write the corresponding nouns, which
end in *–ence.*

adolescent, _____ , _____

confident, _____ , _____

1

absEnt, absEnce
competEnt, competEnce
correspondEnce, correspondEnt
dependEnce, dependEnt

3

Copy the nouns below, and write the corresponding adjectives, which
end in *–ent.*

convenience (Be careful not to omit any letters.)

_____ , _____

eminence, _____ , _____

2

adolescent, adolescence
confident, confidence

4

Copy the adjectives below, and write the corresponding nouns.

evident, _____ , _____

excellent, _____ , _____

3

convenience, convenient
eminence, eminent

5

Copy the nouns below, and write the corresponding adjectives.

existence, _____ , _____

impudence, _____ , _____

4

evident, evidence
excellent, excellence

6

If we know that a word has forms ending in both *–nce* and *–nt* and if
we can spell either of them, we _____ (*can* or *cannot*?) also spell
the other.

5

existence, existent
impudence, impudent

7

In Frames 7–12, the words we have studied are used in pairs within sentences. Write in full each incomplete word.

a. Whenever you are [abs] _____, I remember that [abs] _____ makes the heart grow fonder.

b. [Adol] _____ is a joyful time for many young persons, but for others the [adol] _____ years are difficult.

8

Follow the instructions for Frame 7.

a. I know that he is [comp] _____; no one has ever denied his [comp] _____.

b. Because I am [conf] _____ of my own ability, my parents have [conf] _____ in me.

9

Follow the instructions for Frame 7.

a. Carrying water up the hill was not very [conv] _____, but having water to drink was more important than mere [conv] _____.

b. She likes geometry so much that she even discusses [corresp] _____ angles in her [corresp] _____.

10

Follow the instructions for Frame 7.

a. The [dep] _____ of one idea upon another is shown in a [dep] _____ clause.

b. My father is an [emin] _____ man, but our neighbors are unaware of his [emin] _____.

11

Follow the instructions for Frame 7.

a. It was [evid] _____ that this judge was not interested in hearing all the [evid] _____.

b. The [excel] _____ of fishing as a hobby is due in part to the fact that either inexpensive or [excel] _____ equipment may be used.

6

can

7

a. absent, absence
b. adolescence, adolescent

8

a. competent, competence
b. confident, confidence

9

a. convenient, convenience
b. correspondent, correspondence

10

a. dependence, dependent
b. eminent, eminence

12

Follow the instructions for Frame 7.

a. The [exist] _____ of bacteria where none had been [exist] _____ before could not be denied.

b. You are an [impud] _____ rascal, but I needn't endure your [impud] _____ .

13

Write the *–nt* form required by each definition, using a word studied in this unit. The first letters are given.

a. very good, [ex] _____
b. not present, [ab] _____
c. youthful, [ad] _____
d. existing, [ex] _____
e. smart-alecky, [imp] _____
f. clear; apparent, [ev] _____
g. high and mighty, [em] _____
h. corresponding, [cor] _____
i. easy to get or use, [con] _____
j. sure of oneself, [con] _____
k. able to do work well, [com] _____
l. reliant on someone else, [de] _____

14

Write the *–nce* form required by each definition, using a word studied in this unit.

a. state of being away, [ab] _____
b. high position, [em] _____
c. letter writing, [cor] _____
d. unusually good quality, [ex] _____
e. period before adulthood, [ad] _____
f. ease of securing or using, [con] _____
g. state of being, [ex] _____
h. reliance on another, [de] _____
i. ability to perform, [com] _____
j. facts helping to prove, [ev] _____
k. insolence, [im] _____
l. self-reliance, [con] _____

15

Study each word that you misspelled in Frames 7–14. Look hard at the part of the word that caused you trouble. Write each misspelled word correctly three times. Check your spellings against the list above Frame 1.

11

a. evident, evidence
b. excellence, excellent

12

a. existence, existent
b. impudent, impudence

13

a. excellent   g. eminent
b. absent   h. correspondent
c. adolescent   i. convenient
d. existent   j. confident
e. impudent   k. competent
f. evident   l. dependent

14

a. absence   g. existence
b. eminence   h. dependence
c. correspondence   i. competence
d. excellence   j. evidence
e. adolescence   k. impudence
f. convenience   l. confidence

UNIT 28 · Words ending in *–ence* or *–ent* (III)

WORDS TREATED

independence	insistent	patience	permanent	prominence	silent
independent	magnificence	patient	persistence	prominent	violence
innocence	magnificent	penitence	persistent	residence	violent
innocent	obedience	penitent	presence	resident	
insistence	obedient	permanence	present	silence	

---

1   innocEnt—innocEnce   residEnce—residEnt

       patiEnce—patiEnt   insistEnt—insistEnce

The examples above illustrate the fact that many adjectives ending in *–ent* have corresponding nouns ending in *–ence*. If you know how to spell either one, you should have no trouble with the other.

Copy the eight words at the top of this frame. Capitalize each *e* that is capitalized above.

————————, ————————   ————————, ————————

————————, ————————   ————————, ————————

2

Copy the adjectives below, and write the corresponding nouns, which end in *–ence.*

independent, ————————, ————————

magnificent, ————————, ————————

3

Copy the nouns below, and write the corresponding adjectives, which end in *–ent.*

obedience, ————————, ————————

penitence, ————————, ————————

persistence, ————————, ————————

4

Copy the adjectives below, and write the corresponding nouns.

present, ————————, ————————

permanent, ————————, ————————

prominent, ————————, ————————

1

innocEnt—innocEnce
patiEnce—patiEnt
residEnce—residEnt
insistEnt—insistEnce

2

independent, independence
magnificent, magnificence

3

obedience, obedient
penitence, penitent
persistence, persistent

5

Copy the nouns below, and write the corresponding adjectives.

silence, _____, _____

violence, _____, _____

6

If we know that a word has forms ending in both *–nce* and *–nt* and if we can spell either of them, we _____ (*can* or *cannot*?) also spell the other.

7

In Frames 7–12, the words we have studied are used in pairs within sentences. Write in full each incomplete word.

a. When the Declaration of [Ind] _____ was signed, it meant that the colonies were [ind] _____ of Great Britain.

b. The defendant kept saying that he was [inno] _____ but that he had no way to prove his [inno] _____.

8

Follow the instructions for Frame 7.

a. Why must you be so [insist] _____? Your stubborn [insist] _____ is hurting your cause.

b. Never had I seen so [magnif] _____ a sight! I shall always remember the [magnif] _____ of the Grand Canyon.

c. If [obed] _____ is a virtue, every child should learn to be [obed] _____.

9

Follow the instructions for Frame 7.

a. Please be [pat] _____. [Pat] _____ is often necessary.

b. George never seemed very [penit] _____ about his crime. Perhaps he was not capable of [penit] _____.

c. Stick to it a while longer! Be [persist] _____! [Persist] _____ may lead you to the treasure yet.

4

present, presence
permanent, permanence
prominent, prominence

5

silence, silent
violence, violent

6

can

7

a. Independence, independent
b. innocent, innocence

8

a. insistent, insistence
b. magnificent, magnificence
c. obedience, obedient

10

Follow the instructions for Frame 7.

a. Although he answered "[Pres] _____" when the roll was called, his [pres] _____ was of his body only.

b. Women call them "[perm] _____" waves, but their so-called [perm] _____ actually lasts only a few weeks or months.

11

Follow the instructions for Frame 7.

a. His [prom] _____ in our community is considerable. In fact, he is one of our most [prom] _____ citizens.

b. At that time his real [resid] _____ was in Wyoming, although he was called the [resid] _____ poet of the University of Montana.

12

Follow the instructions for Frame 7.

a. The forest was quiet, almost [sil] _____, at noon. Such [sil] _____ was unusual.

b. Western movies usually show acts of [viol] _____ performed by [viol] _____ men.

13

Write in full the –nt form required by each definition, using words studied in this unit. The first letters are given.

a. standing alone, [ind] _____
b. persistent; urgent, [ins] _____
c. following orders, [ob] _____
d. regretful, [pen] _____
e. lasting forever, [perm] _____
f. living at, [res] _____
g. furious; forceful, [viol] _____
h. not guilty, [inn] _____
i. splendid, [mag] _____
j. enduring calmly, [pat] _____
k. not absent, [pres] _____
l. well known, [prom] _____
m. going on resolutely, [persi] _____
n. quiet, [sil] _____

9

a. patient, Patience
b. penitent, penitence
c. persistent, Persistence

10

a. Present, presence
b. permanent, permanence

11

a. prominence, prominent
b. residence, resident

12

a. silent, silence
b. violence, violent

14

Write in full the *-nce* form required by each definition, using words studied in this unit. The first letters are given.

a. act of fury or force, [viol] _____

b. quietness, [sil] _____

c. place where one lives, [res] _____

d. a going on resolutely, [pers] _____

e. lasting quality, [perm] _____

f. state of being well known, [prom] _____

g. regret, [pen] _____

h. opposite of absence, [pres] _____

i. a following of orders, [ob] _____

j. calm endurance, [pat] _____

k. constant urging, [ins] _____

l. splendor, [mag] _____

m. a standing alone, [ind] _____

n. opposite of guilt, [inn] _____

13

a. independent
b. insistent
c. obedient
d. penitent
e. permanent
f. resident
g. violent

h. innocent
i. magnificent
j. patient
k. present
l. prominent
m. persistent
n. silent

15

Study each word that you misspelled in Frames 7–14. Look carefully at the part of the word that caused you trouble. Write each misspelled word correctly three times. Check your spellings against the list above Frame 1.

14

a. violence
b. silence
c. residence
d. persistence
e. permanence
f. prominence
g. penitence

h. presence
i. obedience
j. patience
k. insistence
l. magnificence
m. independence
n. innocence

UNIT 29 · Words ending in *–ence* or *–ent* (IV)

WORDS TREATED

audience	consistent	influence
circumference	consistence (consistency)	sentence
coincidence	essence	superintendent
conscience	experience	

1

What English word do you suppose came from the Latin *audientia*?
(Hint: It is a noun sometimes used to refer to a group of persons.)

_____

2

The *e* in Latin *audientia* accounts for the first *e* in the English *audience*.

a. What English noun came from Latin *circumferentia*?

_____

b. What English noun came from Latin *conscientia*?

_____

3

Explain why *circumference* and *conscience* each have *e* before the *n* in the last syllable.

_____

_____

4   experience   sentence

Even if you have never studied Latin, perhaps you can now figure out the Latin words from which *experience* and *sentence* came.

a. The Latin ancestor of *experience* was _____ (What?).

b. The Latin ancestor of *sentence* was _____ (What?).

5

a. What English noun do you suppose has come from Latin *essentia*? _____ (Yes, *essential* does, too, but here we are concerned with words ending in –*nce* or –*nt*.)

b. What English noun came from Latin *influentia?* _____

6   superintendent

Superintendent is the same as a Latin word, except that two letters have been chopped off the end of the Latin word. The Latin word is _____ (What?).

1

audience

2

a. circumference
b. conscience

3   Model:

The *e*'s in *circumferentia* and *conscientia* have been kept.

4

a. *experientia*
b. *sententia*

5

a. essence
b. influence

92

7   coincidence   consistent   consistence (consistency)

Coincidence has an *e* before the *n* in the last syllable because it comes from a Latin verb *coincidere*.

   Consistent is from a Latin verb *consistere*.

   The noun *consistence*, which more often appears in the form *consistency*, is from Medieval Latin *consistentia*.

Copy: When events *coincide* by chance, we speak of a *coincidence*.

_____

_____

Copy: Most people try to be *consistent*, but Emerson warned that "a foolish *consistency* is the hobgoblin of little minds."

_____

_____

_____

6

superintendentia

8

You will not be expected to remember the Latin words we have been discussing, but you will find the English words in this unit easier to spell if you remember that all of them are derived from Latin words that have an _____ (What letter?) near the end.

7

When events *coincide* by chance, we speak of a *coincidence*.

Most people try to be *consistent*, but Emerson warned that "a foolish *consistency* is the hobgoblin of little minds."

9

Spell correctly in full the incomplete word in each sentence, using words studied in this unit.

a. The [aud] _____ rose to sing "The Star Spangled Banner."

b. The [circum] _____ of the circle is twelve inches.

8

e

10

Follow the instructions for Frame 9.

a. My [con] _____ hurts me when I do something I shouldn't.

b. We learn from [exper] _____.

9

a. audience
b. circumference

11

Follow the instructions for Frame 9.

a. A simple [sen] _____ has only one clause.

b. This perfume is called [ess] _____ of roses.

10

a. conscience
b. experience

12

Follow the instructions for Frame 9.

a. I should try to have a good [infl] _____ upon my younger brother.

b. The fact that the two players each hit three home runs on the same day is a [coin] _____.

c. Be [con] _____; don't zig and then zag.

13

Write *superintendent* and *consistency* each three times.

_____, _____,

_____, _____,

_____, _____,

14

To match the definitions below, write in full words studied in this unit. The first letters are given.

a. a person in charge of schools, [sup] _____

b. a happening together by chance, [coin] _____

c. words expressing a thought, [sen] _____

d. persons attending a concert, [aud] _____

e. distance around a circle, [cir] _____

f. a "voice" that tells wrong from right, [con] _____

g. living through an event or events, [exp] _____

h. that which produces an effect, [infl] _____

i. the chief characteristic, [ess] _____

j. repeatedly acting in the same way, [con] _____

15

Study the correct spelling of each word you missed in Frames 9–14. Write each missed word correctly three times. Check your spellings with the list above Frame 1.

11

a. sentence
b. essence

12

a. influence
b. coincidence
c. consistent

13

superintendent
superintendent
superintendent
consistency
consistency
consistency

14

a. superintendent
b. coincidence
c. sentence
d. audience
e. circumference
f. conscience
g. experience
h. influence
i. essence
j. consistent

UNIT 30 · Words ending in –ous

WORDS TREATED

analogous	enormous	mountainous	synonymous
barbarous	famous	ridiculous	tremendous
boisterous	humorous	scandalous	unanimous
disastrous	incredulous	stupendous	vigorous

1

If you wonder whether a word ends in –ous, –eous, –ious, or –uous, the best guide (though not completely reliable) is careful pronunciation.

A word that should be spelled with –ous has at the end something that sounds like *ŭs* (not *yŭs* or *ĭ ŭs* or *ĕ ŭs* or *shŭs* or *shĭ ŭs*).

Say and then write *humorous* and *scandalous*. Listen for the *ŭs*.

_____, _____

2

a. Say and then write *boisterous* and *enormous*.

_____, _____

b. Make up a sentence containing the two words.

_____

_____

3

a. Say and then write *unanimous* and *vigorous*.

_____, _____

b. Make up a sentence containing the two words.

_____

_____

4

a. Say and then write *ridiculous*. Note that the second letter is *i*.

_____

b. Say and then write *disastrous*. Note that there are only three syllables. _____

1

humorous
scandalous

2

a. boisterous, enormous
Model:
b. The *enormous* crowd became *boisterous*.

3

a. unanimous, vigorous
Model:
b. His *vigorous* speech resulted in a *unanimous* vote.

5

a. Say and then write *tremendous*. Note that there is no *i* sound and that *o* and *u* are the only vowels in the last syllable. _____
_____

b. Say and then write *stupendous*. Note that the last six letters are the same as in *tremendous*. _____

4

a. ridiculous
b. disastrous

6

Say and then write *barbarous*, *analogous*, and *synonymous*. (Note that *barbarous* has only three syllables, the first two of which are the same. Note that *synonymous* is *synonym* + *–ous*.)
_____, _____, _____

5

a. tremendous
b. stupendous

7

a. Say and then write *famous*, *incredulous*, and *mountainous*.
_____, _____, _____

b. Copy: The *famous* explorer of *mountainous* regions was *incredulous* when he heard the story.
_____
_____

6

barbarous
analogous
synonymous

8

Complete this passage by writing in full the appropriate words studied in this unit.

The most [hum] _____ happening during our almost [dis] _____ trip occurred when Jack found an [enor] _____ shell. Since we were in [moun] _____ country, this seemed like a [rid] _____ place for it. Bob, who is always clowning and acting [boi] _____, stuck his finger into the shell. Then, with an [incred] _____ look on his face, he said, "I can't get my finger out!" Finally, several [vig] _____ pulls got his finger free.

7

a. famous, incredulous,
mountainous
b. The *famous* explorer of *mountainous* regions was *incredulous* when he heard the story.

9

Follow the instructions for Frame 8.

Few marriage customs that are [anal] _____ to those of civilized countries are observed by this [bar] _____ tribe. It would be the almost [unan] _____ opinion of people who do not know sociology that the customs are [scand] _____. If the tribe were not so remote, it would be [fam] _____ for its display of [trem] _____ athletic activity during a marriage ceremony. With a [stup] _____ display of strength, one bridegroom swam and crawled his way up the *bladigem*, a word that is [syn] _____ with *rapids*.

8

humorous
disastrous
enormous
mountainous
ridiculous
boisterous
incredulous
vigorous

10

Match each synonym below with a word we studied in this unit. The first letters are supplied. Write the complete word.

a. very great, [tre] _____
b. funny, [hum] _____
c. unbelievably odd, [rid] _____
d. causing great damage, [dis] _____
e. comparable, [ana] _____
f. savage, [bar] _____
g. noisily playful, [boi] _____
h. of the same meaning, [syn] _____

11

Follow the instructions for Frame 10.

a. huge, [eno] _____
b. well-known, [fam] _____
c. not believing, [inc] _____
d. having mountains, [moun] _____
e. shameful, [scan] _____
f. amazing; immense, [stup] _____
g. completely in agreement, [unan] _____
h. strong; active, [vig] _____

12

Study each word that you misspelled in Frames 8–11. Write it correctly three times. Check your answers against the list above Frame 1.

9

analogous
barbarous
unanimous
scandalous
famous
tremendous
stupendous
synonymous

10

a. tremendous
b. humorous
c. ridiculous
d. disastrous
e. analogous
f. barbarous
g. boisterous
h. synonymous

11

a. enormous
b. famous
c. incredulous
d. mountainous
e. scandalous
f. stupendous
g. unanimous
h. vigorous

UNIT 31 · Plurals with *—oes*

WORDS TREATED

echoes	potatoes
embargoes	tomatoes
heroes	torpedoes
Negroes	vetoes

1

Plurals of words that end in *o* can be very annoying. *Radio*, for example, must be pluralized *radios*. *Hero* must be pluralized *heroes*. The plural of *cargo* may be either *cargos* or *cargoes*. The plural of buffalo may be *buffalo*, *buffalos*, or *buffaloes*.

If you can think of any words ending in *o* that you do not know how to make plural, write those words.

_____

_____

_____

2

Fortunately, there is a fairly easy way to master these troublesome words. The English language has only eight fairly common *o*-words that *must* be pluralized with *–es*. You will be safe with all the others just by adding *–s*, even though some of them have *–es* as a second possibility.

In other words, if you remember just the _____ (How many?) plurals that end in *–oes*, you can spell the plurals of any of the hundred or so words that end in *o*.

3

This unit is intended to help you to remember the eight *–oes* words. You will be required to write all of them a number of times. Here they are:

> echoes embargoes heroes Negroes
> potatoes tomatoes torpedoes vetoes

Copy the eight words.

_____, _____, _____, _____,

_____, _____, _____,

_____

4

Copy this nonsense sentence:

Embargoes on the *echoes* of *torpedoes*, as well as *vetoes* by *Negroes*, resulted in the eating of *potatoes* and *tomatoes* by *heroes*.

_____

_____

_____

1

(Any answer ending in *o* is correct.)

2

eight

3

echoes	potatoes
embargoes	tomatoes
heroes	torpedoes
Negroes	vetoes

5

Write in full the unfinished words.

a. [Po] _____ grow under the ground.
b. [To] _____ grow on vines above the ground.
c. [He] _____ should be brave.
d. [Tor] _____ are usually cigar-shaped.

6

Write in full the unfinished words.

a. [Em] _____ prevent certain shipments.
b. Few [Ne] _____ live in Stockholm.
c. [Ve] _____ keep Congressional bills from becoming law.
d. [Ec] _____ are caused by reflection of sound.

7

Write the one of our eight words that best fits each definition.

a. reflected sounds, _____
b. blacks, Afro-Americans, _____
c. starchy tubers, _____
d. red or yellow juicy fruits, _____

8

Write the one of our eight words that best fits the definition.

a. orders by a government forbidding ships to enter or leave its ports,

_____

b. large explosive shells capable of traveling under their own power,

_____

c. rejections of bills passed by a lawmaking body, _____
d. persons admired for great deeds, _____

9

a. Write a sentence of your own using the words *Negroes* and *echoes*.

_____
_____

b. Write a sentence of your own using the words *potatoes* and *tomatoes*.

_____
_____

4

Embargoes on the *echoes* of *torpedoes*, as well as *vetoes* by *Negroes*, resulted in the eating of *potatoes* and *tomatoes* by *heroes*.

5

a. Potatoes
b. Tomatoes
c. Heroes
d. Torpedoes

6

a. Embargoes
b. Negroes
c. Vetoes
d. Echoes

7

a. echoes
b. Negroes
c. potatoes
d. tomatoes

8

a. embargoes
b. torpedoes
c. vetoes
d. heroes

10

a. Write a sentence of your own using the words *embargoes* and *vetoes*.

_____

_____

b. Write a sentence of your own using the words *heroes* and *torpedoes*.

_____

_____

11

Write ten times any of our eight words that you misspelled in Frame 9 or 10. Check your spellings against the list above Frame 1.

9

(Check your spelling:
   Negroes
   echoes
   potatoes
   tomatoes)

10

(Check your spelling:
   embargoes
   vetoes
   heroes
   torpedoes)

UNIT 32 · Plurals with *–es*

WORDS TREATED

addresses	clothes	Joneses	speeches
beaches	foxes	quizzes	watches
bushes	geniuses	scratches	witches
churches	grasses	screeches	wolves

1

a. Say *bush* to yourself. How many syllables does that word have?

_____

b. Say *bushes* to yourself. How many syllables does that word have?

_____

2

Most nouns, as you know, form their plurals by the addition of *–s*: *boy—boys, girl—girls, cousin—cousins.* In those words the plural has the same number of syllables as the singular has.

   In making *bush* plural, however, we have to say an extra syllable. In the spelling of the plural to show the extra syllable, we add the vowel *e* as well as the usual *–s*.

Write the plural of *bush*. _____

1

a. one
b. two

3

In general, when we have to add a syllable to make a plural, we use *–es* instead of just *–s*. The plurals of words that end in *ch, tch, s, x,* and *z* require the extra syllable and therefore end in *–es*.

Write the plurals of *speech* and *screech.*

_____, _____

4

Write the plurals of *church, watch, witch, scratch,* and *beach.*

_____, _____, _____,

_____, _____

5

Write the plurals of *grass, address, genius, Jones,* and *fox.*

_____, _____, _____,

_____, _____

6

The word *quiz* is different from the others in this unit, for it doubles the *z* before the *–es* is added for the plural.

Write the plural of *quiz.* _____

7

The plural of *wolf* is also different from the others because the *f* changes to *v,* and although the plural has *–es,* the word still has only one syllable.

    Clothes is also an oddity, for it too has only one syllable. Besides, we do not have a singular noun *clothe,* and *cloth* is not quite the same thing.

Copy *clothes,* and write the plural of *wolf.*

_____, _____

8

a. Write one short sentence in which you use the plural of *Jones* and the plural of *genius.*

_____

_____

b. Write one short sentence in which you use the plurals of *wolf, fox, grass,* and *bush.*

_____

_____

2

bushes

3

speeches
screeches

4

churches
watches
witches
scratches
beaches

5

grasses
addresses
geniuses
Joneses
foxes

6

quizzes

7

clothes
wolves

9

a. Write one short sentence in which you use *clothes* and the plural of *witch*.

_____

_____

b. Write one short sentence in which you use the plurals of *quiz* and *address*.

_____

_____

10

a. Write one short sentence in which you use the plurals of *scratch* and *beach*.

_____

_____

b. Write one short sentence in which you use the plurals of *speech* and *church*.

_____

_____

c. Write one short sentence in which you use the plurals of *watch* and *screech*.

_____

_____

11

The principle we studied in this unit applies to a number of other words ending in *ch, tch, s, x,* and *z.* Let's see whether you can think of some of them. Write the plural of each word defined below.

a. a container (rhymes with *fox*), _____
b. a jerking motion (rhymes with *church*), _____
c. something sewed on (rhymes with *scratch*), _____

12

Follow the instructions for Frame 11.

a. a shove (rhymes with *bush*), _____
b. a kind of nut tree (rhymes with *speech*), _____
c. a trench (rhymes with *witch*), _____
d. a ditch (rhymes with *bench*), _____
e. a long seat (rhymes with *trench*), _____

---

8   Models:

a. We *Joneses* are all *geniuses.*
b. The *wolves* and the *foxes* hid among the *grasses* and the *bushes.*

9   Models:

a. The *witches* had torn their *clothes.*
b. We took *quizzes* on the *addresses* of Daniel Webster.

10   Models:

a. They got a few *scratches* on the *beaches.*
b. We listened to *speeches* in two *churches.*
c. When they looked at their *watches,* they let out some *screeches.*

11

a. boxes
b. lurches
c. patches

13

Follow the instructions for Frame 11.

a. a bloodsucker (rhymes with *speech*), _____

b. a fruit (rhymes with *beach*), _____

c. a door fastener (rhymes with *scratch*), _____

d. a religious service (rhymes with *grass*), _____

12

a. pushes

b. beeches

c. ditches

d. trenches

e. benches

14

Study each word that you missed in Frames 8–13. Write each misspelled word correctly three times. Check your answers against the list above Frame 1.

13

a. leeches

b. peaches

c. latches

d. masses

UNIT 33 · How to remember *–ery* or *–ary*

WORDS TREATED

–ery Words			*–ary* Words	
cemetery	gallery	stationery	corollary	stationary
confectionery	millinery	very	hereditary	summary
distillery	monastery		imaginary	
every	mystery			

1

Many a writer puts teeth marks on his pencil as he tries to remember whether a word ends in *–ery* or *–ary*. Quite a few pencils may be saved if one recalls that only a very few common words end in *–ery*.

Copy from the preceding sentence one of the few words that end in *–ery*. _____

---

2   every   cemetery   monastery

Three more of the *–ery* words are listed above.

Copy: *Every monastery* had its *very* own *cemetery*.

_____

_____

1

very

---

3 stationery distillery millinery confectionery

Copy: He used *stationery* from the *distillery*, the *confectionery*, and the *millinery* shop.

_____

_____

(Note that this *stationery* refers to writing paper. It may help to recall *lettEr* and *stationEry*.)

---

4 gallery mystery

Frames 1, 2, and 3 listed eight common *–ery* words. The only others in common use are the two above (although some persons may need to know *dysentery, nunnery, gunnery,* and a few more).

Copy: The *mystery* is why he was killed in the shooting *gallery*.

_____

_____

5

Write the ten *–ery* words we have listed at the head of this unit. Study this list until you know instantly that each of these words ends in *–ery*.

_____   _____

_____   _____

_____   _____

_____   _____

---

6 summary imaginary hereditary

We shall study only five of the *–ary* words, the five that are most often misspelled. Three are given above.

Write three very short sentences, each containing one of the three words at the top of this frame.

_____

_____

---

7 corollary stationary

A *corollary* is a statement that is closely related to another statement and that perhaps grows from it. In mathematics, for instance, if we know that four equal angles total 360 degrees, a corollary is that each must be a right angle.

Stationary means not moving. Something is stationary if it stands still. Remember the A's in *stationAry* and *stAnd*.

Copy: As a *corollary*, the object must be *stationary*.

_____

_____

2

Every monastery had its *very* own *cemetery*.

3

He used *stationery* from the *distillery*, the *confectionery*, and the *millinery* shop.

4

The *mystery* is why he was killed in the shooting *gallery*.

5

very	distillery
every	millinery
cemetery	confectionery
monastery	gallery
stationery	mystery

---

6 Models:

Write a short *summary*.
Ghosts are *imaginary*.
Cancer is not *hereditary*.

8

Write in full the word we studied in this unit that best fits each definition. The first letter or letters have been supplied.

a. something hidden or unknown, [my] _____
b. place where liquor, perfume, etc. is made, [dis] _____
c. extremely, [v] _____
d. shortened version, [sum] _____

9

Follow the instructions for Frame 8.

a. the making of hats, [mil] _____
b. a related statement growing from the first, [cor] _____
c. home for the dead, [cem] _____
d. place where candy is made, [con] _____

10

Follow the instructions for Frame 8.

a. not moving, [sta] _____
b. writing paper, [sta] _____
c. home of monks, [mon] _____
d. unreal, [im] _____

11

Follow the instructions for Frame 8.

a. all, [ev] _____
b. inherited, [her] _____
c. a building to display works of art, [gal] _____

12

Choose from the words we studied in this unit the one that best fits each blank. Write the entire word.

Why my aunt decided to go into the [mil] _____ business is a [v] _____ great [mys] _____. She had [ev] _____ reason to distrust her business judgment, since she had already failed with a [con] _____ and with a [sta] _____ shop. In [sum] _____, her chances of success in any business seemed largely [im] _____.

7

As a *corollary*, the object must be *stationary*.

8

a. mystery
b. distillery
c. very
d. summary

9

a. millinery
b. corollary
c. cemetery
d. confectionery

10

a. stationary
b. stationery
c. monastery
d. imaginary

11

a. every
b. hereditary
c. gallery

13

Follow the instructions for Frame 12.

The monks in this [mon] _____ were especially proud of their art [gal] _____ and their [dis] _____ _____ in which they prepared a unique perfume. Buried in their [cem] _____ were the monks who, a century before, had started the art collection. The perfume resulted as a [cor] _____ _____ to another of the monks' enterprises, the growing of rare flowers. Through controlling [her] _____ characteristics of roses, they had perfected one with an unusually appealing odor.

14

Write once more the ten most important words ending in –*ery*. Remember that most other words with a similar sounding ending require –*ary*. (There are several hundred –*ary* words.)

_____   _____
_____   _____
_____   _____
_____   _____
_____   _____

15

Study each word that you missed in Frames 8–14. Again review the –*ery* words. Write correctly three times each word that you missed. Check your spellings against the list above Frame 1.

12

millinery
very
mystery
every
confectionery
stationery
summary
imaginary

13

monastery
gallery
distillery
cemetery
corollary
hereditary

14

very	distillery
every	millinery
cemetery	confectionery
monastery	gallery
stationery	mystery

UNIT 34 • Double, double—that's no trouble

WORDS TREATED

accessible	assassinate	connoisseur	occurrence	succeed	suppress
accommodate	balloon	embarrass	possess	success	suppression
address	commission	goddess	possession	succession	
aggressive	committee	millennium	possessive	successive	

---

1   possess   goddess   occurrence

Look at the three words above to see how they are alike.

Each of them has _____ (How many?) pairs of doubled letters.

2

All the words we shall discuss in this unit have two sets of doubled letters. (One has three).

Copy the following sentences, capitalizing the doubled letters: The *oCCuRRence* upset the *goDDeSS*. Fear seemed to *poSSeSS* her.

_____

_____

3

Three words that rhyme with *possess* are *success*, *suppress*, and *address*.

Copy the following sentence, capitalizing the doubled letters: He had no *suCCeSS* when he tried to *suPPreSS* the governor's *aDDreSS*.

_____

_____

4

Three other rhyming words are *possession*, *succession*, and *suppression*.

Copy the following sentence, capitalizing the doubled letters: The *suPPreSSion* of three revolts in *suCCeSSion* left King Henry in firm *poSSeSSion* of the crown.

_____

_____

5

Aggressive, *possessive*, and *successive* also rhyme. Which of these three words is needed in each blank?

a. Bob was always fighting. He was very _____.

b. He made three _____ winning bets.

c. *His* is the _____ form of *he*.

6

See whether you can write in full each unfinished word, making a double-letter word we have not yet studied.

a. Would it [emb] _____ you if the principal stepped in right now? (Double *r* and double *s*.)

b. He is a kind person, always eager to _____ [odate] a friend. (Double *c* and double *m*.)

7

Follow the instructions for Frame 6.

a. If at first you don't [su] _____, try, try again.

b. The [ba] _____ burst when I stuck a pin into it.

1

two

2

The oCCuRRence upset the goDDeSS. Fear seemed to poSSeSS her.

3

He had no suCCeSS when he tried to suPPreSS the governor's aD-DreSS.

4

The suPPreSSion of three revolts in suCCeSSion left King Henry in firm poSSeSSion of the crown.

5

a. aggressive
b. successive
c. possessive

6

a. embarrass
b. accommodate

8

Follow the instructions for Frame 6.

a. The salesman is paid a [co] _____ on each sale.
b. The chairman called the [co] _____ to order. (Three sets of double letters in this word.)

7

a. succeed
b. balloon

9

Find and copy four words with two sets of double letters in this passage:

"When the millennium comes," the connoisseur of art said, "fine paintings will be much more accessible than they are now. And critics, I hope, will not try to assassinate the reputation of everyone with whose style they do not agree."

_____, _____,

_____, _____,

8

a. commission
b. committee

10

Complete correctly the unfinished words, all of which we have studied in this unit. Fill in only the missing letters.

"You emb_____ me with your praise," the girl said. "I know that I am not really as beautiful as a go_____, nor do I po_____ eyes of heavenly blue. I am sure that your flattery can never su_____. But keep on trying!"

9

millennium
connoisseur
accessible
assassinate

11

Follow the instructions for Frame 10.

The little boy's most prized po_____ was a red ba_____. His a_____ive older brother tried to take it from him. After this o_____ence, the little boy ran to his mother.

10

embarrass
goddess
possess
succeed

12

Follow the instructions for Frame 10.

A mi_____ium from now, distant planets may be a_____ _____ible. But whether conditions there will a_____odate human life is not known.

11

possession
balloon
aggressive
occurrence

13

Follow the instructions for Frame 10.

"To a_____inate is to commit an act of cowardice!" he shouted. "The co_____ion of such an act would be intolerable. As much as anyone else, I favor the su_____ion of tyranny, but no vote by this co___i_____ can make me approve murder!"

12

millennium
accessible
accommodate

14

Follow the instructions for Frame 10.

    After two su_____ive failures to remove the heavy rock, the co_____eur of spirits said, "Ah, the present gods of the cave are very po_____ive. They are not the true heirs. The su_____ion has been broken. The old gods were more reasonable."

15

Look carefully at the correct spelling of each word you missed in Frames 10–14. Notice the right way to spell the part that you had wrong. Say the word slowly to yourself. Write the word correctly three times, and check above Frame 1 to make sure that you spelled it correctly.

13

assassinate
commission
suppression
committee

14

successive
connoisseur
possessive
succession

UNIT 35 · Some words with *-ar*

WORDS TREATED

beggar	familiar	nuclear	polar	similar
burglar	grammar	particular	regular	spectacular
calendar	hangar	peculiar	scholar	
cellar	mustard	pillar	separate	

---

1   scholar

The Latin word for *school* is *schola*. In English we call a person a *scholar* if he has spent much time studying (in school or elsewhere). Our word *scholar* comes from *schola*.

Explain why *scholar* is spelled with an *a*.

---

2   grammar

Our word *grammar* goes back to Latin *grammatica*. The Romans borrowed their word from the Greek *gramma*, which meant a letter or a piece of writing.

Explain why *grammar* is spelled with an *a* in the last syllable.

---

1   Model:

Scholar keeps the *a* from *schola*.

109

3 calendar

We use a *calendar* to give us information about days of the month. The ancient Romans had the word *kalendae*, which meant the first days of the month.

Explain why *calendar* is spelled with an *a* in the last syllable.

_____

4 separate

Our word *separate* has *ar* in the middle. Once more the reason is that the Latin ancestor used an *a*. The Latin word for *separate* was *separatus*.

Write *separate* and *separatus* three times each.

_____, _____ _____,

_____ _____, _____

5 peculiar

Maybe you think there is nothing very peculiar about cattle, but the word *peculiar* goes back to Latin *pecu*, which meant cattle. Then the Romans coined *peculiaris*, pertaining to their own cattle or to anything else owned privately. Today something is peculiar if it has its own private qualities.

Peculiar is spelled with *iar* because it comes from the Latin word _____ (What?).

6 familiar

Familiar is another *iar* word. It is derived from the Latin *familia*, meaning family.

Copy: The people in our own family, which the Romans called *familia*, are most *familiar* to us.

_____

_____

7 cellar particular hangar

Here is more information about the backgrounds of words with –*ar*:

This English word	is derived from	which meant
cellar	Latin *cella*	storeroom
particular	Latin *particula*	small part
hangar (for air-planes)	Medieval Latin *angarium*	shed for shoeing horses

Copy: This *particular hangar* was really a huge *cellar*.

_____

_____

2 Model:

Grammar keeps the *a* from *gramma*.

3 Model:

Calendar keeps the *a* from *kalendae*.

4

separate, *separatus*
separate, *separatus*
separate, *separatus*

5

peculiaris

6

The people in our own family, which the Romans called *familia*, are most *familiar* to us.

8   polar   burglar   nuclear   mustard   regular

This English word	is derived from	which meant
polar	New Latin *polaris*	pertaining to the pole
burglar	Medieval Latin *burglator*	burglar
nuclear	French *nucleaire*	nuclear
mustard	Old French *mostarde*	mustard
regular	Latin *regula*	straightedge

Make up a phrase, like *a polar bear*, for each word.

_____   _____

_____   _____

_____

---

9   similar   spectacular   beggar   pillar

We have looked at fourteen words with *–ar*, and we might also have considered *similar, spectacular, beggar, pillar,* and a few others. You are not expected to remember the Greek, Latin, or French ancestors, but you may best remember the *–ar* spelling if you recall that *–ar* is in each of these words because the older word _____ (*had or did not have?*) an *a* and often an *r*.

10

Using a word we studied or mentioned in this unit, complete each sentence. Write the word in full.

a. I should recognize you. Your face is [fam] _____.

b. That was a [pecul] _____ thing to say.

c. Look up the date on the [cal] _____.

d. He keeps potatoes in his [cel] _____.

11

Follow the instructions for Frame 10.

a. Taxi the airplane from the [hang] _____.

b. Please put [mus] _____ on my hot dog.

c. The [reg] _____ price is two dollars.

d. A [burg] _____ stole her jewels.

12

Follow the instructions for Frame 10.

a. This submarine is propelled by [nuc] _____ power.

b. We flew so far north that we almost made a trans-[po] _____ flight.

c. My [partic] _____ interest is in psychology.

d. We had a lesson in [gram] _____ yesterday.

7

This *particular hangar* was really a huge *cellar*.

---

8   **Models:**

polar expeditions

a sly *burglar*

nuclear fission

yellow as *mustard*

a *regular* occurrence

9

had

10

a. familiar

b. peculiar

c. calendar

d. cellar

11

a. hangar

b. mustard

c. regular

d. burglar

13

Follow the instructions for Frame 10.

a. Give. us [sep] _____ checks, please.

b. I am a student, but I am not yet a [sch] _____.

c. Twins are usually [sim] _____ in appearance.

14

Follow the instructions for Frame 10.

a. Old Faithful is a [spect] _____ sight.

b. He was a poor, crippled [beg] _____.

c. One [pil] _____ in front of the old mansion had fallen.

15

Look carefully at the correct spelling of each word you missed in Frames 10–14. Notice the right way to spell the part that you had wrong. Say the word slowly to yourself. Write the word three times, and check above Frame 1 to make sure that you spelled it correctly.

12

a. nuclear
b. polar
c. particular
d. grammar

13

a. separate
b. scholar
c. similar

14

a. spectacular
b. beggar
c. pillar

UNIT 36 · Words ending in *–yze* or *–ize*

WORDS TREATED

analyze	fertilize	organize	solemnize	systematize
apologize	harmonize	paralyze	specialize	
catalyze	hypnotize	plagiarize	symbolize	
electrolyze	monopolize	realize	sympathize	

---

1   analyze   paralyze

The easiest way to remember whether a word ends in *–yze* or *–ize* is to memorize four words with *–yze.* The others end in *–ize.*

Two of the *–yze* words are frequently used. They are *analyze* and *paralyze.*

Copy: The noun forms of *analyze* and *paralyze* also have *y*'s: *analysis* and *paralysis.*

---

2 catalyze electrolyze

Two less common –*yze* words are used in science. One is *catalyze*, meaning to cause a reaction without making a change in the chemical that triggers the reaction. The other is *electrolyze*, meaning to break into ions by use of an electric current.

Copy: The noun forms of *catalyze* and *electrolyze* are *catalysis* and *electrolysis*.

_____

_____

3

Without looking back at Frames 1 and 2, write the four –*yze* words twice each.

_____, _____, _____, _____,

_____, _____,

_____, _____

---

4 apologize hypnotize monopolize realize

Over four hundred other English words end in –*ize*. Here we shall look at only a few that are often misspelled. (The British use –*ise* for many such words.)

Write: *apologize, hypnotize, monopolize, realize.*

_____, _____,

_____, _____

---

5 solemnize sympathize systematize

Copy: to *solemnize* an occasion, to *sympathize* with a friend, to *systematize* your record-keeping.

_____

_____

_____

---

6 fertilize harmonize organize

Write a phrase starting with *to* for each of the words above.

_____

_____

_____

---

7 plagiarize specialize symbolize

Write the three –*ize* words given above, with your own brief definition of each.

_____

_____

_____

1

The noun forms of *analyze* and *paralyze* also have *y*'s: *analysis* and *paralysis*.

2

The noun forms of *catalyze* and *electrolyze* are *catalysis* and *electrolysis*.

3

analyze, analyze
paralyze, paralyze
catalyze, catalyze
electrolyze, electrolyze

4

apologize
hypnotize
monopolize
realize

5

to *solemnize* an occasion
to *sympathize* with a friend
to *systematize* your record-keeping

---

6 Models:

to *fertilize* a garden
to *harmonize* at the piano
to *organize* a debate

8

The following pairs of sentences are arranged so that the second will mean about the same as the first after the missing word (from those we studied in this unit) has been inserted. Write in full each unfinished word.

a. I must examine the data with care. I must [an] _____ the data.

b. Farmers spread nutritive chemicals on their fields. Farmers [fe] _____ their fields.

9

Follow the instructions for Frame 8.

a. It is illegal to pretend that someone else's writing is one's own. It is illegal to [pl] _____.

b. The two defendants' stories did not agree. The two defendants' stories did not [har] _____.

c. The wedding ceremony was performed. The wedding ceremony was [sol] _____ [d].

d. I am sorry that I offended you. I [ap] _____ for offending you.

e. Platinum will cause a reaction between ammonia and oxygen. Platinum will [cat] _____ a reaction between ammonia and oxygen.

10

Follow the instructions for Frame 8.

a. In college I want to take much work in agronomy. In college I want to [sp] _____ in agronomy.

b. It is necessary to decompose this solution by sending electricity through it. It is necessary to [el] _____ this solution.

c. I do not know how to cause a person to fall into a trance. I do not know how to [hyp] _____ a person.

d. I am sorry that you are having trouble. I [sym] _____ with you.

e. I was not aware that you were here. I did not [re] _____ that you were here.

---

7   Models:

plagiarize: to steal another's words
specialize: to concentrate in
symbolize: to represent

8

a. analyze
b. fertilize

9

a. plagiarize
b. harmonize
c. solemnized
d. apologize
e. catalyze

11

Follow the instructions for Frame 8.

a. Perhaps the witches represent fate. Perhaps the witches [sym] _____ fate.

b. I do not want to take all your time. I do not want to [mon] _____ your time.

c. It is necessary to regularize my study habits. It is necessary to [sys] _____ my study habits.

d. Because of polio, he could not move his legs. Because of polio, his legs were [par] _____ [d].

e. In writing, I should arrange my ideas better. In writing, I should [org] _____ my ideas better.

10

a. specialize
b. electrolyze
c. hypnotize
d. sympathize
e. realize

12

Once more, write the four words we have studied that end in –*yze*.

_____ , _____ , _____ ,

_____

11

a. symbolize
b. monopolize
c. systematize
d. paralyzed
e. organize

13

Choose two of the following words that you remember using recently, and write a sentence with each.

apologize hypnotize monopolize realize
solemnize sympathize systematize fertilize
harmonize organize plagiarize specialize symbolize

_____

_____

12

analyze
paralyze
catalyze
electrolyze

14

Study each word that you misspelled in Frames 8–13. Write each missed word correctly three times. Check your spellings against the list above Frame 1.

13

(Check the spellings. Count your answer right if the two words are spelled correctly.)

UNIT 37 · Words ending in –*uous*

WORDS TREATED

ambiguous	incongruous	superfluous
arduous	ingenuous	
conspicuous	innocuous	
continuous	strenuous	

1 continuous   superfluous

If you wonder whether a word ends in *–uous*, *–eous*, *–ious*, or *–ous*, the best guide (though not completely reliable) is careful pronunciation.

A word that should be spelled with *–uous* generally has at the end sounds like *yo͞o ŭs* or *o͞o ŭs*, as in *continuous* and *superfluous*.

Say *con tin u ous* and *su per flu ous*. (Accent the *tin* and the *per*.) Then write the two words.

_____, _____

---

2   strenuous   ingenuous

a. Say and then write *stren u ous* and *in gen u ous* (which means naive or unsophisticated).

_____, _____

b. Write a sentence with *ingenuous*.

_____

_____

---

3   conspicuous   innocuous

a. Say and then write *con spic u ous* and *in noc u ous* (which means harmless). _____, _____

b. Write a sentence with *innocuous*.

_____

_____

---

4   arduous   ambiguous

a. Say and then write *ar du ous* (meaning difficult) and *am big u ous* (meaning capable of being understood in two or more ways).

_____

b. Copy: It is an *arduous* task to interpret *ambiguous* statements.

_____

_____

---

5   incongruous

Say and then write *in con gru ous* (which means having parts that do not fit well together). _____

1

continuous
superfluous

2

a. strenuous, ingenuous
Model:
b. It is *ingenuous* to assume that everyone has praiseworthy motives.

3

a. conspicuous, innocuous
b. The bites of many snakes are *innocuous*.

4

a. arduous, ambiguous
Model:
b. It is an *arduous* task to interpret *ambiguous* statements.

6

Using the most suitable of the nine words we have studied, write a word to replace each synonym in parentheses.

The _____ [steady] roar of the waterfall did not disturb our sleep, because we were tired after an _____ [difficult] day of hiking. When we awoke, the most _____ _____ [noticeable] sight was the tall column of water. We said nothing, since words would have been _____ [unneeded; too much].

7

Follow the instructions for Frame 6.

One _____ [naive] girl, who did not realize that she was saying anything _____ [with two possible meanings], said that she liked entertaining boys. We laughed at her _____ [harmless] but _____ [having ill-fitted parts] remark, which helped us to forget that we had just endured a _____ [strain-filled] hour.

8

Write in full each unfinished word, choosing the most suitable one of those we have studied in this unit.

a. A thing is [con] _____ if it proceeds without interruption.
b. A thing is [con] _____ if it is easy to see.
c. A thing is [incon] _____ if its parts do not harmonize with each other or their surroundings.

9

Follow the instructions for Frame 8.

a. A person is [in] _____ if he does not understand the ways of the world.
b. A statement is [am] _____ if it can be interpreted in more than one way.
c. A statement is [in] _____ if it will not harm anyone.

10

Follow the instructions for Frame 8.

a. A task is [str] _____ if it requires considerable energy.
b. A task is [ar] _____ if it requires much hard labor.
c. A task is [super] _____ if it need not have been performed.

5

incongruous

6

continuous
arduous
conspicuous
superfluous

7

ingenuous
ambiguous
innocuous
incongruous
strenuous

8

a. continuous
b. conspicuous
c. incongruous

9

a. ingenuous
b. ambiguous
c. innocuous

11

Study each word that you misspelled in Frames 6–10. Note carefully each trouble spot. Write each missed word correctly three times. Check your spellings against the list above Frame 1.

10

a. strenuous
b. arduous
c. superfluous

UNIT 38 · Words with silent *gh*

WORDS TREATED

eight	playwright	thought
eighth	straight	through
eighty	thorough	weigh
neighbor	though	weight

1   straight

A number of Modern English words contain a silent *gh*. Most of these go back to Old English forms in which *gh* or at least *h* was pronounced.

For example, *straight* goes back to Old English *streght*, which was pronounced something like strĕg h t.

Copy: *Straight* is the only common English word ending in *–aight*.

_____

_____

2   eight   eighth   eighty

The Old English forms of *eight*, *eighth*, and *eighty* had no *g*, but the *h* was present and pronounced.

Copy: We saw *eighty-eight* mallards on the *eighth*.

_____

_____

1

Straight is the only common English word ending in *–aight*.

3   neighbor

The Old English spelling of *neighbor* was *neahgebur*, meaning "nigh-dweller," someone who dwells nigh or near.

Copy: The horse *neighed* at our *neighbor*.

_____

_____

2

We saw *eighty-eight* mallards on the *eighth*.

4 weigh weight

Old English *weigh* was spelled *wegan*, and *weight* was spelled *wiht*. The two spellings blended in our *weigh* and *weight*.

Copy: *Weigh* this. What is the *weight*?

_____

_____

5 though thought

Though in Old English was *thogh*, and *thought* was *thoht*. Today both are spelled with *gh*, and *u* has crept in.

Copy: *Though* I *thought* and *thought*,
  Though I *fought* and *fought*,
  I couldn't pay
  For all he *bought*.

_____

_____

_____

_____

6 through thorough

Through in Middle English was *thurgh*. *Thorough* was spelled *thoruh* (as well as several other ways).

Copy: *Through* the *thorough* search he looked *thoughtful*.

_____

_____

7 playwright

In Old English a *wryhta* was a workman, especially a skilled worker or craftsman. A *wryhta* would usually specialize, so that there were (in modern spellings) wheelwrights, millwrights, wainwrights (wagon builders), and so on. *Playwright* is a modern coinage; it means play builder rather than play writer.

Copy: A *playwright*, like a *wheelwright*, builds something.

_____

_____

8

Match each definition with one of the words we studied in this unit. The first letter or letters have been supplied. Write the word in full.

a. seven plus one, [e] _____

b. in one side and out the other, [thr] _____

c. to measure on a scale, [w] _____

d. the person next door, [n] _____

3

The horse *neighed* at our *neighbor*.

4

Weigh this. What is the *weight*?

5

Though I *thought* and *thought*,
Though I *fought* and *fought*,
I couldn't pay
For all he *bought*.

6

Through the *thorough* search he looked *thoughtful*.

7

A *playwright*, like a *wheelwright*, builds something.

9

Follow the instructions for Frame 8.

a. past tense of think, [th] _____

b. not crooked, [str] _____

c. seventy-nine plus one, [e] _____

d. despite the fact that, [th] _____

8

a. eight

b. through

c. weigh

d. neighbor

10

Follow the instructions for Frame 8.

a. next after the seventh, [e] _____

b. the number of pounds, etc., [w] _____

c. painstaking, [th] _____

d. one who makes plays, [play] _____

9

a. thought

b. straight

c. eighty

d. though

11

Write in full each incomplete word, choosing the most suitable from those studied in this unit.

a. He may be right, [th] _____ I doubt it.

b. The allowable [w] _____ of luggage is forty pounds.

c. Four and four are [e] _____.

d. Use a ruler to draw [str] _____ lines.

10

a. eighth

b. weight

c. thorough

d. playwright

12

Follow the instructions for Frame 11.

a. I [th] _____ you would be late.

b. She did a [th] _____ job of cleaning the apartment.

c. George Bernard Shaw was a famous Irish [play] _____.

d. I liked the [e] _____ one better than the ninth.

11

a. though

b. weight

c. eight

d. straight

13

Follow the instructions for Frame 11.

a. How much did the baby [w] _____?

b. Thirty and fifty are [e] _____.

c. He walked [thr] _____ the room without saying a word.

d. I borrowed a cup of sugar from a [n] _____.

12

a. thought

b. thorough

c. playwright

d. eighth

14

Study each word that you misspelled in Frames 8–13. Write each missed word correctly three times. Check your spellings against the list above Frame 1.

13

a. weigh

b. eighty

c. through

d. neighbor

UNIT 39 · Words ending in *-ance* or *-ant*

WORDS TREATED

abundance	attendant	dominant	instant	radiance	significance	vigilant
abundant	balance	elegance	nuisance	radiant	significant	
ambulance	defendant	elegant	observance	repentance	tolerance	
annoyance	distance	ignorance	observant	repentant	tolerant	
appearance	distant	ignorant	predominance	resistance	vengeance	
attendance	dominance	instance	predominant	resistant	vigilance	

---

1   abundance   abundant

The Romans noticed how plentiful almost everything was in the sea. They built some words around this idea. Something that was very plentiful was *ab unda*, which was similar to saying that it was "from the waves" or "from the sea." The reason that we have in English an *a* after the *d* in *abundance* and *abundant* is that these words go back to Latin *ab unda*.

Write *abundance* and *abundant*.

_____ , _____

---

2   attendance   attendant

Equally good explanations exist for most of our other words' ending in *-ance* and *-ant*, but in this unit we shall concern ourselves just with practicing the spelling of a few of them. If you learn to associate a number of these *-ance* or *-ant* words in your mind, their spellings will be easy for you.

Copy: No *attendant* was in *attendance.*

_____

---

3   dominance   dominant   predominance   predominant

Copy: The "*dominant* male" has no *dominance* where the *predominant* female holds *predominance.*

_____

---

4   ignorance   ignorant
　　 distance   distant
　　 elegance   elegant

Write the six words above.

_____ , _____ , _____

_____ , _____ , _____

1

abundance
abundant

2

No *attendant* was in *attendance.*

3

The "*dominant* male" has no *dominance* where the *predominant* female holds *predominance.*

5

Write the *–ance* and *–ant* forms of *vigil*, *resist*, and *repent*.

_____ , _____

_____ , _____

_____ , _____

6

a. Write the *–t* form of *significance*. _____
b. Write the *–ce* form of *tolerant*. _____
c. Write the *–t* form of *instance*. _____
d. Write the *–ce* form of *observant*. _____
e. Write the *–t* form of *radiance*. _____

---

7 defendant   ambulance
   annoyance   appearance
   balance   nuisance
   vengeance

Write the seven words above.

_____ , _____ , _____ ,

_____ , _____ , _____ ,

_____

8

Write in full each unfinished word, choosing the most appropriate one studied in this unit.

a. He knows little. He is [ig] _____ .
b. The [vig] _____ of the secret service men prevented an accident.
c. He was back on his feet in an [in] _____ .
d. What an [el] _____ dining room!
e. This spray makes curtains fire [res] _____ .

9

Follow the instructions for Frame 8.

a. Walnuts were [abun] _____ .
b. A sinner should be [rep] _____ .
c. We need to be [tol] _____ of persons whose backgrounds differ from ours.
d. [Att] _____ at our basketball games is large.
e. For centuries the Roman Empire was the [dom] _____ power.

4

ignorance, ignorant
distance, distant
elegance, elegant

5

vigilance, vigilant
resistance, resistant
repentance, repentant

6

a. significant
b. tolerance
c. instant
d. observance
e. radiant

7

defendant
ambulance
annoyance
appearance
balance
nuisance
vengeance

8

a. ignorant
b. vigilance
c. instant
d. elegant
e. resistant

10

Follow the instructions for Frame 8.

a. Among the vivid and beautiful colors of the fall season, the reds are [predom] _____.

b. In the [dist] _____ we could hear a church bell.

c. The [signif] _____ of his attitude is hard to understand.

d. Watch where you are going! Be [obs] _____.

e. She was as [rad] _____ as all brides are supposed to be.

11

If the –t form of a word is given, write the –ce form. If the –ce form is given, write the –t form.

a. abundant, _____

b. dominant, _____

c. ignorant, _____

d. resistant, _____

e. vigilance, _____

f. elegant, _____

g. instant, _____

h. repentant, _____

12

Follow the instructions for Frame 11.

a. tolerant, _____

b. abundance, _____

c. predominant, _____

d. significance, _____

e. radiant, _____

f. distant, _____

g. attendance, _____

h. observant, _____

13

Match each synonym with the most suitable word studied in this unit. Write the word in full.

a. something bothersome, [nu] _____

b. a person on trial, [def] _____

c. vehicle for carrying injured persons, [amb] _____

d. to make even, [bal] _____

e. revenge, [ven] _____

f. that which annoys, [ann] _____

g. outward look, [app] _____

9

a. abundant
b. repentant
c. tolerant
d. Attendance
e. dominant

10

a. predominant
b. distance
c. significance
d. observant
e. radiant

11

a. abundance   e. vigilant
b. dominance   f. elegance
c. ignorance   g. instance
d. resistance   h. repentance

12

a. tolerance   e. radiance
b. abundant   f. distance
c. predominance   g. attendant
d. significant   h. observance

14

Study each word that you misspelled in Frames 8–13. Write it correctly three times. Check your spellings against the list above Frame 1.

13

a. nuisance
b. defendant
c. ambulance
d. balance
e. vengeance
f. annoyance
g. appearance

UNIT 40 · Contractions

WORDS TREATED

aren't	hasn't	isn't	she'll	we'll
can't	haven't	it's	they'll	weren't
didn't	he'd	mustn't	they're	won't
doesn't	he'll	shan't	wasn't	you'll
don't	I'll	she'd	we'd	you're

---

1   didn't

Sometimes, especially in reporting conversation, we need to write contractions. A contraction combines two words and leaves out one or more letters.

For instance, *did* and *not* are contracted to *didn't.*

The apostrophe in *didn't* replaces _____ (What letter?), which is left out.

1

o

---

2   isn't   aren't   wasn't   weren't

a. In each of the words above, the apostrophe _____ (*is* or *is not?*) in the place of the omitted letter.

b. Write *is not, are not, was not, were not,* and the contractions of each. Follow this example to remind yourself that the apostrophe replaces the missing letter: is not, isn't

_____ , _____   _____ , _____

_____ , _____   _____ , _____

2

a. is
b. is not, isn't   was not, wasn't
   are not, aren't were not, weren't

---

3   doesn't   don't   haven't   hasn't   mustn't

a. Tell what the apostrophe replaces in each of the above words.

_____

b. Write *does not, do not, have not, has not, must not,* and the contraction of each, using the same plan you followed in Frame 2.

_____ , _____   _____ , _____

_____ , _____   _____ , _____

_____ , _____

4   can't   shan't   won't

a. *Can't* is a contraction of *can not*. The apostrophe replaces _____ (How many?) letters.

b. *Shan't* is a contraction of *shall not*. The apostrophe replaces _____ (How many?) letters in _____ (How many?) different places.

c. *Won't* is a contraction of *woll not*. (*Woll* is an old spelling of *will*.) The apostrophe replaces _____ (How many?) letters in _____ (How many?) different places.

d. Write *can't, shan't, won't*.

_____, _____, _____

---

5   it's   you're   they're

The words above are three of the most often misspelled words in the English language.

a. *It's* stands for _____ (What?). *You're* stands for _____ (What?). *They're* stands for _____ (What?).

b. Write the contraction that could be used in *It is too late*. _____

c. Write the contraction that could be used in *You are right*. _____

d. Write the contraction that could be used in *They are here*. _____

---

6   he'd   she'd   we'd

In the contractions above, the apostrophe may replace four letters, if the meaning is *he would*, etc: _____ (What four letters?).

---

7   I'll   you'll   she'll   he'll   we'll   they'll

The words above are contractions of a pronoun and *shall* or *will*.

Write *I shall, you will, she will, he will, we shall, they will*, and the contraction of each, using the same plan you followed in Frame 2.

_____, _____   _____, _____

_____, _____   _____, _____

_____, _____   _____, _____

8

Write the contraction of each of the following:

a. did not, _____   e. is not, _____

b. do not, _____   f. are not, _____

c. does not, _____   g. was not, _____

d. can not, _____   h. were not, _____

3

a. *o* (or *the omitted letter*)

b. does not, doesn't   has not, hasn't
do not, don't   must not, mustn't
have not, haven't

4

a. two

b. three, two

c. three, two

d. can't, shan't, won't

5

a. it is, you are, they are

b. It's

c. You're

d. They're

6

woul

7

I shall, I'll   he will, he'll
you will, you'll   we shall, we'll
she will, she'll   they will, they'll

9

Write the contraction of each of the following:

a. have not, _____

b. has not, _____

c. must not, _____

d. shall not, _____

e. will not, _____

f. he would, _____

g. he will, _____

h. I shall, _____

10

Write the contraction of each of the following:

a. she would, _____

b. we would, _____

c. you will, _____

d. we shall, _____

e. they will, _____

f. she will, _____

11

Write contractions of the words in brackets.

[It is] _____ a dark night. [You are] _____ alone in the house. Your parents should have been back by now, but [they are] _____ not home yet. You hear a rustling sound, and wonder whether [it is] _____ a mouse. [You are] _____ not really afraid of mice, but [they are] _____ not your favorite friends.

12

Study each word that you misspelled in Frames 8–11. Note that the apostrophe always replaces omitted letters. Write each missed word correctly three times. Check your answers against the list above Frame 1.

8

a. didn't

b. don't

c. doesn't

d. can't

e. isn't

f. aren't

g. wasn't

h. weren't

9

a. haven't

b. hasn't

c. mustn't

d. shan't

e. won't

f. he'd

g. he'll

h. I'll

10

a. she'd

b. we'd

c. you'll

d. we'll

e. they'll

f. she'll

11

It's

You're

they're

it's

You're

they're

UNIT 41 · Possessives of nouns

WORDS TREATED

(possessives of all nouns, plus the possessive pronouns *hers, his, its, ours, theirs, yours*)

1

man woman

a. Does *man* end in *s*? _____

b. Does *woman* end in *s*? _____

2

a man's watch   a woman's scarf

To form the possessive of *man* or *woman* or any other noun that does not end in *s*, we add the mark and the letter shown above in *man's* and *woman's*.

The mark is an _____ (What?) and the letter is an __ (What letter?).

3

boys   ladies

a. Does *boys* end in *s*? _____
b. Does *ladies* end in *s*? _____

4

two boys' shirts   several ladies' purses

To form the possessive of *boys* or *ladies* or any other noun that ends in *s*, we make the change shown above. That is, we add only an _____ (What mark?).

5

You will have no trouble with the possessives of nouns if you remember the two things we have noticed:

a. If the noun does not end in *s*, make it possessive by adding _____ _____ (What two things?).
b. If the noun ends in *s*, make it possessive by adding only an _____ _____ (What?).

6

Mr. Jones' hat or Mr. Jones's hat

When a singular name of a person, like *Mr. Jones*, ends in *s*, we may form the possessive in either of the two ways. That is, we may use only an _____ (What mark?), or we may use an _____ (What mark?) and an _____ (What letter?).

7

Remember that we have been discussing nouns only. Possessive pronouns (*yours, his, hers, its, ours, theirs*) should not be written with apostrophes.

Write a sentence using both *yours* and *ours*.
_____

1

a. no
b. no

2

apostrophe
s

3

a. yes
b. yes

4

apostrophe

5

a. apostrophe and *s*
b. apostrophe

6

apostrophe
apostrophe
s

8

girl   girls   dog   dogs

Write the possessive of each word above.

_____, _____, _____, _____

9

fox   foxes   wolf   wolves

Write the possessive of each word above.

_____, _____, _____, _____

10

child   children   men   women

Write the possessive of each word above. If you have any doubts, look at Frame 2 again.

_____, _____, _____,

_____

11

Write two acceptable possessive forms of *Dickens.*

_____, _____

12

they   you   we   it   he   her

Write the possessive pronoun corresponding to each pronoun above. Use the *s* form if there is more than one. Review Frame 7 if you are in doubt.

_____, _____, _____, _____, _____, _____

13

If you misspelled any words in Frames 8–12, look back at the first seven frames to see why you made the mistake. Write a phrase, such as *a girl's shoes,* for each word that you missed.

---

7   Model:

This is *ours,* not *yours.*

8

girl's
girls'
dog's
dogs'

9

fox's
foxes'
wolf's
wolves'

10

child's
children's
men's
women's

11

Dickens'
Dickens's
(Dicken's is wrong.)

12

theirs
yours
ours
its
his
hers

UNIT 42 · Ordinal numbers

WORDS TREATED

eighth	first	nineteenth	thirteenth	twenty-eighth
fifteenth	forty-fourth	ninth	thirtieth	twenty-fourth
fifth	fourth	second	twelfth	twenty-ninth
fifty-fifth	hundredth	third	twentieth	

1

Ordinal numbers are those that show the rank of something, as *first, second, third.* (The others, such as *one, two, three,* are called *cardinal* numbers.)

The following ordinal numbers are formed simply by adding *th* to the base word:

fourth	fourteenth
sixth	sixteenth
seventh	seventeenth
tenth	eighteenth
eleventh	nineteenth
thirteenth	hundredth

The three of these that cause the most trouble are *fourth, nineteenth,* and *hundredth.* Remember: Write the base word, and add *th.* Write the three troublesome words twice each.

_____, _____

_____, _____

_____, _____

2   first   second   third

The other ordinals are formed in various ways. We write *first* rather than something like *oneth* because of an old word *fyrst,* referring to that which goes before. *Second* goes back to a Latin word meaning follow. *Third* was once pronounced and spelled with the *r* before the *i,* as *bird* also was, but through a linguistic change known as metathesis it became *third.*

Copy: My brothers are in the *first, second,* and *third* grades.

_____

_____

1

fourth, fourth
nineteenth, nineteenth
hundredth, hundredth

3   fifth   twelfth

It is difficult to pronounce the sound of *v* before *th*. For that reason the *v* of *five* and of *twelve* changes to *f* in *fifth* and *twelfth*.

Copy: Is a *fifth* of a *twelfth* the same as a *twelfth* of a *fifth*?

_____

_____

---

4   thirteenth   fifteenth

Note that the first four letters of *thirteenth* and *fifteenth* are the same as the first four letters of *third* and *fifth*, respectively.

Write a sentence using *thirteenth* and *fifteenth*.

_____

_____

---

5   twentieth   thirtieth

Twentieth, thirtieth (and also *fortieth, fiftieth*, etc.) follow the rule about changing *y* to *i* before most suffixes. For example, the *y* of *twenty* becomes an *i* in *twentieth*.

Write *twentieth* and *thirtieth* and the ordinal forms of *sixty* and *seventy*.

_____ , _____ , _____ ,

_____

6

Compound ordinals (such as *thirty-first, forty-fourth*, etc.) will cause no trouble if you remember the hyphen and if you spell the last part in the way you have learned in this unit.

Spell the ordinals of 44, 55, and 69.

_____ , _____ ,

_____

7

Spell the ordinal of each number given.

a. 1, _____   d. 4, _____
b. 2, _____   e. 5, _____
c. 3, _____   f. 8, _____

8

Spell the ordinal of each number given.

a. 9, _____   d. 14, _____
b. 12, _____   e. 19, _____
c. 13, _____   f. 20, _____

2

My brothers are in the *first, second,* and *third* grades.

3

Is a *fifth* of a *twelfth* the same as a *twelfth* of a *fifth*?

---

4   Model:

Visitors arrived on the *thirteenth* and the *fifteenth*.

5

twentieth
thirtieth
sixtieth
seventieth

6

forty-fourth
fifty-fifth
sixty-ninth

7

a. first
b. second
c. third
d. fourth
e. fifth
f. eighth

9

Spell the ordinal of each number given.

a. 24, _____

b. 28, _____

c. 29, _____

d. 30, _____

e. 94, _____

f. 100, _____

10

Study each word you misspelled in Frames 7–9. Note exactly where any trouble spot is. Write each missed word correctly three times. Check your spellings against the list above Frame 1.

8

a. ninth

b. twelfth

c. thirteenth

d. fourteenth

e. nineteenth

f. twentieth

9

a. twenty-fourth

b. twenty-eighth

c. twenty-ninth

d. thirtieth

e. ninety-fourth

f. (one) hundredth

UNIT 43 · Plurals of letters, figures, signs, and words

WORDS TREATED

(plurals of letters, figures, signs, and words referred to as words)

1

There are four *i*'s and four *s*'s in *Mississippi*.

The example above shows how to indicate the plural of a letter. We write the letter, underline it (for italics), and add an _____ _____ (What mark?) and an _____ (What letter?).

2

If we did not use the apostrophe, the reader might be puzzled when he saw something like "There are four *is* in *Mississippi*." Tell why.

3

The number has two 9's in it.

The example above shows how to indicate the plural of a figure. Tell how.

1

apostrophe

s

2   Model:

The *is* looks like the word *is*.

4

These typewriters have no &'s or #'s.

The example above shows how to indicate the plural of a sign. Tell how.

_____

---

3 Model:

Add an apostrophe and *s*.

5

The document was full of *however's* and *therefore's*.
The document was full of *howevers* and *therefores*.

The examples above show that when we are referring to words as words, we may add either an _____ (What mark?) and an _____ (What letter?) or only an _____ (What letter?). Both ways are acceptable, although some teachers and editors prefer the first.

_____

---

4 Model:

Add an apostrophe and *s*.

6

In summary, we have seen that we indicate the plurals of letters, figures, and signs by adding _____ . (What two things?). To pluralize a word referred to as a word, we may do either of two things. What are they?

_____
_____

5

apostrophe
s
s

7

l a M R

Write the plurals of the letters above.

_____, _____, _____, _____

6

an apostrophe and an *s*
We may add an apostrophe and an *s* or only an *s*.

8

7 4 80

Write the plurals of the figures above.

_____, _____, _____

7

l's
a's
M's
R's

9

@ °

Write the plurals of the signs above.

_____, _____

8

7's
4's
80's

10	**9**
and then Assume that the words above are being written about as words. Write the plural of each. Underline them. _____ , _____	@'s °'s
11	**10**
If you missed any of the answers to Frames 7–10, study the first six frames again. Write three times the correct form of each item that you missed.	*and's* (or *ands*) *then's* (or *thens*)

PART TWO

Words Best Learned in Groups

UNIT 44 · Words that use *i* for the schwa sound (I)

WORDS TREATED

accident	definite	intelligent	quantitative	utensil
asinine	evidently	medicine	rarity	
basis	experiment	opportunity	scarcity	
caricature	intelligence	origin	specimen	

---

1 accident experiment intelligent evidently

Many English words contain a sort of "uh" sound that is called a "schwa." The sound of schwa, unfortunately, is spelled in several ways. In this exercise we will concentrate on some words in which the schwa is spelled *i*. Later we will notice other spellings.

Accident, experiment, intelligent, and *evidently* are four words with *i* for the schwa. Pronounce them, noting the schwa sound near the middle of each. Then write *accident, experiment, intelligent,* and *evidently* twice each. Capitalize the *i*'s to emphasize them.

_____ , _____   _____ , _____

_____ , _____   _____ , _____

---

2 intelligence rarity scarcity

Note the *i* in *rarity* and *scarcity*. Note also that *intelligence*, like the related *intelligent*, uses *i* for the schwa.

Copy: *Intelligence* is not really a *rarity*, but there's a *scarcity* of wise use of it.

_____

_____

---

3 origin definite

Note that *origin* has two *i*'s, just as the related word *original* has.

Note that the two *i*'s in *definite* correspond to the first two *i*'s in *definition*.

Copy: *original definition*
      definite origin

_____ _____

_____ _____

1

accIdent, accIdent
experIment, experIment
intellIgent, intellIgent
evIdently, evIdently

2

Intelligence is not really a *rarity*, but there's a *scarcity* of wise use of it.

---

4 quantitative caricature

Copy these sentences:

a. A *quantitative* measurement gives the *quantity*, or amount, of something.

_____

_____

b. A drawing that exaggerates one or more features is a *caricature*.

_____

_____

5 basis utensil

Note that the next-to-last letter in *basis* and *utensil* is an *i*.

Copy: This *utensil* will become the *basis* of your housekeeping.

_____

_____

6 opportunity specimen

The ending *–ity* appears in many English words, including *opportunity*. With very few exceptions, the sound of *uh tee* at the end of a word is spelled with *–ity*.

   Specimen is related to *species*.

Copy: Astronauts had an *opportunity* to collect many *specimens* of moon rocks.

_____

_____

7 medicine asinine

Remember that *medicine* has an *i* after the *d*, just as *medical* and *medicinal* have.

   Asinine, which means foolish, comes from the Latin word for donkey-like, *asininus*. (In Latin a donkey was *asinus*.)

Copy: No *medicine* can keep a fool from being *asinine*.

_____

_____

8

Match each definition with one of the words we studied in this unit. The first letters have been supplied. Write the word in full.

a. chance, [op] _____

b. foundation, [ba] _____

c. pertaining to amount, [quan] _____

d. high in brain power, [int] _____

e. mental ability, [int] _____

3

original definition
definite origin

4

a. A *quantitative* measurement gives the *quantity*, or amount, of something.

b. A drawing that exaggerates one or more features is a *caricature*.

5

This *utensil* will become the *basis* of your housekeeping.

6

Astronauts had an *opportunity* to collect many *specimens* of moon rocks.

7

No *medicine* can keep a fool from being *asinine*.

9

Follow the instructions for Frame 8.

a. something not intended, [acc] _____

b. scarceness, [rar] _____

c. the source or beginning, [or] _____

d. a pan, [ut] _____

10

Follow the instructions for Frame 8.

a. attempt to discover something, [exp] _____

b. an exaggerated drawing, [car] _____

c. certain, [def] _____

d. preparation taken to relieve illness, [med] _____

11

Follow the instructions for Frame 8.

a. clearly, [ev] _____

b. opposite of plenty, [sca] _____

c. extremely foolish, [as] _____

d. an example, [spec] _____

12

Write each incomplete word in full, choosing the most suitable from those studied in this unit.

A [car] _____ drawn by an [int] _____ _____ artist may become, either through intention or by [acc] _____, the [ba] _____ for the public's opinion of an individual. Although I have no [def] _____ proof, I suspect that the [or] _____ of many persons' opinions of a President lies in political cartoons.

13

Follow the instructions for Frame 12.

a. I tried to perform an [ex] _____ in chemistry today, but since the litmus paper did not change color, [ev] _____ I failed.

b. Since this dime was minted in small quantities, it is now a [rar] _____ .

c. Every [ut] _____ in the kitchen was dirty.

d. That was an [as] _____ remark.

8

a. opportunity
b. basis
c. quantitative
d. intelligent
e. intelligence

9

a. accident
b. rarity
c. origin
d. utensil

10

a. experiment
b. caricature
c. definite
d. medicine

11

a. evidently
b. scarcity
c. asinine
d. specimen

12

caricature
intelligent
accident
basis
definite
origin

14

Follow the instructions for Frame 12.

a. This is a rare [spec] _____ of beetle.
b. The [med] _____ tastes bitter.
c. [Op] _____ really knocks many times.
d. The [scar] _____ of food created a problem.
e. In college I shall study [quan] _____ analysis in chemistry.

13

a. experiment, evidently
b. rarity
c. utensil
d. asinine

15

Study each word that you missed in Frames 8–14. Notice the trouble spots, such as the indistinct *i*. Write each missed word correctly three times. Check your spellings against the list above Frame 1.

14

a. specimen
b. medicine
c. Opportunity
d. scarcity
e. quantitative

UNIT 45 · Words that use *i* for the schwa sound (II)

WORDS TREATED

article	eliminate	manifest	primitive	sensitive
attitude	furniture	obstinate	privilege	
comparison	heartily	optimism	readily	
dormitory	incident	optimist	sacrifice	

1   eliminate   obstinate

In this unit we will look at some more words that use an *i* to represent the schwa sound (something like "uh"). Associating them with one another will help you to remember them. Later we will see other spellings for the schwa.

Note that both *eliminate* and *obstinate* have an *i* before the *–nate*.

Write *eliminate* and *obstinate* twice each, capitalizing the *i* before *n* for emphasis.

_____, _____

_____, _____

2   optimist   optimism

The first *i* in *optimist* and in *optimism* is there because these words come from Latin *optimus*, the best.

Copy: *Optimist* and *optimism* are derived from *optimus*.

_____

_____

1

elimInate, elimInate
obstInate, obstInate

3   heartily   readily

Heartily and *readily* are two of the many words in which a *y* is changed to an *i* before a suffix. That is, *hearty* + *−ly* becomes *heartily*, and *ready* + *−ly* becomes *readily*. (See Unit 6 for other examples.)

Copy: I *heartily* agreed, *readily* falling in with his scheme.

———————————————————————
———————————————————————

4   privilege   sacrifice   sensitive

Each of the words above has nine letters, and the middle letter in each is *i*. Some persons misspell *privilege* with ten letters. Note that it is exactly balanced, like the other two: priv i lege.

Draw three little balance scales, with *I* as the central point, to show the balance of the three words listed above.

5   dormitory   furniture   primitive

Three other balanced nine-letter words with an *i* in the middle are *dormitory*, *furniture*, and *primitive*.

Draw balance scales for *dormitory*, *furniture*, and *primitive*.

6   manifest   incident

Manifest and *incident* are not balanced, but the *i* is near the middle. Write *manifest* and *incident* twice each.

——————————— , ———————————
——————————— , ———————————

2

Optimist and *optimism* are derived from *optimus*.

3

I *heartily* agreed, *readily* falling in with his scheme.

4

5

7   comparison   article   attitude

Note the troublesome *i* in each of the words above.

Copy: The *article* concerns a *comparison* of *attitudes*.

_____

_____

8

Match each definition with one of the words we studied in this unit. The first letters have been supplied.

a. a place for sleeping, [dor] _____

b. in a hearty manner, [he] _____

c. one who expects good things, [opt] _____

d. get rid of, [el] _____

e. of early times; simple, [prim] _____

9

Follow the instructions for Frame 8.

a. item in a newspaper, [art] _____

b. a show of similarities and differences, [com] _____

c. stance; position, [att] _____

d. something given up at great cost or pain, [sac] _____

10

Follow the instructions for Frame 8.

a. cheerfulness, [opt] _____

b. plain; evident, [man] _____

c. emotional; easily hurt, [sen] _____

d. without hesitation, [re] _____

11

Follow the instructions for Frame 8.

a. stubborn, [obs] _____

b. special right, [priv] _____

c. equipment for a house, [fur] _____

d. a happening, [inc] _____

6

manifest, manifest

incident, incident

7

The *article* concerns a *comparison* of *attitudes*.

8

a. dormitory

b. heartily

c. optimist

d. eliminate

e. primitive

9

a. article

b. comparison

c. attitude

d. sacrifice

10

a. optimism

b. manifest

c. sensitive

d. readily

12

Write in full each incomplete word, choosing the most suitable from those studied in this unit.

An [opt] _____ takes the [att] _____ that it is a [priv] _____ to be alive. To him it is [man] _____ that everyone should [he] _____ enjoy himself, for it is an [art] _____ of his faith that we live in a wonderful world.

13

Follow the instructions for Frame 12.

a. A strange [inc] _____ happened this morning.
b. The boys slept in a [dor] _____.
c. Can we [elim] _____ jealousy as a motive?
d. Some parents [sac] _____ a great deal to send children to college.
e. The lecturer made a [com] _____ between Mars and Venus.
f. Even today, explorers hope to find other [prim] _____ drawings in caves.

14

Follow the instructions for Frame 12.

a. My skin is [sen] _____ to chlorine.
b. Jarvis [re] _____ accepted the suggestion.
c. Why do women insist on moving [fur] _____?
d. Voltaire satirized eighteenth century [opt] _____, which expressed the belief that this is "the best of all possible worlds."
e. If Jim weren't so [obs] _____, he would apologize.

15

Study each word that you missed in Frames 8–14. Notice the trouble spots, such as the indistinct *i*. Write each missed word correctly three times. Check your spellings against the list above Frame 1.

11

a. obstinate
b. privilege
c. furniture
d. incident

12

optimist
attitude
privilege
manifest
heartily
article

13

a. incident
b. dormitory
c. eliminate
d. sacrifice
e. comparison
f. primitive

14

a. sensitive
b. readily
c. furniture
d. optimism
e. obstinate

UNIT 46 · Words ending in –ible

WORDS TREATED

accessible	eligible	illegible	intelligible	responsible
audible	feasible	incredible	irresistible	sensible
contemptible	flexible	ineligible	permissible	susceptible
digestible	forcible	inexhaustible	possible	tangible

1

It is not easy to remember whether some words end in *–ible* or *–able*, but it helps to study at one time the often misspelled words that have the same ending.

Usually, if we start with something that is not a whole word, like *suscept* or *feas*, the ending is *–ible*. (There are exceptions.)

Write the words you get when you add *–ible* to *suscept* and *feas*.

_____, _____

2

Usually, too, if we add an ending to a root ending in *ns*, the spelling is *–ible*.

Add *–ible* to *sens* and *respons*.

_____, _____

1
susceptible
feasible

3

Usually *–ible* is what we add to a root ending in *ss*.

Add *–ible* to *poss*, *permiss*, and *access*.

_____, _____, _____

2
sensible
responsible

4

If the root ends in soft *c* or soft *g*, *–ible* is the likely ending.

Add *–ible* to *forc*, *tang*, and *intellig*.

_____, _____, _____

3
possible
permissible
accessible

5

These words also illustrate the principle you learned in Frame 4: *illegible*, *eligible*, and *ineligible*.

Copy *illegible* (as in *illegible handwriting*), *eligible* (as in *an eligible bachelor*), and *ineligible* (as in *an ineligible player*).

_____, _____, _____

4
forcible
tangible
intelligible

---

6 Add *–ible* to these roots: *contempt, flex, incred, irresist.* _____, _____, _____, _____	**5** illegible eligible ineligible
7 Add *–ible* to these roots: *aud, digest, inexhaust.* _____, _____, _____	**6** contemptible flexible incredible irresistible
8 Match each of the following definitions with a synonym we studied in this unit. The first letters have been supplied. Write each word in full. a. with force, [forc] _____ b. impossible to be read, [illeg] _____ c. easily influenced, [sus] _____ d. worthy of contempt, [con] _____ e. capable of being touched, [tang] _____	**7** audible digestible inexhaustible
9 Follow the instructions for Frame 8. a. capable of being heard, [aud] _____ b. not capable of being resisted, [irre] _____ c. able to be bent, [flex] _____ d. capable of being done easily, [feas] _____ e. showing good sense, [sen] _____	**8** a. forcible b. illegible c. susceptible d. contemptible e. tangible
10 Follow the instructions for Frame 8. a. capable of being accomplished, [poss] _____ b. obliged to account for, [respon] _____ c. allowed, [permiss] _____ d. capable of being understood, [intell] _____ e. not capable of being believed, [incred] _____	**9** a. audible b. irresistible c. flexible d. feasible e. sensible

11

Follow the instructions for Frame 8.

a. properly qualified, [elig] _____

b. the opposite of word *a*, [inel] _____

c. easy to reach, [acce] _____

d. capable of being digested, [di] _____

e. not capable of being tired out, [inexh] _____

12

Choose from the words we studied in this unit the one that best fits each blank. The first letters have been supplied. Write the whole word.

Is it [po] _____ that dogs are superior to people? They can hear sounds not [au] _____ to human ears. They can eat foods that people do not consider [di] _____. Young dogs have seemingly [inex] _____ energy. Their bodies are more [fle] _____ than human bodies. They can wag their tails in an [irre] _____ manner.

13

Follow the instructions for Frame 12.

a. The burglar considered it [fe] _____ to make a [for] _____ entry through the cellar door.

b. Two of our players who were [inel] _____ because of low grades have now become [el] _____.

c. The boy told an [incr] _____ story about meeting two Indian chiefs.

d. A liar is a [cont] _____ person.

e. The gun with fingerprints provided [tan] _____ evidence.

14

Follow the instructions for Frame 12.

a. The drunkard did not say anything [sen] _____ or even [intel] _____.

b. The soldier was told that it was not [per] _____ to sign his name in such an [ille] _____ way.

c. Are you [sus] _____ to poison ivy?

d. If the ring is lost, you are [res] _____.

e. Do not put medicine in a place [acc] _____ to children.

10

a. possible
b. responsible
c. permissible
d. intelligible
e. incredible

11

a. eligible
b. ineligible
c. accessible
d. digestible
e. inexhaustible

12

possible
audible
digestible
inexhaustible
flexible
irresistible

13

a. feasible, forcible
b. ineligible, eligible
c. incredible
d. contemptible
e. tangible

15

Study each word that you misspelled in Frames 8–14. Write each missed word correctly three times. Check your answers against the list above Frame 1.

14

a. sensible, intelligible
b. permissible, illegible
c. susceptible
d. responsible
e. accessible

UNIT 47 · Words with *or*

WORDS TREATED

accelerator	benefactor	favorite	inventor	percolator	spectator
author	competitor	governor	labor	portray	sponsor
authoritative	compulsory	humor	metaphor	scissors	
authority	doctor	humorist	motor	senator	

---

1   author   authority   authoritative

In this unit we shall consider various frequently misspelled words containing *or*. Most of these words, as we shall see, come from Latin words that have *or*. If you associate with other *or* words the ones that give you trouble, you may remember them easily.

The three words at the top of this frame are derived from Latin *auctor*, meaning originator or creator.

Copy the three words. _____ , _____ ,
_____

---

2   doctor   senator

Doctor and *senator* are taken directly from Latin, without change of spelling. In Latin, however, *doctor* meant one who teaches. A Roman senator was a member of the *senatus*, or senate.

Write one sentence containing both *doctor* and *senator*.

1

author
authority
authoritative

---

3   humor   humorist

Humor is spelled exactly like Latin *humor*, but the Latin word meant moisture or fluid. Old-time physiologists thought that the body contained four kinds of fluid and that a person's disposition, or "humor," depended upon which fluid he possessed in greatest amount. Then *humor* came to mean a whimsical or comical disposition, and finally changed to the present meaning: a sense of the ridiculous.

Humorist adds the suffix *–ist* which means one who. A humorist, then, is one who has a sense of the ridiculous.

Write a sentence using both *humor* and *humorist*.

2   Model:

The *doctor* reported that the *senator's* health was excellent.

4   favorite   scissors

Although *favorite* comes from French *favorit*, which goes back to Italian *favorire*, to favor, all three words may be traced to Latin *favor*, with a meaning similar to that of English *favor*.

Scissors is another example of a word with *or* in its Latin ancestor, though its spelling otherwise is not much like *cisorium*, which was the Late Latin word for a cutting instrument.

Write a sentence using both *favorite* and *scissors*.

_____

_____

5   labor   portray

Labor is the same in spelling and meaning as its Latin ancestor, *labor*.

Portray, however, uses an *or* because those letters are in the Old French word *portraire*, from which the English borrowed it.

Copy: The *labor* leader was *portrayed* favorably.

_____

_____

6   metaphor   compulsory   accelerator

Metaphor can be traced through French and Latin to Greek *metaphora*, a "carrying over" or "transfer." When we use the *metaphor* "Joan is an angel," we transfer to Joan some of the qualities of an angel.

Compulsory, which means required, comes from Medieval Latin *compulsorius*. That word is based on the Latin word for *compel*. One is *compelled* to do that which is *compulsory*.

Accelerator is pure Latin: *accelerator*.

Copy: Using a *metaphor*, the sales director said, "It is *compulsory* for us to step on the *accelerator*."

_____

_____

7   benefactor   governor   sponsor   percolator
**   competitor   inventor   motor   spectator**

The remaining words we shall study all end in *or*, which means one who or that which.

Write each of the eight words in the following list.

benefactor—one who helps others _____

competitor—one who competes _____

governor—one who governs _____

inventor—one who invents _____

sponsor—one who supports _____

motor—that which moves something _____

percolator—that which percolates _____

spectator—one who watches _____

3   Model:

I do not enjoy the *humor* of some *humorists*.

4   Model:

He tried to cut linoleum with my *favorite scissors*.

5

The *labor* leader was *portrayed* favorably.

6

Using a *metaphor*, the sales director said, "It is *compulsory* for us to step on the *accelerator*."

8

From the words we studied in this unit, select and write in full the one that best fits each definition. The beginning letter or letters have been supplied.

a. writer, [a] _____
b. required, [com] _____
c. physician, [doc] _____
d. instrument for making coffee, [per] _____
e. top official of a state, [gov] _____
f. engine, [mo] _____
g. device for regulating speed, [ac] _____
h. person who looks at, [spec] _____

9

Follow the instructions for Frame 8.

a. one who invents, [in] _____
b. an expert in a subject, [auth] _____
c. one who competes, [com] _____
d. one who supports, [spon] _____
e. figure of speech, [met] _____
f. work, [la] _____
g. sense of the ridiculous, [h] _____

10

Follow the instructions for Frame 8.

a. one who does a good deed, [bene] _____
b. to picture, [por] _____
c. two-edged cutting instrument, [sci] _____
d. one who has a sense of
   the ridiculous, [hum] _____
e. member of the senate, [sen] _____
f. based on facts, [auth] _____
g. best-liked, [fav] _____

11

From the words we studied in this unit, select and write in full the one that makes sense for each unfinished word.

a. When Mother was ill, her [fav] _____ [doc] _____ was not in the clinic.
b. The [sen] _____ announced that he no longer favored [com] _____ military training.
c. For coffee lovers, a [perc] _____ is a great [bene] _____ of humanity.

7

benefactor
competitor
governor
inventor
sponsor
motor
percolator
spectator

8

a. author
b. compulsory
c. doctor
d. percolator
e. governor
f. motor
g. accelerator
h. spectator

9

a. inventor   e. metaphor
b. authority   f. labor
c. competitor   g. humor
d. sponsor

10

a. benefactor   e. senator
b. portray   f. authoritative
c. scissors   g. favorite
d. humorist

12

a. The [au] _____ of this book of poems is unusually fond of [met] _____ [s].

b. The [inv] _____ of this [mo] _____ deserves much praise.

c. What a sense of [hu] _____ Lincoln had!

13

Follow the instructions for Frame 11.

a. Now for a word from our [sp] _____.

b. The [gov] _____ of our state is a born fighter, a great [com] _____.

c. The Secretary of [La] _____ should be an [auth] _____ _____ on the needs of workers.

14

Follow the instructions for Frame 11.

a. If those who best know a subject [por] _____ it favorably, their words will be considered [auth] _____.

b. The [hum] _____ said that modern maps change so rapidly that the most important possessions of mapmakers are paste and [sc] _____.

c. Each [spec] _____ watched with interest.

d. Press the [acc] _____ before turning the key.

15

Study each word that you misspelled in Frames 8–14. Look back at Frames 1–7 to see why the word is spelled as it is. Write each missed word correctly three times. Check your spellings against the list above Frame 1.

11

a. favorite, doctor
b. senator, compulsory
c. percolator, benefactor

12

a. author, metaphors
b. inventor, motor
c. humor

13

a. sponsor
b. governor, competitor
c. Labor, authority

14

a. portray, authoritative
b. humorist, scissors
c. spectator
d. accelerator

UNIT 48 · Words ending in –al

WORDS TREATED

actual	colloquial	moral	principal
annual	dual	original	several
biennial	medical	pedestal	substantial
capital	medieval	political	testimonial

1   actual   medical   original   substantial

A number of English words end in *–al*. As a rule, these words are shortened from Latin words that ended in *–alis*. In Latin the words at the top of this frame were spelled *actualis, medicalis, originalis,* and *substantialis.*

Copy the four words from the top of the frame and their Latin ancestors.

_____, _____

_____, _____

_____, _____

_____, _____

---

2   moral   political   medieval

Two of the easy *–al* words are *moral* and *political. Medieval* is sometimes spelled in a more difficult way *(mediaeval)*, but the simpler spelling *medieval* is generally used today.

Copy: The *moral* and *political* beliefs of the *medieval* period differed in many ways from ours.

_____

_____

---

3   several   pedestal   testimonial   colloquial

The first three of the words above are rather easy. The fourth, *colloquial,* is used especially to describe informal language, as in *Most of us use colloquial English in talking with our friends.* (The *loqu* part is also found in *loquacious,* meaning talkative: *a loquacious person.*)

Copy: The senators stood by the *pedestal* and delivered *several colloquial testimonials.*

_____

_____

---

4   annual   biennial

Annual comes from Latin *annualis,* meaning once a year. *Biennial* comes from Latin *biennium,* meaning two years. This difference in derivation accounts for the different spellings. (Another word, *biannual,* is sometimes used to mean twice a year, but *semiannual* seems less confusing for this purpose.)

Copy: An *annual* flower must be replanted *annually;* a *biennial* flower, *biennially.*

_____

_____

1

actual, *actualis*
medical, *medicalis*
original, *originalis*
substantial, *substantialis*

2

The *moral* and *political* beliefs of the *medieval* period differed in many ways from ours.

3

The senators stood by the *pedestal* and delivered *several colloquial testimonials.*

---

5 dual duel

An automobile with dual carburetors has two carburetors. *Dual* comes from Latin *dualis*, meaning double or pertaining to two; the Latin word for *two* is *duo*. (*Dual* should not be confused with *duel*, meaning a fight. The *el* in *duel* is retained from an Early Latin form of *bellum*, war.)

Copy: If something has a *dual* purpose, it has a double purpose.

_____

_____

6 capital capitol

Whenever you need to write the word pronounced *capital*, the chances are perhaps twenty to one that you need the *–al* spelling. The only use for the spelling with *–ol* is for a legislative building. (Some students associate the *o* in *dome* with the *o* in *capitol* because such a building often has a dome.) So *capital* is the word you need in *capital letter*, *capital punishment*, *capital in the bank*, and *capital of a state*.

Copy the four examples just given.

_____ , _____

_____ , _____

7 principal

Principal, from Latin *principalis*, is the usual spelling of this word. (The word that is confused with it, *principle*, is needed just to refer to a rule or law. Some students remember the *le* of *rule* and the *le* of *principle*.) So *principal* is the word you need in *principal of a school*, *the principal parts*, and *principal* (money) *that draws interest*.

Copy the three examples just given.

_____

_____

_____

8

Write in full the word we studied in this unit that best fits each definition. The first letters have been supplied.

a. a statement about the value of something, [test] _____
b. a few, [sev] _____
c. pertaining to politics, [pol] _____
d. chief or most important, [prin] _____

4

An *annual* flower must be planted *annually*; a *biennial* flower, *biennially*.

5

If something has a *dual* purpose, it has a double purpose.

6

capital letter
capital punishment
capital in the bank
capital of a state

7

principal of a school
the principal parts
principal (money) that draws interest

9

Follow the instructions for Frame 8.

a. a stand on which something may be mounted, [ped] _____

b. first, [orig] _____

c. pertaining to the Middle Ages, [med] _____

d. double, [du] _____

10

Follow the instructions for Frame 8.

a. pertaining to medicine, [med] _____

b. informal, as language, [col] _____

c. once a year, [an] _____

d. a city that is the head of government for a state or country, [cap]
_____

11

Follow the instructions for Frame 8.

a. real, [act] _____

b. every two years, [bi] _____

c. good in character or conduct, [mor] _____

d. solid; considerable, [subs] _____

12

Write in full the word we studied in this unit that is most suitable
for each blank. The beginning letters have been supplied.

The Class of 1960 holds an [an] _____ reunion. Many
of these men and women have become [subs] _____
citizens. [Sev] _____ are in the [med] _____
profession, at least two have high [pol] _____ ambi-
tions, and one is the [prin] _____ of a school.

13

Follow the instructions for Frame 12.

a. A plant that lives for two years is called a [bi] _____ .

b. My mother wrote a [test] _____ about how
good the medicine was.

c. Don't think of an author as someone on a [ped] _____ .

d. What will be the [ac] _____ cost to the buyer?

e. The actor played a [du] _____ role in the play.

8

a. testimonial
b. several
c. political
d. principal

9

a. pedestal
b. original
c. medieval
d. dual

10

a. medical
b. colloquial
c. annual
d. capital

11

a. actual
b. biennial
c. moral
d. substantial

12

annual
substantial
several
medical
political
principal

14

Follow the instructions for Frame 12.

a. Does this novel have any [mor] _____ significance?

b. Why are there two [cap] _____ letters in *O'Brien*?

c. The stranger talked easily, in a highly [col] _____ manner.

d. Did the [med] _____ period end about 1500 A.D.?

e. I'd like to write an [orig] _____ story.

15

Study each word that you misspelled in Frames 8–14. Note the trouble spot. Write each missed word correctly three times. Check your spellings against the list above Frame 1.

13

a. biennial

b. testimonial

c. pedestal

d. actual

e. dual

14

a. moral

b. capital

c. colloquial

d. medieval

e. original

UNIT 49 · One and two

WORDS TREATED

across	centennial	omission	professor
artillery	dilemma	opossum	recommend
Britannica	harass	parallel	toboggan
career	necessary	profession	trespass

---

1   across   dilemma

This unit concerns a number of words that cause trouble because people do not remember which letter is doubled. All the words in this unit have doubled letters at or near the end and various single letters earlier.

For example, *across* has its doubled letters at the end, and *dilemma* has them near the end.

Write: *acroSS* and *dileMMa*.

_____ , _____

---

2   harass   trespass

Write the two words above, which have the doubled letters at the end. Capitalize the doubled letters.

_____ , _____

1

acroSS

dileMMa

---

3   professor   profession   omission

Write the three words above, noting their two *s*'s near the end. Capitalize the doubled letters.

_____ , _____ , _____

---

4   necessary   opossum

Write the two words above, noting their two *s*'s near the end. Capitalize the doubled letters.

_____ , _____

---

5   artillery   parallel

Write the two words above, noting the two *l*'s near the end. Capitalize the doubled letters.

_____ , _____

---

6   centennial   Britannica

Write the two words above, noting the two *n*'s near the end. Capitalize the doubled letters.

_____ , _____

---

7   toboggan   career   recommend

Write the three words above, capitalizing the doubled letters.

_____ , _____ , _____

8

Choose from the words we studied in this unit the ones that best complete each sentence. Write each word in full.

a. The [pro] _____ found an [op] _____ in the trap.

b. It is [nec] _____ that the rails of a railroad track be exactly [par] _____ .

9

Follow the instructions for Frame 8.

a. He had a long and successful [car] _____ in the medical [pro] _____ .

b. We could hear the [art] _____ booming [ac] _____ the bay.

2

haraSS
trespaSS

3

profeSSor
profeSSion
omiSSion

4

neceSSary
opoSSum

5

artiLLery
paraLLel

6

centeNNial
BritaNNica

7

toboGGan
carEEr
recoMMend

8

a. professor, opossum
b. necessary, parallel

10

Follow the instructions for Frame 8.

a. The committee responsible for the [cen] _____ celebration faced a strange [dil] _____ .

b. To [ful] _____ this assignment, you should consult sources besides the *Encyclopaedia* [*Brit*] _____ .

11

Follow the instructions for Frame 8.

a. The station wagon will be crowded, so I [rec] _____ the [om] _____ of the [tob] _____ .

b. We do not want to [har] _____ anyone, but we cannot allow you to [tres] _____ .

12

Write the complete word from this unit that best fits each definition. The first letters are supplied.

a. on the other side, [ac] _____

b. college teacher, [pro] _____

c. occupation, [pro] _____

d. at the same distance apart, [par] _____

e. essential, [nec] _____

f. action through life, [car] _____

g. hundredth anniversary, [cen] _____

h. puzzling situation, [dil] _____

13

Follow the instructions for Frame 12.

a. annoy, [har] _____

b. act of leaving out, [om] _____

c. a small mammal, [op] _____

d. enter property illegally, [tre] _____

e. sled without runners, [to] _____

f. speak in favor of, [re] _____

g. a well-known encyclopedia, [*Bri*] _____

h. cannon, [ar] _____

14

In the future, when you need to write one of the words studied in this unit, try to associate it with one or two of the other words so that you will remember the double letters near the end.

Study each word that you misspelled in Frames 8–13. Write each missed word correctly three times. Check your answers against the list above Frame 1.

9

a. career, profession

b. artillery, across

10

a. centennial, dilemma

b. fulfill, *Britannica*

11

a. recommend, omission, toboggan

b. harass, trespass

12

a. across	e. necessary
b. professor	f. career
c. profession	g. centennial
d. parallel	h. dilemma

13

a. harass	e. toboggan
b. omission	f. recommend
c. opossum	g. *Britannica*
d. trespass	h. artillery

UNIT 50 · Words ending in *—le*

WORDS TREATED

angle	icicle	noble	simple
bridle	inveigle	pickle	spectacle
ennoble	ladle	receptacle	vehicle
fable	morale	ridicule	

---

1   angle   bridle   noble

English words ending in *le* came from a variety of sources. For example, *angle* is from Latin *angulus;* *bridle* (as in *to bridle a horse*) is from Old English *bridlian*; *noble* is from Latin *nobilis*.

Write one short sentence about the *angles* in a triangle, another about the *bridle* of a horse, and a third about a *noble* gesture.

_____

_____

_____

---

1   Models:

A triangle has three inside *angles*.
The *bridle* was made of new leather.

His *noble* gesture went unnoticed.

---

2   icicle   vehicle

Although *icicle* and *vehicle* end with the same four letters, they are derived differently. *Icicle* comes from Old English *is* (ice) and *ikel* (stick of ice); *vehicle* comes from a French word, *vehicule*.

Copy: Long *icicles* hung from the *vehicle*.

_____

2

Long *icicles* hung from the *vehicle*.

---

3   ladle   pickle

Ladle and *pickle* both existed in earlier English, as names for many other commonplace objects did. *Ladle* used to be spelled *hlaedel*; it comes from an Old English verb *hladan*, to load or drain. *Pickle* in Middle English was sometimes spelled *pykyl*.

Copy: With the *ladle* he dipped up some sliced *pickles*.

_____

_____

3

With the *ladle* he dipped up some sliced *pickles*.

---

4   simple   fable

A *fable* is a *simple* story, often with animal characters. Both words come from Latin.

Write *a simple fable* three times.

_____, _____,

_____

5   ridicule   morale

Ridicule comes from Latin through French; it goes back to a Latin verb meaning to laugh. *Morale* comes from the French. *Morale* is a noun, meaning emotional condition with reference to confidence or enthusiasm: The *morale* of the troops was high. (It should not be confused with the adjective *moral*, as in *moral standards*.)

Copy: My sister's *ridicule* lowered my *morale*.

_____

_____

6   ennoble   inveigle

To *ennoble* is to make noble. Note the double *n*. To *inveigle* is to lead by trickery: The spider tried to *inveigle* the fly into his parlor.

Copy: It hardly *ennobles* a man to *inveigle* a child into stealing.

_____

_____

7   spectacle   receptacle

Note that both *spectacle* and *receptacle* end in *acle*: Put your *spectacles* into this *receptacle*.

Copy: What a *spectacle*! The *receptacle* was only three feet deep!

_____

_____

8

Match each definition with one of the words we studied in this unit. The first letter or letters have been supplied. Write each word in full.

a. container, [rec] _____
b. emotional condition, [mor] _____
c. not complicated, [sim] _____
d. stick of ice, [ic] _____
e. any corner of a triangle, [an] _____

9

Follow the instructions for Frame 8.

a. conveyance, [ve] _____
b. scorn, [rid] _____
c. story, often with animal characters, [f] _____
d. of high birth, [no] _____
e. cucumber in vinegar, [pi] _____

4

a simple fable
a simple fable
a simple fable

5

My sister's *ridicule* lowered my *morale*.

6

It hardly *ennobles* a man to *inveigle* a child into stealing.

7

What a *spectacle*! The *receptacle* was only three feet deep!

8

a. receptacle   d. icicle
b. morale   e. angle
c. simple

10

Follow the instructions for Frame 8.

a. strap for guiding a horse, [br] _____
b. to make noble, [en] _____
c. to lead by trickery, [in] _____
d. a great sight, [sp] _____
e. large, cup-shaped spoon, [l] _____

11

Write in full each incomplete word, choosing the most suitable from those studied in this unit.

a. This dill [p] _____ is huge!
b. He told the [fa] _____ about the fox and the grapes.
c. Our old car is no longer a comfortable [ve] _____.
d. It is heartless to [rid] _____ a handicapped person.

12

Follow the instructions for Frame 11.

a. Dip out the soup with this [la] _____.
b. Dad tried to [in] _____ the mule into moving by holding an ear of corn before it.
c. Giving generously to the poor will [en] _____ a man, my uncle believes.
d. I have never seen a funnier [sp] _____.

13

Follow the instructions for Frame 11.

a. Many [no] _____ men have died for their country.
b. First I had to learn to put the [br] _____ on the horse.
c. Turn at a right [an] _____.

14

Follow the instructions for Frame 11.

a. An inkwell was a glass [rec] _____ for holding ink.
b. One long [ic] _____ hung from the roof.
c. The [mor] _____ of the civilians sank rapidly.
d. Nothing is as [sim] _____ as it appears to be.

9

a. vehicle	d. noble
b. ridicule	e. pickle
c. fable	

10

a. bridle
b. ennoble
c. inveigle
d. spectacle
e. ladle

11

a. pickle
b. fable
c. vehicle
d. ridicule

12

a. ladle
b. inveigle
c. ennoble
d. spectacle

13

a. noble
b. bridle
c. angle

15

Study each word that you misspelled in Frames 8–14. Write an original sentence including each missed word. Check your spellings against the list above Frame 1.

14

a. receptacle
b. icicle
c. morale
d. simple

UNIT 51 · Words ending in *–able*

WORDS TREATED

acceptable	conceivable	desirable	imaginable	memorable
available	considerable	despicable	inevitable	peaceable
believable	dependable	enviable	inseparable	probable
chargeable	deplorable	fashionable	irritable	taxable

1

It is not easy to remember whether some words end in *–able* or *–ible,* but it helps to study at one time the often-misspelled words that have the same ending.

Usually, if we start with a whole word, like *accept* or *depend,* the ending is *–able.*

Write the words you get when you add *–able* to *accept* and *depend.*

_____, _____

2

Now write the words you get when you add *–able* to *avail, consider, fashion,* and *tax.*

_____, _____,

_____, _____

1

acceptable
dependable

3

Sometimes *–able* is added to a word that ends in *e.* When that happens the *e* is usually omitted. (See Units 11 and 12 for more words that drop the *e.*)

Add *–able* to *desire* and *imagine.* Drop the *e.*

_____, _____

2

available
considerable
fashionable
taxable

4

Conceive, believe, and *deplore* are among the other words that drop the final *e* before adding *–able.*

Write the words you get when you add *–able* to *conceive, believe,* and *deplore.*

_____, _____, _____

5

When a word ends in a soft *c* sound or a soft *g* sound, like *peace* or *charge,* the final *e* is kept before *–able,* because otherwise the *c* or *g* would seem hard.

Add *–able* to *peace* and *charge.* Keep the *e.*

_____, _____

6

Here are some miscellaneous words that end in *–able:*

    inevitable   inseparable   despicable

Copy: It was *inevitable* that the two boys would be almost *inseparable* after they had fought together against the *despicable* bully.

_____

_____

_____

7

Here are four more *–able* words:

    enviable   irritable   probable   memorable

Make up one or two sentences using those four words.

_____

_____

_____

8

Match each of the following definitions with a synonym we studied in this unit. The first letters have been supplied. Write the word in full.

a. capable of being imagined, [im] _____

b. not capable of being separated, [insep] _____

c. not warlike, [peac] _____

d. capable of being conceived, [conc] _____

e. to be deplored, [de] _____

3

-desirable
imaginable

4

conceivable
believable
deplorable

5

peaceable
chargeable

6

It was *inevitable* that the two boys would be almost *inseparable* after they had fought together against the *despicable* bully.

---

7   **Model:**

It is *probable* that he became *irritable* because of the *enviable* excellence of his opponent's *memorable* address.

9

Follow the instructions for Frame 8.

a. capable of being envied, [env] _____
b. not avoidable, [inev] _____
c. capable of being charged, [char] _____
d. capable of being believed, [bel] _____
e. capable of being desired, [des] _____

10

Follow the instructions for Frame 8.

a. capable of being irritated, [irr] _____
b. more than likely, [prob] _____
c. hateful, [despic] _____
d. capable of being accepted, [acc] _____
e. capable of being depended upon, [dep] _____

11

Follow the instructions for Frame 8.

a. ready or near at hand, [ava] _____
b. fairly large, [consid] _____
c. in fashion, [fash] _____
d. capable of being taxed, [tax] _____
e. worthy of being remembered, [mem] _____

12

Choose from the words we studied in this unit the one that best fits each blank. The first letters have been supplied. Write the whole word.

Hank Aaron had an [env] _____ career in baseball, but it was [inev] _____ that some day he must retire. It is hardly [conc] _____, and certainly not [prob] _____, that any single player will break many of his records. Although his hitting was most [mem] _____, his fielding was also always [depend] _____.

13

Follow the instructions for Frame 12.

a. Is this kind of dress still [fash] _____?
b. Your story is hardly [bel] _____; I have [consid] _____ doubt that it is accurate.
c. My father became [irr] _____ when he learned that this income was [tax] _____.
d. A person who mistreats a child is [despic] _____.
e. Is it [acc] _____ to wear a green tie with a blue shirt?

8

a. imaginable
b. inseparable
c. peaceable
d. conceivable
e. deplorable

9

a. enviable
b. inevitable
c. chargeable
d. believable
e. desirable

10

a. irritable
b. probable
c. despicable
d. acceptable
e. dependable

11

a. available
b. considerable
c. fashionable
d. taxable
e. memorable

12

enviable
inevitable
conceivable
probable
memorable
dependable

14

Follow the instructions for Frame 12.

a. Damon and Pythias were such good friends that they were [insep] _____ .

b. It is [depl] _____ that no [peac] _____ solution has been found.

c. It would be more [desir] _____ if the cost were [charg] _____ to the company.

d. This is the most exciting movie [imag] _____ .

e. Have you an extra sleeping bag [avail] _____ ?

13

a. fashionable
b. believable; considerable
c. irritable, taxable
d. despicable
e. acceptable

15

Study each word that you misspelled in Frames 8–14. Write each missed word correctly three times. Check your answers against the list above Frame 1.

14

a. inseparable
b. deplorable, peaceable
c. desirable, chargeable
d. imaginable
e. available

UNIT 52 · Words that use *a* for the schwa sound

WORDS TREATED

amateur	character	hesitancy	miracle	relative
anniversary	dictionary	imperative	narrative	secretary
asparagus	emphasize	lavatory	obstacle	stomach
casualty	equivalent	magazine	propaganda	testament

1   dictionary   secretary   anniversary

No easy way exists to remember the words in which the schwa sound (like an "uh") is used. Sometimes an *a* represents this sound. Perhaps the best way to remember those words with *a* for the schwa is to try to associate a number of them with one another. For example, the three words at the top of this frame all end in *–ary*. If you remember the *–ary* in one of them, it may help you to remember it in the others.

Write a single sentence using the words *dictionary*, *secretary*, and *anniversary*.

_____

_____

2   obstacle   miracle   character

Each of the three words above has an indistinct *a* followed by a *c*.
Write a single sentence using the words *obstacle*, *miracle*, and *character*.

_____

_____

3   propaganda   asparagus

Perhaps *propaganda* and *asparagus* have little in common except an indistinct *a* followed by a *g*.
Write a sentence telling about the *propaganda* issued by some growers of *asparagus*.

_____

_____

4   amateur   relative   testament

The three words above all have the same rhythm. The first syllable of each is accented, and the indistinct *a* comes near the middle.
Write a sentence about a *relative* of yours who was an *amateur* lawyer and who drew up his own last will and *testament*.

_____

_____

5   magazine   emphasize   casualty

The three words above also are similar to each other in rhythm. Again the indistinct *a* is near the middle.
Write a sentence in which you use *magazine*, *emphasize*, and *casualty*.

_____

_____

6   narrative   equivalent   hesitancy

Perhaps it will help you if you associate *narrative* with *narrate*, *equivalent* with *value*, *hesitancy* with *hesitate*.
Write *narrate*, *narrative*, *equivalent*, *value*, *hesitancy*, *hesitate*.

_____, _____

_____, _____

_____, _____

1   Model:

He gave his *secretary* a *dictionary* on her *anniversary*.

2   Model:

The *miracle* is that his poor *character* is not a great *obstacle*.

3   Model:

The *asparagus* growers released much *propaganda* about the healthfulness of their product.

4   Model:

A *relative* of mine, although he was only an *amateur* lawyer, prepared his own last will and *testament*.

5   Model:

The *magazine* articles *emphasize* that such a high *casualty* rate can be avoided.

imperative   lavatory   stomach

A Latin word related to *imperative* is *imperátor*, "emperor, commander." Associate *lavatory* with Lava soap. And associate the *a* in *stomach* with *ache*.

Fill in the missing words in the following sentences.

The boy's _____ was churning. It was _____ _____ that he find a _____ at once.

8

Write in full the unfinished words in the following passage, choosing from those you have studied in this unit.

Mr. Clanton's [sec] _____ was a woman of strong [char] _____. Without [hes] _____ she would [emph] _____ to her employer that it was [imper] _____ to buy a [dict] _____, to remember his wife's [anniv] _____, to purchase better soap for the [lav] _____, or to discharge the incompetent [rel] _____ whom he had lately hired.

9

Follow the instructions for Frame 8.

A [nar] _____ in this [mag] _____ concerns an [am] _____ athlete who could overcome every [obst] _____ except his liking for [asp] _____. He ate so much of it that it is a [mir] _____ that he did not become a [cas] _____. He worried a little and drew up his last will and [test] _____ but kept on munching the succulent stalks. His coach issued [prop] _____ to the effect that other vegetables possess [equiv] _____ amounts of vitamins. But his [st] _____ craved only [asp] _____.

10

Match each definition below with a synonym that we have studied in this unit. The first letters are given. Write each word in full.

a. word book, [dic] _____
b. story, [nar] _____
c. wonderful, unexpected happening, [mir] _____
d. long green vegetable, [asp] _____

6

narrate, narrative
equivalent, value
hesitancy, hesitate

7

stomach
imperative
lavatory

8

secretary	dictionary
character	anniversary
hesitancy	lavatory
emphasize	relative
imperative	

9

narrative	casualty
magazine	testament
amateur	propaganda
obstacle	equivalent
asparagus	stomach
miracle	asparagus

11

Follow the instructions for Frame 10.

a. person injured or killed in an accident, [cas] _____
b. equal in value, size, meaning, etc., [equiv] _____
c. something in the way, [obst] _____
d. not professional, [am] _____
e. instructions for disposing of one's money or property after death, [test] _____
f. a bodily organ, [st] _____

12

Follow the instructions for Frame 10.

a. woman who does not mind being dictated to, [sec] _____
b. systematic spreading of ideas, [prop] _____
c. person in a story, [char] _____
d. periodical publication, [mag] _____
e. doubt or indecision, [hes] _____

13

Follow the instructions for Frame 10.

a. to stress, [emph] _____
b. kin, [rel] _____
c. essential; compulsory, [imp] _____
d. bathroom, [lav] _____
e. yearly return of a date, [ann] _____

14

Study each word that you misspelled in Frames 8–13. Try to associate it with other words using *a.* Write each missed word correctly three times. Check your answers against the list above Frame 1.

10

a. dictionary
b. narrative
c. miracle
d. asparagus

11

a. casualty
b. equivalent
c. obstacle
d. amateur
e. testament
f. stomach

12

a. secretary
b. propaganda
c. character
d. magazine
e. hesitancy

13

a. emphasize
b. relative
c. imperative
d. lavatory
e. anniversary

UNIT 53 · Words ending in –*ious*

WORDS TREATED

atrocious	curious	gracious	laborious	religious	superstitious
cautious	delicious	harmonious	mysterious	repetitious	suspicious
conscientious	facetious	impervious	precarious	sacrilegious	various
conscious	fictitious	ingenious	pretentious	supercilious	

1

If you wonder whether a word ends in *–ious*, *–eous*, *–uous*, or *–ous*, the best guide (though not always reliable) is careful pronunciation.

A word that should be spelled with *–ious* generally has at the end something that sounds like *yŭs*. (Some persons make it sound more like *i ŭs*.) In words ending in *–cious* or *–tious* the sound may be *shŭs* or *shĭ ŭs*.

Say and then write *mysterious* and *cautious*. (Listen for the *yŭs* or *ĭ ŭs* sound.)

_____, _____

2

a. Say and then write *various*, *curious*, *laborious*, and *precarious*.

_____, _____, _____,

_____

b. Copy: *Various curious* onlookers watched his *laborious* efforts in his *precarious* position.

_____

_____

3

a. Say and then write *delicious*, *gracious*, *atrocious*, and *suspicious*.

_____, _____, _____,

_____

b. Try to make up a sentence using all four words.

_____

_____

4

a. Say and then write *superstitious* and *fictitious*.

_____, _____

b. Make up a sentence using *superstitious* and *fictitious*.

_____

_____

5

a. Say and then write *facetious*, *pretentious*, and *repetitious*.

_____, _____,

_____

b. Copy: We made *facetious* remarks about his *pretentious, repetitious* lectures.

_____

_____

1

mysterious
cautious

2

a. various, curious, laborious, precarious

b. *Various curious* onlookers watched his *laborious* efforts in his *precarious* position.

3

a. delicious, gracious, atrocious, suspicious

Model:

b. Although our host was *gracious* and the food was *delicious*, we were *suspicious* that he might have an *atrocious* motive.

4

a. superstitious, fictitious

Model:

b. Some of the stories about the *superstitious* natives were *fictitious*.

6

a. Say and then write *conscious* and *conscientious*.

_____, _____

b. Copy: I am *conscious* of the fact that you are trying to be *conscientious*.

_____

_____

7

a. Say and then write *religious, harmonious,* and *ingenious*.

_____, _____, _____

b. Copy: He was *ingenious* enough to show that his *religious* beliefs and mine were *harmonious*.

_____

_____

8

a. Say and then write *impervious, sacrilegious* (which comes from *sacrilege*), and *supercilious*.

_____, _____,

_____

b. Copy: *Impervious* means not penetrable. *Sacrilegious* means disrespectful of holy things. *Supercilious* means haughty.

_____

_____

_____

9

In Frames 9–14 write in full each unfinished **word**, choosing the best answer from the words studied in this unit.

a. [Var] _____ answers were given by the class.

b. I was knocked out; I was not [con] _____ for an hour.

c. I am [cur] _____ about the reasons for your decision.

10

Follow the instructions for Frame 9.

a. John is prompt and works hard. He is very [con] _____.

b. This cake is [del] _____.

c. The [lab] _____ task was difficult to complete.

d. The story is not true. It is entirely [fictit] _____.

5

a. facetious, pretentious, repetitious

b. We made *facetious* remarks about his *pretentious, repetitious* lectures.

6

a. conscious, conscientious

b. I am *conscious* of the fact that you are trying to be *conscientious*.

7

a. religious, harmonious, ingenious

b. He was *ingenious* enough to show that his *religious* beliefs and mine were *harmonious*.

8

a. impervious, sacrilegious, supercilious

b. *Impervious* means not penetrable. *Sacrilegious* means disrespectful of holy things. *Supercilious* means haughty.

9

a. Various

b. conscious

c. curious

11

Follow the instructions for Frame 9.

a. Modern music is not always [harm] _____.

b. Your solution is clever. It shows you are [ingen] _____.

c. [Myst] _____ sounds came from the cave.

d. Lincoln was a deeply [rel] _____ man, even though he did not go to church regularly.

12

Follow the instructions for Frame 9.

a. It was [sacri] _____ to make such a remark in the cathedral.

b. I am often [sus] _____ of people who flatter me, but I love them.

c. His crime was [atroc] _____.

d. Always be [caut] _____ with campfires.

13

Follow the instructions for Frame 9.

a. The armor could not be dented. It was [imper] _____ to all blows.

b. A woman who wears too much jewelry is considered to be [preten] _____.

c. A wisecrack is a [face] _____ remark.

d. "Oh, [grac] _____!" she exclaimed.

14

Follow the instructions for Frame 9.

a. Sleeping on the edge of a cliff is [prec] _____.

b. The speaker was [rep] _____: he kept saying the same things over and over.

c. A person who sneers at another is [superc] _____.

d. [Superst] _____ people do not necessarily believe in ghosts.

15

Study carefully each word you misspelled in Frames 9–14. Write each missed word correctly three times. Check your spellings against the list above Frame 1.

10

a. conscientious
b. delicious
c. laborious
d. fictitious

11

a. harmonious
b. ingenious
c. Mysterious
d. religious

12

a. sacrilegious
b. suspicious
c. atrocious
d. cautious

13

a. impervious
b. pretentious
c. facetious
d. gracious

14

a. precarious
b. repetitious
c. supercilious
d. Superstitious

UNIT 54 · Words with *ain*

WORDS TREATED

acquaint	captain	disdain	refrain
acquaintance	certain	entertain	villain
bargain	certainly	mountain	villainous
Britain	certainty	pertain	

---

1   entertain   refrain   pertain

a. Each of the three words above ends in ———— (What three letters?).

b. Copy: Please *refrain* from *entertaining* thoughts that *pertain* to escape.

---

2   acquaint   acquaintance

Note the *ain* in each of the two words above. While you are looking, note also the *c* near the beginning of *acquaint* and *acquaintance*.

Copy: I'll *acquaint* you clearly with one fact: I don't like your old *acquaintance*.

---

3   certain   certainly   certainty

Try to remember that *certain* and its relatives also have *ain*, even though the pronunciation of these words does not reveal that fact.

Copy: A *certain* man *certainly* feels *certainty*!

---

4   villain   Britain

Villain and *Britain* are two very often misspelled words. It will help if you associate them with *entertain* and other words in which the *ain* is more distinctly pronounced.

Copy: Will you *entertain* a *villain* who is not from Great *Britain*?

1

a. *ain*

b. Please *refrain* from *entertaining* thoughts that *pertain* to escape.

2

I'll *acquaint* you clearly with one fact: I don't like your old *acquaintance*.

3

A *certain* man *certainly* feels *certainty*!

---

5   villain   +   ous = villainous

If you can spell *villain*, then *villainous* should be easy.
Write *villainous* twice.

_____ , _____

6   captain   mountain

Two other troublesome *ain* words are those above. Once more, associate them in your mind with words like *entertain* and *refrain*.

Copy: Oh, *Captain*, dear *Captain*, please *refrain* from climbing the
    mountain!

_____

_____

7   bargain   disdain

Bargain also may be associated with *entertain* and the like, even though the *ain* in it is less distinctly pronounced.

In *disdain*, note the two *d*'s. Say the word, pronouncing both *d*'s. This word is sometimes misspelled because it is mispronounced.

Copy: Never *disdain* a *bargain*, but distrust it.

_____

_____

8

Write the missing letters in each of the unfinished words in the following passage, choosing the most appropriate one of the words treated in this unit.

    When we were in Great Br_____, we made the ac_____
_____ of a cer_____ cap_____ in the navy. As a
seaman, he had dis_____ for moun_____s, and he cer_____
ly did not mind showing it. His constant re_____ was "Water
and flat land for me!"

9

Follow the instructions for Frame 8.

    The only vil_____ with whom I have ever knowingly been
ac_____ed liked to ent_____ his friends by singing
some ribald ballads that per _____ ed to his own exploits. It is a
cer _____ ty that this vil _____ ous gentleman would have
sold his own mother into slavery if he thought he could make a good
bar_____.

4

Will you *entertain* a *villain* who is
not from Great *Britain*?

5

villainous
villainous

6

Oh, *Captain*, dear *Captain*, please
refrain from climbing the *mountain*!

7

Never *disdain* a *bargain*, but distrust it.

8

Britain
acquaintance
certain
captain
disdain
mountains
certainly
refrain

10

Match each of the following definitions with the most appropriate one of the words you have studied in this unit. The beginning letters have been supplied. Write each word in full.

a. sure, [cer] _____
b. a wicked person, [vil] _____
c. islands west of Europe, [Br] _____
d. a very high hill, [mo] _____

11

Follow the instructions for Frame 10.

a. surely, [cer] _____
b. to belong or be associated with, [per] _____
c. wicked, [vil] _____
d. to make familiar, [ac] _____

12

Follow the instructions for Frame 10.

a. to amuse, [en] _____
b. a good trade or exchange, [bar] _____
c. sureness, [cer] _____

13

Follow the instructions for Frame 10.

a. a regularly repeated verse, [re] _____
b. a commander of a ship, [cap] _____
c. a person known to one, [ac] _____
d. to scorn or look down on, [dis] _____

14

Study each word that you misspelled in Frames 8–13. Note especially the *ain* spelling. Write each missed word correctly three times. Check your spellings against the list above Frame 1.

9

villain
acquainted
entertain
pertained
certainty
villainous
bargain

10

a. certain
b. villain
c. Britain
d. mountain

11

a. certainly
b. pertain
c. villainous
d. acquaint

12

a. entertain
b. bargain
c. certainty

13

a. refrain
b. captain
c. acquaintance
d. disdain

UNIT 55 · Two and one

1 occasion accelerate

This unit concerns a number of words that cause trouble because people do not remember which letter is doubled. All the words in this unit are alike in that the doubled letters come near the beginning.

For example, *occasion* and *accelerate* both have double *c* near the beginning.

Copy: On *occasion*, the driver would *accelerate* sharply.

_____

_____

2 accumulate accident moccasin

a. What do the three words above have in common?
b. Copy: He *accumulates* evidence about *accidents* with cottonmouth *moccasins*.

_____

_____

3 grammatical immediate imminent commemorate

a. Copy: What is the difference in meaning between *immediate* and *imminent*?

_____

_____

b. Copy: Jespersen, a Dane, was *commemorated* in 1960 for his *grammatical* analysis of English.

_____

_____

1

On *occasion*, the driver would *accelerate* sharply.

2

a. double *c* near the beginning
b. He *accumulates* evidence about *accidents* with cottonmouth *moccasins*.

4 baggage aggravate exaggerate

a. Copy: *Baggage* and *luggage* are similar in spelling.

_____

b. Copy: To *aggravate* my displeasure, he *exaggerated* the size of his fish.

_____

_____

---

5 allot apparent collateral

Copy: It is *apparent* that you should not *allot* much attention to *collateral* evidence.

_____

_____

_____

(Note: *a lot*, as in "a lot of time," is written as two words. So, of course, is *a little*: "a little time.")

---

6 apparatus appetite correlate

Write the three words above, noting the double letters in each.

_____, _____, _____

---

7 abbreviate battalion illiterate

Write the three words above, noting the double letters in each.

_____, _____, _____

8

Write in full the word we studied in this unit that best matches each definition. The letters given are the *last* ones in the word.

a. stretch the truth, _____ [erate]
b. soft slipper, _____ [sin]
c. not able to read or write, _____ [erate]
d. near, _____ [nent]

9

Follow the instructions for Frame 8.

a. relate with something else, _____ [elate]
b. honor the memory, _____ [orate]
c. accompanying but less important, _____ [ateral]
d. military unit of two or more companies, _____ [lion]
e. luggage, _____ [age]

3

a. What is the difference in meaning between *immediate* and *imminent*?

b. Jespersen, a Dane, was *commemorated* in 1960 for his *grammatical* analysis of English.

4

a. *Baggage* and *luggage* are similar in spelling.

b. To *aggravate* my displeasure, he *exaggerated* the size of his fish.

5

It is *apparent* that you should not *allot* much attention to *collateral* evidence.

6

apparatus
appetite
correlate

7

abbreviate
battalion
illiterate

8

a. exaggerate
b. moccasin
c. illiterate
d. imminent

10

Follow the instructions for Frame 8.

a. obvious, _____ [ent]

b. desire for food, _____ [tite]

c. complex machinery for a special purpose, _____ [atus]

d. coming at once, _____ [diate]

11

Follow the instructions for Frame 8.

a. give shares of, _____ [ot]

b. make worse, _____ [vate]

c. shorten, _____ [viate]

d. unintentional and unfortunate happening, _____ [dent]

12

Follow the instructions for Frame 8.

a. pertaining to grammar, _____ [ical]

b. collect little by little, _____ [ulate]

c. speed up, _____ [erate]

d. a particular time, _____ [sion]

13

Write in full the word studied in this unit that makes the best sense in each blank. This time only the first letter has been supplied.

a. "This is a sad [o] _____," said the minister. "The [a] _____ that took this child's life should have been prevented."

b. The driver began to [a] _____, and a crash seemed [i] _____.

c. Each soldier in the [b] _____ hoped that he would [a] _____ enough points to be sent home.

14

Follow the instructions for Frame 13.

a. This monument will [c] _____ the inventor of [a] _____ for storing sunlight.

b. Perhaps you think that I lie or at least [e] _____, but I have such an [a] _____ that I could eat a raw goat.

c. One [i] _____ result will be [a] _____: fewer children will be [i] _____.

9

a. correlate

b. commemorate

c. collateral

d. battalion

e. baggage

10

a. apparent

b. appetite

c. apparatus

d. immediate

11

a. allot

b. aggravate

c. abbreviate

d. accident

12

a. grammatical

b. accumulate

c. accelerate

d. occasion

13

a. occasion, accident

b. accelerate, imminent

c. battalion, accumulate

15

In the future, when you need to write one of the words used in this unit, try to associate it with one or two of the other words so that you will remember the double letters near the beginning.

Study each word that you misspelled in Frames 8–14. Write each missed word correctly three times. Check your answers against the list above Frame 1.

14

a. commemorate, apparatus
b. exaggerate, appetite
c. immediate, apparent, illiterate

UNIT 56 · Words with the vowel *y*

WORDS TREATED

analysis	hypnosis	mystery	syphilis
bicycle	hypocrite	paralysis	tricycle
cylinder	hysterical	symbol	tyranny
hymn	motorcycle	symptom	

---

1 hymn

Perhaps as a child you learned that the vowels are *a, e, i, o, u,* and sometimes *y.* Although modern linguists believe that that statement is an oversimplification, it helps if you remember that *y* is used as a vowel in some words. Often the vowel *y* is at the end, as in *hungry* or *opportunity,* but it seldom causes trouble there. We shall look at a few words in which *y* appears elsewhere.

A choir may sing a *hymn.* Note that *y* is used like an *i* in this word. (Note also the silent *n.*) The Greek word from which *hymn* comes is *hymnos.*

Copy: *Hymn* comes from Greek *hymnos.*

---

2 bicycle

Bicycle is composed of *bi,* from a Latin word meaning two, and *cycle,* from Latin *cyclus* and Greek *kyklos,* meaning circle or wheel. The *y,* then, is due to the Latin and Greek ancestors.

Write *bicycle* and then the corresponding name for a three-wheeled vehicle and the name for a cycle with a motor.

_____ , _____ , _____

1

Hymn comes from Greek *hymnos.*

---

3 cylinder

Cylinder also goes back to the Greek, this time to *kylindein,* to roll. Use *cylinder* (or *cylinders*) in a sentence.

2

bicycle
tricycle
motorcycle

---

4   **hypnosis**   **hypocrite**

Hypnosis is derived from Greek *hypnos,* sleep.

   Hypocrite in Greek was *hypokrites,* an actor or deceiver. Once more, then, the Greeks are responsible for the *y's.*

Write a single sentence using both *hypnosis* and *hypocrite.*

_____

_____

_____

5   **hysterical**   **mystery**

Hysterical goes back to still another Greek word, *hysterikos,* of the womb (because women are supposedly more often hysterical than men are).

   Mystery is from Greek *mysterion,* secrets or secret rites.

Write a single sentence using both *hysterical* and *mystery.*

_____

_____

_____

6   **symbol**   **symptom**

A symbol is a token of something else. Thus our flag is a symbol of our country. The *y* is in this word because it comes from Greek *symbolon,* or token. The Greek *symptoma,* the ancestor of *symptom,* explains not only the *y* but also the two *m's* in that word.

Use *symbol* and *symptom* each in a short sentence.

_____

_____

_____

7   **paralysis**   **analysis**

Paralysis, like the related words *paralyze* and *paralytic,* goes back to Greek *paralyein,* to disable. *Analysis* goes back to Greek *analyein,* to dissolve.

Copy: While suffering *paralysis*
       He underwent *analysis.*

_____

_____

8   **tyranny**   **syphilis**

Syphilis and *tyranny,* as well as *syphilitic, tyrant,* and *tyrannous,* may serve as final examples of the troublesome words with *y* as a vowel. Like the other words we have noticed, *tyranny* goes back to Greek, but *syphilis* was the title of a Renaissance poem about love.

Copy: A *tyrant* is *tyrannous* or *tyrannical* and rules with *tyranny.*

_____

_____

A person with *syphilis* is by definition *syphilitic.*

_____

_____

3   **Model:**

The engine is now hitting on only three *cylinders.*

4   **Model:**

When he was under *hypnosis,* he declared that he was a *hypocrite.*

5   **Model:**

The fact that she was *hysterical* did not help to solve the *mystery.*

6   **Models:**

A dollar bill is a *symbol* of possessions.

The first *symptom* was a high fever.

7

While suffering *paralysis*
He underwent *analysis.*

9

Choose from the words we studied in this unit the one that best fits each definition. The beginning letter or letters have been supplied. Write the complete word.

a. religious song, [h] _____
b. an artificially induced sleep, [h] _____
c. strict and often harsh government, [t] _____
d. a reduced power of motion or feeling, [par] _____
e. a venereal disease, [s] _____

10

Follow the instructions for Frame 9.

a. two-wheeled vehicle, [b] _____
b. two-wheeled vehicle with a motor, [m] _____
c. token or emblem, [s] _____
d. excited beyond control, [h] _____

11

Follow the instructions for Frame 9.

a. three-wheeled vehicle, [tr] _____
b. a long, round object with flat ends, [c] _____
c. one who pretends to be better than he is, [h] _____
d. something difficult to account for, [m] _____
e. examination of the parts, [anal] _____

12

Choose from the words we studied in this unit the one that best fits each sentence. Write the word in full.

a. She laughed so hard that I thought she would become [h] _____
_____.
b. I rode off on my [b] _____.
c. The French Revolution was only in part a protest against the [t] _____ of French kings.
d. We shall now sing the first [h] _____ in the book.
e. The disease was diagnosed as [s] _____.

13

Follow the instructions for Frame 12.

a. My little sister was riding her [tr] _____.
b. A cone has only one-third the volume of an equally tall [c] _____.
c. Don't be a [h] _____. We know that you really detest Fred.
d. The crown is a [s] _____ of the king's authority.

8

A *tyrant* is *tyrannous* or *tyrannical* and rules with *tyranny*.
A person with *syphilis* is by definition *syphilitic*.

9

a. hymn
b. hypnosis
c. tyranny
d. paralysis
e. syphilis

10

a. bicycle
b. motorcycle
c. symbol
d. hysterical

11

a. tricycle
b. cylinder
c. hypocrite
d. mystery
e. analysis

12

a. hysterical
b. bicycle
c. tyranny
d. hymn
e. syphilis

14

Follow the instructions for Frame 12.

a. This detective story is called "The [M] _____ of the Lost Lavaliere."

b. Ken roared up on his [mo] _____ and dismounted hurriedly.

c. The accident caused partial [par] _____ in his left leg.

d. Doctors sometimes use [h] _____ in treating patients; in such a sleep, the patients may provide important clues for a diagnosis.

e. The chemist made an [a] _____ of the unknown compound.

13

a. tricycle
b. cylinder
c. hypocrite
d. symbol

15

Study each word you missed in Frames 9–14. Write each missed word correctly three times. Check your spellings against the list above Frame 1.

14

a. Mystery
b. motorcycle
c. paralysis
d. hypnosis
e. analysis

UNIT 57 · When *ph = f*

WORDS TREATED

alphabet	diphthong	paragraph	phlegm	physical	telephone
catastrophe	emphasis	phase	phobia	physician	
diaphragm	emphatic	phenomenon	photograph	physiology	
diphtheria	pamphlet	philosophy	phrase	telegraph	

1

The Greek letter φ was called *phi*. In classic Greek, it was pronounced about like the *ph* in *uphill*. The Romans wrote *ph* instead of φ. Gradually the sound changed, perhaps because the sound of *p* followed by the sound of *h* is rather hard to pronounce. Finally it was sounded as *f*, as it is in modern English.

You may guess from the preceding paragraph that English words spelled with a *ph* instead of *f* are derived from _____ (What language?).

2

A large dictionary lists several hundred English words that start with *ph*. Here are some of the more common ones:

       phase phrase philosophy physiology
  physical phenomenon phlegm phobia physician

Write these nine words that start with *ph*.

_____, _____, _____,

_____, _____, _____,

_____, _____, _____

3

Some persons misspell *diphtheria* and *diphthong* because they mispronounce the words. Notice that the first syllable is *diph*, which most careful speakers pronounce *dĭf*.

Say and then write *diphtheria* and *diphthong*.

_____, _____

4

Here are some more words with *ph* near the beginning or the middle:

    diaphragm (Note the silent *g*.)
    pamphlet (*ph* = *f*)
    alphabet (*Alpha* and *beta* are the first letters in Greek.)
    emphasis, emphatic
    telephone (literally "far sound")

Write the six words just listed.

_____, _____, _____,

_____, _____, _____

5

Here are a few words with *ph* at or near the end:

    catastrophe
    telegraph (literally "far writing")
    paragraph (literally "writing beside")
    photograph (literally "writing with light")

Copy: *Graph*, which is found in *telegraph*, *paragraph*, and *photograph*, means writing. It was almost a *catastrophe* when I said it meant sound.

_____

_____

_____

1

Greek

2

phase	phenomenon
phrase	phlegm
philosophy	phobia
physiology	physician
physical	

3

diphtheria
diphthong

4

diaphragm	emphasis
pamphlet	emphatic
alphabet	telephone

6

From words we studied in this unit, choose the one that best fits each sentence. Write the word in full.

a. One disease that has almost disappeared is [di] _____.

b. I got this [pam] _____ from the library.

c. Since he had no telephone, I tried to [tele] _____ him.

7

Follow the instructions for Frame 6.

a. I could write only one short [para] _____ on that subject.

b. An example of a [di] _____ is *ou*.

c. The thirteenth letter in the [al] _____ is *m*.

d. The death of a President can result in [cat] _____.

8

Follow the instructions for Frame 6.

a. I hurried to answer the ringing [tele] _____.

b. When he speaks, he puts too much [em] _____ on unimportant words like *and*.

c. A small [dia] _____ controls the amount of light entering the microscope.

d. The President sent an [em] _____ message to the Secretary of State.

9

To match each definition below, write in full words we have studied beginning with *ph*.

a. science of the functions and activities of living things, _____

b. study of truth or of principles underlying truth, _____

c. stage of development, _____

d. thick discharge from nose or throat, _____

e. picture made with a camera, _____

5

Graph, which is found in *telegraph*, *paragraph*, and *photograph*, means writing. It was almost a *catastrophe* when I said it meant sound.

6

a. diphtheria

b. pamphlet

c. telegraph

7

a. paragraph

b. diphthong

c. alphabet

d. catastrophe

8

a. telephone

b. emphasis

c. diaphragm

d. emphatic

10

Follow the instructions for Frame 9.

a. short group of words, _____

b. doctor, _____

c. unreasonable and lasting fear, _____

d. of the body, _____

e. extraordinary thing or person, _____

9

a. physiology

b. philosophy

c. phase

d. phlegm

e. photograph

11

To match the following definitions, write words we have studied that contain *ph* but do not begin with it.

a. A, B, C, etc., [al] _____

b. great disaster, [cat] _____

c. to send a written message rapidly, [tel] _____

d. instrument for speaking to someone at a distance, [tel] _____

_____

10

a. phrase

b. physician

c. phobia

d. physical

e. phenomenon

12

Follow the instructions for Frame 11.

a. a set of related sentences (usually), [par] _____

b. thin membrane, [dia] _____

c. special force or stress, [em] _____

11

a. alphabet

b. catastrophe

c. telegraph

d. telephone

13

Follow the instructions for Frame 11.

a. forcefully spoken, [em] _____

b. small paperbound book, [pam] _____

c. disease of the throat, [di] _____

d. two vowel sounds pronounced in one syllable, [di] _____

12

a. paragraph

b. diaphragm

c. emphasis

14

Study carefully each word you misspelled in Frames 6–13. Write each missed word correctly three times. Check your answers against the list above Frame 1.

13

a. emphatic

b. pamphlet

c. diphtheria

d. diphthong

UNIT 58 · Words that use *e* for the schwa sound

WORDS TREATED

benefit	category	competition	interest	repetition	treacherous
bulletin	ceremony	corner	lavender	represent	vinegar
cafeteria	challenge	enumerate	operate	supplement	
catechism	comedy	implement	penetrate	tendency	

---

1   repetition   competition

The schwa sound (like an "uh") is represented by an *e* in many words. Such words may best be remembered if a number of them are associated.

Repetition and *competition* are two such words. Note the *et* followed by the *it* in each.

Copy: Let's send a petition.
       Such fine *competition*
       Deserves *repetition*.

_____

_____

_____

---

2   operate   enumerate   penetrate

Write a short sentence with each word above. Capitalize the indistinct *e* to emphasize it.

_____

_____

_____

---

3   category   ceremony   catechism

Write each word twice. Capitalize the indistinct *e* to emphasize it.

_____ , _____

_____ , _____

_____ , _____

---

4   corner   lavender   represent   implement

Note especially the two *e*'s of *lavender*, as well as the *e*'s in the other words.

Copy: I *represent* the *implement* dealer in the *lavender* store on the *corner*.

_____

_____

1

Let's send a petition.
Such fine *competition*
Deserves *repetition*.

---

2   Models:

Can you *opErate* a crane?
EnumErate your reasons.
The drill *penEtrated* a foot of rock.

3

catEgory, catEgory
cerEmony, cerEmony
catEchism, catEchism

5   benefit   bulletin   comedy   vinegar

Note the indistinct *e* in each word.

Copy: The *bulletin* said that a *comedy* for the *benefit* of the spices and *vinegar* fund would be presented.

_____

_____

6   interest   treacherous   supplement

Copy: Let me *supplement* my question: Why so much *interest* in such a *treacherous* fellow?

_____

_____

_____

7   tendency   challenge   cafeteria

Write a short sentence with each word above. Capitalize the indistinct *e*.

_____

_____

_____

8

Match each definition with one of the words we studied in this unit. The first letters have been supplied. Write each word in full.

a. an eating place, [caf] _____

b. to list one by one, [enum] _____

c. acid for flavoring, [vin] _____

d. pale purple, [lav] _____

e. tool, [imp] _____

f. a repeating, [rep] _____

g. class or group, [cat] _____

9

Follow the instructions for Frame 8.

a. not to be trusted, [tre] _____

b. inclination, [ten] _____

c. amusing play, [com] _____

d. place where streets meet, [cor] _____

e. short news item, [bul] _____

f. manage, [op] _____

g. call to fight, [chal] _____

4

I *represent* the *implement* dealer in the *lavender* store on the *corner*.

5

The *bulletin* said that a *comedy* for the *benefit* of the spices and *vinegar* fund would be presented.

6

Let me *supplement* my question: Why so much *interest* in such a *treacherous* fellow?

7   Models:

I have a *tendEncy* to eat too much. Should I *challEnge* that answer? Meet me in the *cafEteria*.

8

a. cafeteria   e. implement

b. enumerate   f. repetition

c. vinegar   g. category

d. lavender

10

Follow the instructions for Frame 8.

a. formal activity, [cer] _____

b. questions and answers, [cat] _____

c. money paid for use of money, [int] _____

d. pierce, [pen] _____

e. rivalry, [com] _____

f. stand for, [rep] _____

g. to be good for, [ben] _____

h. to add to, [sup] _____

11

Write in full each incomplete word, choosing the most suitable from those studied in this unit.

A [caf] _____ makes decisions harder for me than a restaurant. In a restaurant the menu [enum] _____ [s] all the delicacies, and I do not face the [chal] _____ of seeing them before me: the luscious leafy salads with oil and [vin] _____ and the array of desserts in red and yellow and [lav] _____. All the foods [int] _____ me, and the [rep] _____ of identical dishes whets my appetite.

12

Follow the instructions for Frame 11.

a. This crime falls into the legal [cat] _____ called "torts."

b. The teacher repeated the assignment for my [ben] _____.

c. He has a [ten] _____ to stretch the truth.

d. Dad can [op] _____ almost any business at a profit.

e. Don't paint yourself into a [cor] _____.

13

Follow the instructions for Frame 11.

a. Icy pavements are [treach] _____.

b. In this equation, let X [rep] _____ the son's age.

c. The [imp] _____ for cutting is called an adz.

d. The child repeated the [cat] _____ that he had learned at church.

e. In major league baseball, [com] _____ is keen.

9

a. treacherous   e. bulletin
b. tendency   f. operate
c. comedy   g. challenge
d. corner

10

a. ceremony   e. competition
b. catechism   f. represent
c. interest   g. benefit
d. penetrate   h. supplement

11

cafeteria
enumerates
challenge
vinegar
lavender
interest
repetition

12

a. category
b. benefit
c. tendency
d. operate
e. corner

14

Follow the instructions for Frame 11.

a. This play is a [com] _____, not a tragedy.
b. Everyone was ready for the wedding [cer] _____.
c. This drill will not [pen] _____ metal.
d. A news [bul] _____ was broadcast five minutes ago.
e. The city asked the federal government to [sup] _____ its funds for welfare.

15

Study each word that you missed in Frames 8–14. Notice the trouble spots, such as the indistinct *e*. Write each missed word correctly three times. Check your spellings against the list above Frame 1.

13

a. treacherous
b. represent
c. implement
d. catechism
e. competition

14

a. comedy
b. ceremony
c. penetrate
d. bulletin
e. supplement

UNIT 59 · Some words ending in *–el*

WORDS TREATED

angel	excel	personnel
cancel	expel	sentinel
compel	level	
duel	nickel	

1   angel

Note the *el* ending of *angel*. In pictures, an *angel* usually has wings. The word is derived from Greek *angelos*, messenger, and Mercury, the messenger of the gods, had wings on his feet.

Write a sentence with *angel*.

_____

_____

2   duel

Duel, which means a fight between two persons, is derived from Latin *duo*, two.

Write a sentence with *duel*.

_____

_____

1   Model:

She thought that her boy friend was an *angel*, but now he has fallen.

3   **level**   **cancel**

Write *level* and *cancel* three times each. Note the second *c* in *cancel*.

_____, _____, _____

_____, _____, _____

---

4   **nickel**

The spellings for the name of the coin *nickel* and for the metallic element *nickel* are the same.

Copy: How much *nickel* is there in a *nickel*?

_____

_____

---

5   **personnel**   **excel**

Personnel refers to a group of persons: military *personnel* or the *personnel* of an office.

    Note the single *l* in *excel*.

Copy: Our *personnel excel*. Do your *personnel excel*?

_____

_____

---

6   **compel**   **expel**

Note the single *l* in *compel* and in *expel*.

Copy: "You *compel* me to *expel* you," said the erudite bouncer.

_____

_____

---

7   **sentinel**

Sentinel goes back to the Italian *sentinella*. Note the *i* before the *n*. Write a sentence using *sentinel*.

_____

_____

8

Match each definition with one of the words we studied in this unit. The beginning letter or letters have been supplied. Write each word in full.

a. smooth; even, [l] _____

b. a group of persons, [per] _____

c. to force out, [ex] _____

d. a chemical element, [ni] _____

e. heavenly being, [an] _____

---

2   **Model:**

Fighting *duels* was once a college sport in Germany.

3

level, level, level
cancel, cancel, cancel

4

How much *nickel* is there in a *nickel*?

5

Our *personnel excel*. Do your *personnel excel*?

6

"You *compel* me to *expel* you," said the erudite bouncer.

---

7   **Model:**

A *sentinel* must never sleep at his post.

9

Follow the instructions for Frame 8.

a. to force, [com] _____

b. watchman, [sen] _____

c. a fight between two persons, [d] _____

d. to eliminate or mark out, [can] _____

e. to be superior, [ex] _____

10

Write in full each incomplete word, choosing the most suitable from those studied in this unit.

While other military [per] _____ watched, the soldier who had been the [sen] _____ challenged Jacques to a [d] _____, even though Jacques was known to [ex] _____ as a swordsman. "You will [com] _____ me to kill you," said Jacques quietly.

11

Follow the instructions for Frame 10.

a. Land in Illinois is very [le] _____.

b. The principal threatened to [ex] _____ Jim from school.

c. It was necessary to [can] _____ the flight.

d. He died and became an [an] _____.

e. This alloy contains much [ni] _____.

12

Study each word that you misspelled in Frames 8–11. Write a sentence using each word you missed. Check your spellings against the list above Frame 1 to make sure you are now spelling correctly.

8

a. level

b. personnel

c. expel

d. nickel

e. angel

9

a. compel

b. sentinel

c. duel

d. cancel

e. excel

10

personnel

sentinel

duel

excel

compel

11

a. level

b. expel

c. cancel

d. angel

e. nickel

UNIT 60 · Foreign plurals

WORDS TREATED

aides-de-camp	analyses	criteria	noms de plume	syntheses
algae	axes	diagnoses	oases	theses
alumnae	bases	emphases	parentheses	
alumni	crises	hypotheses	phenomena	

1 alga, algae   alumna, alumnae

A number of English words borrowed from other languages keep the plurals they have in those languages. Several of these are Latin words with the singular ending in *a*. The plurals of these are likely to end in *ae*.

    Algae are mainly plants or scum growing in water.

    Alumnae are female graduates of a school.

Write an original sentence using *algae* and another using *alumnae*.

_____

_____

2 alumnus, alumni

Some other Latin words ended in *us*, with the plural in *i*. Some of the borrowed English words of this variety now have two alternative plurals; thus *fungus* may be pluralized as either *fungi* or *funguses*.

    Alumnus, however, meaning a male graduate, keeps the plural *alumni*. (This spelling is also used to refer to a combination of male and female graduates.)

Copy: *Alumni* are male, and *alumnae* are female.

_____

3 analysis, analyses   axis, axes   basis, bases

Other words from Greek or Latin had endings in *is*, with the plural *es*. So we write *an analysis, two analyses; an axis, two axes; a firm basis, some firm bases* (pronounced bā′ sēz).

Write the plurals of *analysis, axis, basis*.

_____ , _____ , _____

4 crisis, crises   diagnosis, diagnoses
emphasis, emphases   hypothesis, hypotheses

A *crisis*, several *crises*; a *diagnosis*, two *diagnoses*; this *emphasis*, these *emphases*; that *hypothesis*, those *hypotheses*.

Write the plurals of *crisis, diagnosis, emphasis, hypothesis*.

_____ , _____ , _____ ,

_____

5 oasis, oases   parenthesis, parentheses
thesis, theses   synthesis, syntheses

An *oasis*, two *oases*; a *parenthesis*, some *parentheses*; this *thesis*, these *theses*; a *synthesis*, several *syntheses*.

Write the plurals of *oasis, parenthesis, thesis, synthesis*.

_____ , _____ , _____ ,

_____

1 Models:

Algae flourished in the warm water. The *alumnae* marched in a procession.

2

Alumni are male, and *alumnae* are female.

3

analyses
axes
bases

4

crises
diagnoses
emphases
hypotheses

6   criterion, criteria   phenomenon, phenomena

Some Greek words ending in *on* had plurals in *a*. *Criteria* and *phenomena* are two of these plurals that have been kept in English. Remember: one *criterion*, two *criteria*; a *phenomenon*, several *phenomena*.

Write the plurals of *criterion* and *phenomenon*.

_____, _____

7   aide-de-camp, aides-de-camp
          nom de plume, noms de plume

From French we have taken *aide-de-camp* and its plural *aides-de-camp*, who are a general's helpers. French also gives us *nom de plume* (pen name) and its plural, *noms de plume*.

Write the plurals of *aide-de-camp* and *nom de plume*. Note that the first is hyphenated.

_____, _____

8

Match each definition with one of the plurals we studied in this unit. The first letters have been supplied. Write each word in full.

a. girl graduates, [al] _____
b. water plants, [alg] _____
c. moments of decision, [cri] _____
d. studies of symptoms, [diag] _____
e. a general's helpers, [aide] _____
f. rare things or events, [phen] _____

9

Follow the instructions for Frame 8.

a. pen names, [nom] _____
b. green spots in a desert, [oas] _____
c. male graduates, [al] _____
d. separations into parts for study, [anal] _____
e. stresses, [emph] _____
f. theories, [hypoth] _____

10

Follow the instructions for Frame 8.

a. graduate research studies, [the] _____
b. standards for judging, [crit] _____
c. ( ), [par] _____
d. straight lines around which bodies revolve, [ax] _____
e. foundations, [bas] _____
f. combinations of parts, [syn] _____

5

oases
parentheses
theses
syntheses

6

criteria
phenomena

7

aides-de-camp
noms de plume

8

a. alumnae
b. algae
c. crises
d. diagnoses
e. aides-de-camp
f. phenomena

9

a. noms de plume
b. oases
c. alumni
d. analyses
e. emphases
f. hypotheses

11

Write in full each incomplete word, choosing the most suitable from those studied in this unit. Use plural forms only.

a. Pearl Buck wrote under several [nom] _____ .
b. Both doctors' [diag] _____ were inconclusive.
c. Unimportant or incidental remarks are sometimes punctuated with [par] _____ .
d. We must test both [hyp] _____ carefully.

12

Follow the instructions for Frame 11.

a. "Fellow [al] _____ ," the speaker began her address to the graduates of the Female Seminary.
b. Many small [oas] _____ are in the Sahara.
c. Two of the doctoral [the] _____ have been approved by the dean.
d. Mars and Venus, like Earth, revolve on their [ax] _____ .
e. Chemical [anal] _____ must be made meticulously.

13

Follow the instructions for Frame 11.

a. What will be the [crit] _____ for deciding the winner?
b. What will be the [bas] _____ for decision?
c. Seaweeds and other [alg] _____ were abundant.
d. Analyses are the opposite of [syn] _____ .

14

Follow the instructions for Frame 11.

a. Two [aide] _____ hurried into the officers' tent.
b. The President has two new international [cri] _____ to worry about.
c. Such [phen] _____ as sunspots still puzzle astronomers.
d. The university appealed to its [alum] _____ for funds.
e. His principal [emph] _____ were on tariff and international trade.

15

Study each word you misspelled in Frames 8–14. Write both the singular form and the plural form of each missed word correctly three times. Check your spellings against the list above Frame 1.

10

a. theses
b. criteria
c. parentheses
d. axes
e. bases
f. syntheses

11

a. noms de plume
b. diagnoses
c. parentheses
d. hypotheses

12

a. alumnae
b. oases
c. theses
d. axes
e. analyses

13

a. criteria
b. bases
c. algae
d. syntheses

14

a. aides-de-camp
b. crises
c. phenomena
d. alumni
e. emphases

UNIT 61 · Some troublesome words in grammar

WORDS TREATED

adjective	clause	gerund	participle	pronoun
adverb	conjunction	infinitive	phoneme	
apostrophe	exclamatory	modifier	predicate	
appositive	expletive	morpheme	preposition	

1   adjective   adverb

The words in this unit are not alike except that all are used in grammar. We shall note some of their peculiarities.

Latin *adjectivus* means that which is added. An *adjective* is added to a noun or its equivalent.

Ad in Latin means to. An *adverb*, which usually modifies a verb, does something *to* the verb.

Write a sentence with each word: *adjective, adverb.*

_____

_____

2   infinitive   expletive   appositive

Infinitive is simply the English spelling of Latin *infinitivus*. Note the syllables: in fin i tive.

There is a good reason why *expletive* is spelled as it is. It is a word used like *there* in the preceding sentence, which fills out the beginning of the sentence when the subject comes later. It comes from Latin *explere*, to fill out. Therefore the fifth letter is an *e*.

An *appositive* is placed next to something else with the same meaning. Latin *appositivus* means placed next to.

Write a sentence with each word: *infinitive, expletive, appositive.*

_____

_____

_____

_____

3   phoneme   morpheme

A *phoneme* is a speech sound. It comes from Greek *phone*, sound, just as *telephone* does.

A *morpheme* (like *'s* in *John's* or *–ed* in *asked*) helps us to understand the form and meaning of a word. Greek *morphe* means form.

Write each word twice: *phoneme, morpheme.*

_____ , _____

_____ , _____

---

1   Models:

Is *green* an *adjective* in this sentence?

In "Come quickly," *quickly* is an *adverb*.

---

2   Models:

An *infinitive* usually starts with *to*.
The word *there* is often an *expletive*.
An *appositive* renames a thing or person.

4   gerund   participle   preposition

A *gerund* is a verb form used as a noun. The word comes from Latin *gerundium*. Note the *r* and the *u*.

Participle, a verb form often used as an adjective, comes from Latin through French. Note the *le* ending.

Preposition is literally *pre-position*, a position before. A preposition usually is in a position before a noun.

Copy: A *gerund* but probably not a *participle* may be the object of a *preposition*.

_____

_____

5   clause   predicate

Clause, from Latin *clausula*, refers to a word group with a subject and a predicate.

Predicate is based on a Latin word meaning to proclaim. The predicate of a sentence "proclaims" the action.

Copy: The *predicate* in this *clause* is incomplete.

_____

6   apostrophe   exclamatory   conjunction

Apostrophe comes from Latin *apostrophus*, omitting of a letter. An apostrophe often shows where a letter was omitted.

Exclamatory is based on Latin *exclamare*, to cry out. Note the *ory* ending.

You know what a *junction* is on a highway: a place where roads join. *Con + junction = conjunction*, a word that joins two parts of a sentence.

Write a sentence with each word: *apostrophe, exclamatory, conjunction*.

_____

_____

_____

7   pronoun   modifier

In Latin, *pro* means for. A *pronoun* usually stands for a noun.

A *modifier*, like *tall* in *tall boy* or *swiftly* in *run swiftly*, sets limits to the thing being described. Thus *tall boy* limits our thinking by ruling out short boys and boys of average height. The Latin ancestor of *modifier* means to set limits.

Copy: This *pronoun* needs a *modifier*.

_____

3

phoneme, phoneme
morpheme, morpheme

4

A *gerund* but probably not a *participle* may be the object of a *preposition*.

5

The *predicate* in this *clause* is incomplete.

6   Models:

Don't omit the *apostrophe*.
Halt! is an *exclamatory* sentence.
And is used as a *conjunction*.

8

Match each definition with one of the words we studied in this unit. The first letters have been supplied.

a. punctuation mark in *they're*, [ap] _____
b. words with subject and predicate, [cl] _____
c. verb form used as noun, [ge] _____
d. a speech sound, [ph] _____

9

Follow the instructions for Frame 8.

a. word used for a noun, [pr] _____
b. word that modifies a noun, [ad] _____
c. word that modifies a verb, [ad] _____
d. a "filler-out" in a sentence, [exp] _____
e. a word or part of a word having specific form, [mor] _____
_____

10

Follow the instructions for Frame 8.

a. an adjective or an adverb, [mod] _____
b. in a loud manner, [exc] _____
c. a word like *and* or *because*, [con] _____
d. verb form used as an adjective, [par] _____
e. a word like *to* or *of*, [pre] _____

11

Follow the instructions for Frame 8.

a. a verb or verb phrase plus modifiers, [pred] _____
b. what *Fred* is in *my brother Fred*, [ap] _____
c. what *to tell* is, [inf] _____

12

Write in full each incomplete word, choosing the most suitable from those studied in this unit.

a. Three of the forms of verbs are the [in] _____, the [ge] _____, and the [pa] _____.
b. An [adj] _____ and an [adv] _____ are both [mod] _____ [s].

7

This *pronoun* needs a *modifier*.

8

a. apostrophe
b. clause
c. gerund
d. phoneme

9

a. pronoun
b. adjective
c. adverb
d. expletive
e. morpheme

10

a. modifier
b. exclamatory
c. conjunction
d. participle
e. preposition

11

a. predicate
b. appositive
c. infinitive

13

Follow the instructions for Frame 12.

a. A complete [cl] _____ must have a [pre] _____.
b. A [ph] _____ is a small, distinct speech sound.
c. The [mo] _____ [s] in *taller* are *tall* and *er*.
d. *For* is a [pre] _____ in the phrase *for dinner* and a [con] _____ in *I ran, for I was afraid.*

12

a. infinitive, gerund, participle
b. adjective, adverb, modifiers

14

Follow the instructions for Frame 12.

a. Do not put an [ap] _____ in a possessive [pro] _____.
b. The word *there* at the beginning of a sentence is often an [ex] _____.
c. In *Earth's satellite, the moon,* the word *moon* is an [ap] _____.
d. The sentence *Stop or I'll shoot!* is [ex] _____.

13

a. clause, predicate
b. phoneme
c. morphemes
d. preposition, conjunction

15

Study each word that you misspelled in Frames 8–14. The comments in Frames 1–7 may help you review. Write each missed word correctly three times. Check your spellings against the list above Frame 1.

14

a. apostrophe, pronoun
b. expletive
c. appositive
d. exclamatory

UNIT 62 · Some troublesome words in literature

WORDS TREATED

allegory	epigram	lyric	poem	soliloquy
ballad	iambic	novel	quatrain	sonnet
biography	imagery	pentameter	rhyme	tetrameter
epic	limerick	personification	simile	

1   poem   novel

The words in this unit are not alike except that all are used in discussion of literature. We shall note some of their peculiarities.

Poem is often misspelled because it is mispronounced. Say it as two syllables: po em.

Novel comes from French *nouvelle* or Italian *novella*. It is the same as the adjective *novel* meaning new; once a novel was a new kind of literature.

Write a sentence with each word: *poem, novel*.

_____

_____

2   quatrain   rhyme

Quatrain, a four-line stanza, comes from the French *quatre*, four. Note that both *refrain* and *quatrain* end in *rain*.

Rhyme was formerly *rime*. Then, influenced by *rhythm*, the spelling *rhyme* became general. Today both *rhyme* and *rime* are used, with *rhyme* regarded as the more elegant.

Copy: After each *quatrain* comes a *refrain* with an intricate *rhyme*.

_____

_____

3   lyric   epic   iambic

Lyric goes back finally to Greek *lyra*, lyre. A lyric was originally intended to be sung to the accompaniment of a lyre.

Epic also goes back to Greek. In Greek an *epos* was a tale or song. An epic is a long tale that was once recited or sung.

Iambic, from Greek *iambos*, refers to verse consisting of an unstressed syllable followed by a stressed syllable, as in the word *be sides*.

Copy: Both the *lyric* and the *epic* were written in *iambic* verse.

_____

_____

4   tetrameter   pentameter

In Greek, *tetra* means four, *penta* means five, and *meter* means measure. A tetrameter line has four "feet" or measures, and a pentameter has five.

Copy the preceding sentence.

_____

_____

1   Models:

Do you like my *poem*?
Have you finished your *novel* yet?

2

After each *quatrain* comes a *refrain* with an intricate *rhyme*.

3

Both the *lyric* and the *epic* were written in *iambic* verse.

5 ballad   imagery   simile

Ballad is related to *ballet* and to *ball* (dance). It is a story-telling song that has sometimes been sung during a dance.

Imagery is simply *image + ry*. It refers to the images or pictures that figurative language suggests.

Simile comes from Latin *similis*, similar. A simile points out a similarity between two apparently unlike things.

Copy: This *ballad* has been praised for its *imagery*, especially its *similes*.

_____

_____

6 epigram   limerick   soliloquy

Epigram, from Greek *epigramma*, is a bright thought concisely expressed.

Limerick is named for a county in Ireland. Note that the fourth letter is *e*.

Note the last three letters of *soliloquy: quy* (a very unusual combination in English).

Copy: Pope is famous for *epigrams*.
     Can you compose a *limerick*?
     I recited Hamlet's *soliloquy*.

_____

_____

_____

7 biography   personification   allegory   sonnet

Biography is related to *biology*. *Biology* is literally "words about life," and *biography* is "writing about a person's life."

Personification is related to *personify*. Personification refers to giving a thing the characteristics of a person.

Allegory has not changed its meaning from the days of Greek *allegoria*, description of one thing as if it were something else.

Sonnet is the diminutive of Old French *son*, song. Therefore a sonnet is literally "a little song."

Copy: This *sonnet* is based on *personification*. The *biography* of the author says that he liked *allegory*.

_____

_____

4

A *tetrameter* line has four "feet" or measures, and a *pentameter* has five.

5

This *ballad* has been praised for its *imagery*, especially its *similes*.

6

Pope is famous for *epigrams*.
Can you compose a *limerick*?
I recited Hamlet's *soliloquy*.

8

Match each definition with one of the words studied in this unit. The first letter or letters have been given. Write each word in full.

a. pictures, figurative language, [im] _____
b. five-line humorous poem, [lim] _____
c. making a thing seem like a person, [per] _____
_____
d. four-foot line, [tet] _____
e. words of similar sounds, [r] _____

9

a. verse, [po] _____
b. long story in poetic form, [e] _____
c. story told in terms of something else, [al] _____
d. story of a person's life, [bi] _____

10

Follow the instructions for Frame 8.

a. fourteen-line poem, [son] _____
b. speech, in drama, by one person alone, [sol] _____
c. a bright thought, briefly expressed, [ep] _____
d. story-telling song, [bal] _____
e. long fictional story, [no] _____

11

Follow the instructions for Frame 8.

a. comparison using *like* or *as*, [sim] _____
b. five-foot line, [pen] _____
c. characterized by an unstressed plus a stressed syllable, [i] _____
_____
d. four-line stanza, [qu] _____
e. pertaining to poetry that was once sung, [l] _____

12

Write in full each incomplete word, choosing the most suitable from those studied in this unit.

a. A [son] _____ consists of fourteen [i] _____ [pen] _____ lines with a definite [r] _____ scheme.
b. This [l] _____ poem consists of six [qu] _____ [s] or a total of twenty-four [tet] _____ lines.

7

This *sonnet* is based on *personification*. The *biography* of the author says that he liked *allegory*.

8

a. imagery
b. limerick
c. personification
d. tetrameter
e. rhyme (or rime)

9

a. poem
b. epic
c. allegory
d. biography

10

a. sonnet
b. soliloquy
c. epigram
d. ballad
e. novel

11

a. simile
b. pentameter
c. iambic
d. quatrain
e. lyric

13

Follow the instructions for Frame 12.

a. An [e] _____ poem by Homer is filled with much military [im] _____.

b. The refrain of this famous [po] _____ is "Where are the snows of yesteryear?"

c. This story, although intended as a [bi] _____ of the general, reads more like fiction; no [no] _____ could be more exciting.

14

Follow the instructions for Frame 12.

a. An [ep] _____, because of its brevity, may be only a [sim] _____.

b. We laughed at the [lim] _____ about the young lady from Niger.

c. Saying that a cloud weeps is an example of [per] _____ _____.

d. *Pilgrim's Progress* is a famous [al] _____.

e. "Sir Patrick Spens" is my favorite old [bal] _____.

f. He recited the famous [sol] _____ from *Hamlet*.

15

Study each word that you misspelled in Frames 8–14. The comments in Frames 1–7 may help you to review. Write each missed word correctly three times. Check your answers against the list above Frame 1.

12

a. sonnet, iambic, pentameter, rhyme (or rime)

b. lyric, quatrains, tetrameter

13

a. epic, imagery

b. poem

c. biography, novel

14

a. epigram, simile

b. limerick

c. personification

d. allegory

e. ballad

f. soliloquy

UNIT 63 · Some troublesome words in music

WORDS TREATED

ballet	choir	oboe	prelude	soprano
baritone	clarinet	octave	saxophone	tenor
cadence	encore	orchestra	serenade	violin
cello	ensemble	piano	sonata	xylophone

1 saxophone xylophone

The words in this unit are not alike except that all are used in music. We shall note some of their peculiarities.

Note that the fourth letter of both *saxophone* and *xylophone* is an *o*.

Note also that *xylophone* is one of the few English words starting with an *x*. *Xylo* is from Greek *xylon*, wood, plus *phone*, sound; the sound of a xylophone is made by striking wooden bars. *Saxophone* is named for its inventor, Antoine Sax.

Use *saxophone* and *xylophone* in a sentence.

_____

_____

2 tenor soprano baritone

Note the single *n* in *tenor*. *Tenor* is spelled like its Latin ancestor *tenor*, a holding; a tenor voice often takes and holds the principal part.

Soprano is an Italian word meaning highest. Note the *o–a–o* arrangement of vowels and the single *n*.

Baritone (which may permissibly be spelled *barytone*) goes back through French and Italian to Greek words meaning heavy tone.

Use *tenor*, *soprano*, and *baritone* in a sentence.

_____

_____

3 piano cello violin

Piano, in Italian, means soft. The steel wires of a piano are struck softly by felt-covered hammers.

Cello is the shortened form of Italian *violoncello*, which means a little contrabass. *C* in Italian is often pronounced *ch*.

Violino, the Italian ancestor of *violin*, means little viola. Note that *violin* ends in *in*.

Use *piano*, *cello*, and *violin* in a sentence.

_____

_____

1 Model:

I played the *saxophone;* Martin, the *xylophone.*

2 Model:

The *tenor*, the *soprano*, and the *baritone* were quarreling.

4   orchestra   oboe   clarinet

Orchestra comes from a Greek word, also spelled *orchestra*, that meant a place for dancers. The *e* and the last two letters give the most trouble.

A French musical instrument is called an *hautbois*, pronounced about like *o bwa*. The Italians borrowed the name, simplifying the spelling and pronunciation to *oboe*. We should thank the Italians.

Clarinet is shortened from French *clarinette*, which goes back to the Latin *clarus*, clear.

Use *orchestra*, *oboe*, and *clarinet* in a sentence.

_____

_____

5   choir   serenade   ensemble

Choir comes from a French spelling of Latin *chorus*. Note that the *o* is before the *i*.

The French borrowed the Italian *serenata* and changed the spelling to *sérénade*. The English borrowed the French spelling, simply dropping the accent marks. Note that the fourth letter is *e*.

Although *ensemble* retains the French pronunciation *ahn som b'l*, the fourth letter in *ensemble* is an *e*.

Use *choir*, *serenade*, and *ensemble* in a sentence.

_____

_____

6   encore   ballet   prelude

Encore and *ballet* are two other words that retain their French pronunciations and therefore seem, to us, to be spelled oddly. Note the *en* of *encore* and the *et* of *ballet*.

Prelude, also from French, goes back to the Latin words meaning to play before.

Use *encore*, *ballet*, and *prelude* in a sentence.

_____

_____

7   sonata   octave   cadence

Sonata, a fairly long musical composition for one or two instruments, is an Italian word. Note the vowels: *so na ta*.

Octave comes from Latin *octava*, an eighth.

In music a *cadence* is a trill or some other concluding strain. Note the two *c*'s.

Write each word twice: *sonata*, *octave*, *cadence*.

_____ , _____

_____ , _____

_____ , _____

3   Model:

The *piano* was out of tune, the *cello* had a broken string, and none of us could play the *violin*.

4   Model:

Our *orchestra* was short of *oboes* and *clarinets*.

5   Model:

The *choir* and orchestra as an *ensemble* presented a *serenade*.

6   Model:

The orchestral *prelude* was lovely, but the *ballet* was so well performed that the audience demanded an *encore*.

8

Match each definition with one of the words we studied in this unit. The first letter or letters have been given. Write each word in full.

a. something played first, [pre] _____
b. performance of all voices and instruments, [en] _____
c. a woodwind instrument, [cl] _____
d. a stringed instrument, [v] _____
e. male voice between bass and tenor, [ba] _____

9

Follow the instructions for Frame 8.

a. percussion instrument with wooden bars, [x] _____
b. a concluding strain, [ca] _____
c. a call for a repetition, [en] _____
d. a group of singers, [ch] _____
e. a band stressing stringed instruments, [or] _____

10

Follow the instructions for Frame 8.

a. instrument with 88 keys, [p] _____
b. high male voice, [t] _____
c. wind instrument with bent tube, [s] _____
d. high female voice, [s] _____
e. large stringed instrument, [c] _____

11

Follow the instructions for Frame 8.

a. an interval of eight, [oc] _____
b. composition for one or two instruments, [s] _____
c. theatrical dance, [b] _____
d. music sung under a lady's window, [s] _____
e. slender woodwind instrument, [o] _____

12

Write in full each incomplete word, choosing the most suitable from those studied in this unit.

a. Two woodwinds, the [cl] _____ and the [o] _____,
   had the major parts in the prelude.
b. The [p] _____ [s] _____ was beautifully played,
   all the way through the final [ca] _____.

7

sonata, sonata
octave, octave
cadence, cadence

8

a. prelude
b. ensemble
c. clarinet
d. violin
e. baritone

9

a. xylophone
b. cadence
c. encore
d. choir
e. orchestra

10

a. piano
b. tenor
c. saxophone
d. soprano
e. cello

11

a. octave
b. sonata
c. ballet
d. serenade
e. oboe

13

Follow the instructions for Frame 12.

a. Two of the male voices, a [t] _____ and a [ba] _____
_____, were outstanding.

b. The little boy hammered away on a [x] _____,
while his sister coaxed mournful sounds from an alto [sa] _____
_____.

c. The [ce] _____ played the same melody as the [v] _____
but an [oc] _____ lower.

14

Follow the instructions for Frame 12.

a. The [or] _____ and the [ch] _____ make a splendid [ens] _____.

b. The crowd applauded, trying to induce the lovely [s] _____
to sing an [en] _____.

c. The ardent lover decided to take his guitar and [ser] _____
_____ the [b] _____ dancer.

15

Study each word that you misspelled in Frames 8–14. The comments
in Frames 1–7 may help you to overcome any trouble spots. Write
each missed word correctly three times. Check your spellings against
the list above Frame 1.

12

a. clarinet, oboe
b. piano, sonata, cadence

13

a. tenor, baritone
b. xylophone, saxophone
c. cello, violin, octave

14

a. orchestra, choir, ensemble
b. soprano, encore
c. serenade, ballet

UNIT 64 · Some troublesome words in science

WORDS TREATED

acoustics	barometer	luminous	osmosis	respiration
alloy	biologist	meteor	oxidation	sterilization
aluminum	chemistry	opaque	protoplasm	turbine
atom	cyclone	orbit	radioactive	

---

1   atom   orbit

The words in this unit are not alike except that all are used in
science. We shall note some of their peculiarities.

Atom has one *t* and an *o* because it comes from Greek *atomos*,
meaning indivisible.

Orbit is spelled with an *i* because its ancestors were French *orbite*
and Latin *orbita*, meaning a track made by a wheel.

Write a short sentence with each word: *atom, orbit.*

_____

_____

2 respiration sterilization oxidation

Respiration, which means breathing, is from Latin *re* + *spirare*, to breathe again.

Sterilization comes from Latin *sterilis*, which accounts for the the first two *i*'s. In bacteriology, *sterilization* refers to getting rid of living microbes.

Although *oxidation* refers to combining with oxygen, *oxidation* is spelled with an *i* rather than a *y*. The reason is that it is derived from French *oxide*.

Use each word, *respiration*, *sterilization*, and *oxidation*, in a sentence.

_____

_____

_____

3 chemistry osmosis aluminum

Chemistry is related to the earlier *alchemy*, which was influenced by Greek and Latin words. Note the *i*.

Osmosis, which refers to mixing of two liquids through a membrane, makes no change in the Latin spelling, *osmosis*.

Aluminum (generally spelled *aluminium* by the British) comes from Latin *aluminis*, alum.

Use each word, *chemistry*, *osmosis*, and *aluminum*, in a sentence.

_____

_____

_____

4 luminous turbine

Luminous goes back to Latin *luminosus*. Note the *i*.

A *turbine* is a rotary engine driven by fluid under pressure. It comes from Latin *turbinis*, that which spins.

Write each word twice: *luminous*, *turbine*.

_____, _____

_____, _____

5 opaque alloy meteor

Opaque, which means not reflecting or giving out light, used to be spelled *opake*, but the French spelling replaced the simpler one.

Alloy, with two *l*'s, comes from French *aloi*, with only one. The older Latin *alligare*, however, has two *l*'s.

Meteor can be traced back to Greek *meteoron*, something high in the air. Note the two *e*'s.

Use *opaque*, *alloy*, and *meteor* each in a short sentence.

_____

_____

_____

1 Models:

An *atom* is smaller than a molecule. Another space ship was sent into *orbit*.

2 Models:

The baby's *respiration* was uneven. Babies' bottles require *sterilization*. *Oxidation* results in rust.

3 Models:

In *chemistry* we learned about *osmosis*.

Now we are studying *aluminum* oxide.

4

luminous, luminous
turbine, turbine

6   acoustics   barometer   cyclone

Acoustics, the science of sound, is the English spelling of Greek *akoustikos*, pertaining to hearing. Note the single *c* and the *ou*.

Greek *baros* means weight and *meter* means measure. A barometer measures the weight, or pressure, of air.

Cyclone is related to *bicycle* and other words with *cycle*. It comes from Greek *kyklos*, circle. Winds in a cyclone move circularly.

Use *acoustics*, *barometer*, and *cyclone* each in a short sentence.

_____

_____

_____

7   radioactive   protoplasm   biologist

Radioactive is easy to spell: *radio* + *active*.

Protoplasm, from Greek *protos* (first) and *plasma* (form), refers to the basic form of living matter.

Greek *bios* means life, and *logos* means word. A *biologist* writes or speaks words about living things.

Use *radioactive*, *protoplasm*, and *biologist* in a single sentence.

_____

_____

8

Match each definition with one of the words studied in this unit. The first letter or letters have been given. Write each word in full.

a. silver-white metal, [al] _____

b. combination of metals, [al] _____

c. combination with oxygen, [ox] _____

d. circular path, [or] _____

e. rotary engine, [t] _____

9

Follow the instructions for Frame 8.

a. heavenly body, [me] _____

b. circular wind, [c] _____

c. an expert on living things, [bi] _____

d. small particle, [a] _____

e. elimination of living micro-organisms, [ster] _____

10

Follow the instructions for Frame 8.

a. method of mixing liquids, [os] _____

b. emitting light, [lum] _____

c. instrument useful in weather forecasting, [bar] _____

d. basis of life, [pro] _____

e. breathing, [res] _____

5   Models:

The curtain is *opaque*.
What *alloy* is hardest?
Did you see the *meteor*?

6   Models:

The *acoustics* are excellent.
Is the *barometer* steady?
Which direction do winds move in a *cyclone*?

7   Model:

The *biologist* found that the *protoplasm* had become *radioactive*.

8

a. aluminum
b. alloy
c. oxidation
d. orbit
e. turbine

9

a. meteor
b. cyclone
c. biologist
d. atom
e. sterilization

11

Follow the instructions for Frame 8.

a. science for analysis of substances, [ch] _____
b. not transparent, [op] _____
c. science of sound, [ac] _____
d. emitting particles or rays, [ra] _____

10

a. osmosis
b. luminous
c. barometer
d. protoplasm
e. respiration

12

Write in full each incomplete word, choosing the most suitable from those studied in this unit.

a. In [ch] _____ class we first studied the structure of the hydrogen [at] _____.
b. As he was a [bi] _____, he was much interested in [pro] _____.
c. We could hear little because the [ac] _____ were poor.

11

a. chemistry
b. opaque
c. acoustics
d. radioactive

13

Follow the instructions for Frame 12.

a. The [al] _____ was composed of [alu] _____ and zinc.
b. [Ox] _____, resulting from long exposure to the weather, had made the [tu] _____ rusty and useless.
c. A [me] _____, like the comet which may be its parent, travels in a rather regular [or] _____.
d. A tornado is popularly, but not quite accurately, called a [cy] _____.

12

a. chemistry, atom
b. biologist, protoplasm
c. acoustics

14

Follow the instructions for Frame 12.

a. Before conducting his experiment with [os] _____, the chemist took special pains with the [ster] _____ of his equipment.
b. Although we had expected that the flying saucer would be [lum] _____, to our surprise it was [op] _____.
c. We had to dispose of our reliable [bar] _____ because its presence in the fallout area had made it [rad] _____.
d. The patient's pulse and [res] _____ were both rapid.

13

a. alloy, aluminum
b. Oxidation, turbine
c. meteor, orbit
d. cyclone

15

Study each word that you misspelled in Frames 8–14. The comments in Frames 1–7 may help you to remember the correct spellings. Write each missed word correctly three times. Check your spellings against the list above Frame 1.

14

a. osmosis, sterilization
b. luminous, opaque
c. barometer, radioactive
d. respiration

UNIT 65 · Some troublesome words in social science

WORDS TREATED

alien	census	fiscal	legislative	precinct
ambassador	communism	geography	naturalization	suburbs
bipartisan	democracy	inauguration	poll	
caucus	executive	judicial	preamble	

---

1   census   caucus

The words in this unit are not much alike except that all are used in social science. We shall try to note some of their peculiarities.

Census comes from Latin *censere*, meaning to value or tax. We generally use *census* to mean a population count.

Caucus probably comes from an Algonquian Indian word. It refers to a small political meeting.

Use each word in a sentence: *census, caucus.*

_____

_____

---

2   inauguration   naturalization

In Rome an *augur* was a soothsayer or prophet. His predictions determined when important political events, like the crowning of a ruler, took place. We no longer pay attention to *augurs*, but *inauguration* comes from that word.

Naturalization is related to *nature*, which comes from the Latin *natus*, born. When a person becomes a citizen by *naturalization*, he acquires the privileges of a person born in the nation.

Use each word in a sentence: *inauguration, naturalization.*

_____

_____

1   Models:

The *census* shows a population of almost a million.
The Republicans held a *caucus.*

3   poll   democracy   bipartisan

Poll comes from a Dutch word, *polle*, meaning head. A *poll*, at least figuratively, is a counting of heads, a vote.

Democracy comes from two Greek words, *demos*, people, and *kratein*, to rule. In a *democracy* the people rule.

Bipartisan comes from the Latin *bi*, two, and *pars*, part. In a bipartisan policy, both parts (or parties) are in agreement.

Copy: In a *democracy,* both *polls* and occasional *bipartisan* action are essential.

_____

_____

4   suburbs   precinct   preamble

Suburbs means, literally, "under the city." We use it, of course, to mean the area around the city.

Latin *praecinctum* means encompassing or including. In local American politics, a *precinct* includes a small part of a city or county.

Latin *praeambulus* means walking before. In modern writing, a *preamble* goes before, like the Preamble to the Constitution.

Use each word in a sentence: *suburbs, precinct, preamble.*

_____

_____

_____

5   alien   legislative   executive

Alien comes from Latin *alius*, other. An *alien* comes from some other land.

Legis, of the law, and *lator*, a proposer, are the Latin ancestors of *legislator* and *legislative*. A *legislative* body proposes and makes laws.

Latin *ex*, out, and *sequi*, follow, are the ancestors of *executive*. An *executive* "follows out" or carries out the regulations of a country or a company.

Copy: An *alien* cannot be elected to a *legislative* or an *executive* position.

_____

_____

2   Models:

The *inauguration* took place in January.

He has his first *naturalization* papers.

3

In a *democracy,* both *polls* and occasional *bipartisan* action are essential.

4   Models:

Suburbs are growing rapidly.

The third *precinct* voted for Gray.

Let us study the *preamble* first.

6 judicial communism ambassador

Judicial comes from Latin *judicialis*, which in turn was based on *judex*, judge. The *judicial* branch of government consists of courts and judges.

Communism is related to *community*. Both words go back to Latin *communis*, common.

Ambassador, as befits a word with international associations, has come to English through several languages: French, Italian, and Provençal.

Write each word twice: *judicial, communism, ambassador.*

_____, _____

_____, _____

_____, _____

---

7 geography fiscal

Geo, from Greek, means earth; *graph*, which appears also in such words as *biography*, means writing. *Geography* is literally "writing about the earth."

Fiscal, from Latin *fiscalis*, means pertaining to money. *Fiscal* policies, for example, are policies pertaining to money.

Write a short sentence with each word: *geography, fiscal.*

_____

_____

8

Match each definition with one of the words we studied in this unit. The first letters have been given. Write each word in full.

a. a population count, [cen] _____

b. installation of an official, [in] _____

c. a vote, [po] _____

d. areas near a city, [sub] _____

9

Follow the instructions for Frame 8.

a. foreign, [al] _____

b. study of the earth, [ge] _____

c. pertaining to courts, [jud] _____

d. small political meeting, [ca] _____

e. way to become a citizen, [nat] _____

5

An *alien* cannot be elected to a *legislative* or an *executive* position.

6

judicial, judicial
communism, communism
ambassador, ambassador

---

7 Models:

I studied the *geography* of Africa.
The city government is having *fiscal* trouble.

8

a. census
b. inauguration
c. poll
d. suburbs

10

Follow the instructions for Frame 8.

a. government by the people, [dem] _____
b. small political area, [pre] _____
c. pertaining to lawmaking, [leg] _____
d. Marxian socialism, [com] _____
e. pertaining to money, [fis] _____

9

a. alien
b. geography
c. judicial
d. caucus
e. naturalization

11

Follow the instructions for Frame 8.

a. pertaining to two parties, [bi] _____
b. words going before, [pre] _____
c. branch of government that includes the President, [ex] _____
_____
d. a representative abroad, [amb] _____

10

a. democracy
b. precinct
c. legislative
d. communism
e. fiscal

12

Write in full each incomplete word, choosing the most suitable from those studied in this unit.

a. [Fis] _____ decisions are made by the [leg] _____ _____ bodies.
b. The new [amb] _____ to France enjoys [bi] _____ support in Congress.
c. The latest [cen] _____ shows that three thousand people live in this [pre] _____ .

11

a. bipartisan
b. preamble
c. executive
d. ambassador

13

Follow the instructions for Frame 12.

a. The [Pre] _____ to the Constitution is a famous document in the history of [dem] _____ .
b. The [in] _____ of the new chief [ex] _____ _____ will occur in January.
c. The [p] _____ showed that the city was more strongly Democratic than the [sub] _____ were.

12

a. Fiscal, legislative
b. ambassador, bipartisan
c. census, precinct

14

Follow the instructions for Frame 12.

a. It was found that only one [al] _____ in ten favored [com] _____ over democracy.
b. A [ca] _____ was held involving those who favored the proposed [nat] _____ bill.
c. The [jud] _____ decision necessarily took into consideration the [ge] _____ of the state.

13

a. Preamble, democracy
b. inauguration, executive
c. poll, suburbs

15

Study each word that you misspelled in Frames 8–14. The information in Frames 1–7 may help you. Write each missed word correctly three times. Check your spellings against the list above Frame 1.

14

a. alien, communism
b. caucus, naturalization
c. judicial, geography

UNIT 66 · Some troublesome words in mathematics

WORDS TREATED

area	decimal	exponent	octagonal	rectangle
arithmetic	diameter	geometry	perimeter	sphere
binomial	equation	hypotenuse	perpendicular	symmetry
circumference	equiangular	oblique	quadratic	tangent
conical	equilateral	obtuse	radius	trigonometry

---

1   geometry   trigonometry   symmetry

The words in this unit are not much alike except that all are used in mathematics. We shall note some of their peculiarities.

The three words at the top of this frame all end in *metry*, meaning measurement.

Geo, from the Greek word for earth, plus *metry*, equals *geometry*, a way to measure the earth.

Trigono, from the Greek word for triangle, plus *metry*, equals *trigonometry*, measuring by triangles.

Sym, from the Greek word for with or same, plus *metry*, equals *symmetry*, the same or even measurements.

Write a sentence containing *geometry, trigonometry,* and *symmetry*.

---

2   decimal   conical   binomial

The suffix *–al* means pertaining to.

Decim, from the Latin word *decem*, ten, plus *–al*, equals *decimal*, pertaining to tens.

Conical goes back to Greek *konikos*. *Conical* means pertaining to a cone or shaped like a cone.

Bi in Latin refers to two. *Nomos* is Greek for number. A *binomial* expression in algebra has two numbers or terms, like 3x + 2y.

Use each word in a sentence: *decimal, conical, binomial*.

1   Model:

I enjoy the *symmetry* of many drawings in *geometry* and *trigonometry*.

3 arithmetic quadratic equation

Arithmetic is the English spelling of Greek *arithmetikos*.

    Quadratic, from Latin, refers to the square of a number.

    Equation is related to the words *equal*, *equate*, and *equator*. In an *equation*, the parts on the two sides are equal.

Write a single sentence containing *arithmetic*, *quadratic*, and *equation*.

_____

_____

_____

4 perimeter circumference area

Peri, the Greek word meaning around, and *meter*, meaning measure, give *perimeter*, the distance around.

    Circum, the Latin word meaning around, attached to another Latin word meaning to carry, gives *circumference*, the distance around a circle.

    Area makes no spelling change in the Latin word for a large piece of level ground. We define *area* as the extent of a surface.

Write each word in a sentence: *perimeter*, *circumference*, *area*.

_____

_____

_____

5 sphere radius diameter

The *sph* in *sphere* is due to the *sph* in the Greek ancestor, *sphaira*, which meant ball.

    Radius, a Latin word meaning rod or radius, is a straight line from the center of a circle or sphere to the edge.

    Diameter combines Greek *dia*, which meant dividing into two parts, with our old friend *meter*, measure. The *diameter* divides a circle into two equal parts.

Write a sentence containing *sphere*, *radius*, and *diameter*.

_____

_____

6 obtuse oblique hypotenuse

Obtusus, the Latin ancestor of *obtuse*, meant dull. An *obtuse* angle is a "dull" angle; that is, it does not come to a sharp point.

    Oblique, from Latin *obliquus*, means slanting.

    Hypotenuse comes from Greek words meaning to stretch under. The *hypotenuse* of a right triangle is the side opposite the right angle.

Copy: This *oblique* line will complete an *obtuse* angle, so there can be no *hypotenuse*.

_____

_____

2 Models:

Don't forget the *decimal* point.
The flower is *conical*.
We are now studying *binomials*.

3 Model:

Conventional *arithmetic* does not cover *quadratic equations*.

4 Models:

The *perimeter* of the square is ten feet.
The *circumference* of the circle is nine inches.
The *area* is four square feet.

5 Model:

The *radius* is half the *diameter* of a *sphere*.

7   tangent   exponent   rectangle   perpendicular

Tangent, from the Latin verb for touch, refers to a line touching some other line or surface.

Exponent, from Latin words meaning placed outside, refers to a symbol like the 2 in x^2.

Rectus in Latin means right. A *rectangle* has only right angles.

Perpendicular goes back to Latin *perpendiculum,* a plumb line. A *perpendicular* line is a straight line that makes right angles with another line or surface.

Write each word twice: *tangent, exponent, rectangle, perpendicular.*

_____, _____

_____, _____

_____, _____

_____, _____

6

This *oblique* line will complete an *obtuse* angle, so there can be no *hypotenuse.*

---

8   equiangular   equilateral   octagonal

Note the *i* in *equiangular* and *equilateral.*

Note that *octagon* and *octagonal,* like *hexagon* and *hexagonal,* have *a* as the fourth letter.

Copy: Most triangles are not *equiangular* and *equilateral.* An *octagonal* figure always has eight sides.

_____

_____

_____

7

tangent, tangent
exponent, exponent
rectangle, rectangle
perpendicular, perpendicular

9

Match each definition with one of the words we studied in this unit. The first letters have been given. Write the words in full.

a. the study of numbers, [ari] _____
b. extent of a surface, [a] _____
c. measurement by triangles, [trig] _____
d. a ball, [sp] _____
e. numbered by tens, [de] _____
f. distance around, [per] _____
g. slanting, [ob] _____
h. having equal sides, [eq] _____

8

Most triangles are not *equiangular* and *equilateral.* An *octagonal* figure always has eight sides.

10

Follow the instructions for Frame 8.

a. a line that touches a surface, [tan] _____
b. a figure with right angles only, [re] _____
c. line bisecting a circle, [di] _____
d. distance around a circle, [cir] _____
e. symbol written above another and to the right, [ex] _____
f. science of measurement, [ge] _____
g. pertaining to a cone, [con] _____
h. eight-sided, [oc] _____

9

a. arithmetic
b. area
c. trigonometry
d. sphere
e. decimal
f. perimeter
g. oblique
h. equilateral

11

Follow the instructions for Frame 8.

a. line at right angles to another, [per] _____
b. even measurement, [sym] _____
c. larger than a right angle, [ob] _____
d. line opposite right angle in a triangle, [hy] _____
e. half of a diameter, [ra] _____
f. pertaining to a square, [qua] _____
g. statement of equality, [eq] _____
h. pertaining to two numbers, [bi] _____
i. having equal angles, [eq] _____

10

a. tangent
b. rectangle
c. diameter
d. circumference
e. exponent
f. geometry
g. conical
h. octagonal

12

Write in full each incomplete word, choosing the most suitable from those studied in this unit.

a. $X^2 + Y = 6$ is a [qu] _____ [eq] _____.

b. 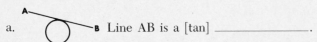 This angle is [ob] _____.

c. ▭ This figure is a [re] _____.

d. ◯ the [cir] _____ of the circle is labeled c, and the [a] _____ is labeled A.

e. If each side of a triangle measures three meters, the triangle is [eq] _____ by definition, but it is also [eq] _____.

11

a. perpendicular
b. symmetry
c. obtuse
d. hypotenuse
e. radius
f. quadratic
g. equation
h. binomial
i. equiangular

13

Follow the instructions for Frame 11.

a. 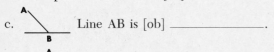 Line AB is a [tan] _____.

b. The "period" in 3.7 is a [de] _____ point.

c. Line AB is [ob] _____.

d. Line AB is [per] _____ to CD.

e. The [per] _____ of the rectangle is six inches.

f. In y^3 the 3 is an [ex] _____.

12

a. quadratic, equation
b. obtuse
c. rectangle
d. circumference, area
e. equilateral, equiangular

14

Follow the instructions for Frame 11.

a. The church steeple was [con] _____ in shape.
b. In [ari] _____ we learned to add and subtract.
c. The earth is not quite a perfect [sp] _____.

d. A—B—C Line AB is a [ra] _____, and AC is a [di] _____
_____.

15

Follow the instructions for Frame 11.

a. Line AB is a [hy] _____.
b. Most high schools have courses in plane and solid [ge] _____
_____, but many do not offer [trig] _____.
c. Eighteenth-century gardens were very regular and even; they were good illustrations of [sym] _____.
d. a + b is an example of a [bi] _____.

16

Study each word that you misspelled in Frames 9–15. Write each missed word correctly three times. Check your spellings against the list above Frame 1.

13

a. tangent
b. decimal
c. oblique
d. perpendicular
e. perimeter
f. exponent

14

a. conical
b. arithmetic
c. sphere
d. radius, diameter

15

a. hypotenuse
b. geometry, trigonometry
c. symmetry
d. binomial

UNIT 67 · Some troublesome words in home economics

WORDS TREATED

acetate	canapé	croquette	meringue	sherbe(r)t
appliqué	chiffon	crouton	mousse	soufflé
au gratin	condiment	embroider	pasteurize	spaghetti
bodice	corduroy	fricassee	puree	sterilize
bouillon	crochet	gingham	purl	synthetic

1   appliqué   canapé   soufflé

Many home economics terms in English are taken directly from French and preserve characteristics of that language. For example, the three words above keep the accent mark above the final *e* and thus show that the *e* (pronounced "ay") is not silent.

    An *appliqué* is a cutout decoration applied to a surface.

    A *canapé* is an appetizer, such as a spread on a cracker.

    A *soufflé* is a fluffy food consisting mainly of eggs beaten and baked.

Copy each word, making the accent mark extra large.

_____ , _____ , _____

---

2   au gratin   bouillon   chiffon   crochet

Four more French words are listed above.

    Au gratin (pronounced "oh grotten") means with cheese: potatoes *au gratin*.

    In *bouillon* (pronounced "boo yon" or "bull yon"), note the placement of the *i* as well as the three consecutive vowels.

    Note the two *f*'s in *chiffon* and the *chet* in *crochet* (pronounced "kro shay").

Copy: He liked beef *bouillon*, eggs *au gratin*, and *chiffon* pie, but all she wanted to do was *crochet*.

---

3   croquette   crouton   fricassee

More French words: A *croquette* is a small cake of diced food fried in deep fat: salmon *croquettes*.

    Croutons, often dropped into soups or on salads, are toasty tidbits named for the French word for crust.

    Fricassee, from the French word for fry, in English refers to stewed pieces of meat served with thick gravy.

Write a sentence with each word: *croquette, crouton, fricassee.*

---

4   meringue   mousse   puree (purée)

Meringue (pronounced "muh rang") is the egg-white topping for pastry.

    Mousse (pronounced like the name of a big animal) is usually a chilled dessert with whipped cream; in French it means froth.

    Puree, which has several pronunciations, is listed in some dictionaries with the French accent over the first *e*, in others without it—so take your choice; it refers to a strained food.

Copy: My *puree* (or *purée*) is tasty, but my *meringue* and my *mousse* are watery.

1

appliqué
canapé
soufflé

2

He liked beef *bouillon*, eggs *au gratin*, and *chiffon* pie, but all she wanted to do was *crochet*.

---

3   Models:

The little coquettes always served him *croquettes*.

I like *croutons* in chicken soup.

Fricassee ends like *Tennessee*.

5　pasteurize　sherbe(r)t　spaghetti

Pasteurize gets its spelling from French scientist Louis *Pasteur*; note the last three letters of his name.

Dictionaries usually spell the second word *sherbet*, but one or two admit *sherbert* as an alternative, and almost all waitresses and menu writers seem to stick in the second *r*. The Turkish *sherbet* and Persian *sharbat*, from which we borrowed the word, show that historically *sherbet* is more defensible.

Americans sometimes overlook the *h* in *spaghetti*, an Italian word that originally meant strings.

Copy: She served *spaghetti*, *sherbet*, and *pasteurized* milk.

_____

_____

6　bodice　embroider　purl

Bodice (the part of a dress extending from shoulder to waist) looks like French but is actually a changed spelling of *bodies*.

Embroider is from French, though we have changed the spelling here, too.

And *purl*, an inverted stitch to give a ribbed effect in knitting, is an English word of unknown origin, once spelled *pyrle*.

Copy: While Janice *purled* one and knitted two, Janet *embroidered* a *bodice* for the carnival.

_____

_____

7　acetate　corduroy　gingham　synthetic

A *synthetic* fiber is a man-made one, in contrast to a natural fiber like wool or cotton.

An example is *acetate*, a fiber also called cellulose acetate.

Corduroy and *gingham* are usually made of cotton. Note the *u* in *corduroy*, and *gha* in *gingham*.

Copy: *Acetate*, a *synthetic* fiber, was unknown to our grandmothers, who sewed *gingham* and *corduroy*.

_____

_____

_____

8　condiment　sterilize

Note that *i* represents the schwa sound (like "uh") in the middle of each of these words.

Copy: In her zeal to *sterilize* everything, she even scalded *condiments* like pepper.

_____

_____

4

My *puree* (or *purée*) is tasty, but my *meringue* and my *mousse* are watery.

5

She served *spaghetti*, *sherbet*, and *pasteurized* milk.

6

While Janice *purled* one and knitted two, Janet *embroidered* a *bodice* for the carnival.

7

Acetate, a *synthetic* fiber, was unknown to our grandmothers, who sewed *gingham* and *corduroy*.

9

Match each definition with the most suitable word studied in this unit. The first letters have been supplied. Write the complete word.

a. artificial, man-made [syn] _____

b. a seasoning, [con] _____

c. an appetizer, [can] _____

d. stewed meat in thick gravy, [fric] _____

10

Follow the instructions for Frame 9.

a. a synthetic fiber, [ac] _____

b. to free from bacteria, [st] _____

c. egg white as pie topping, [m] _____

d. fried meat ball, [cro] _____

11

Follow the instructions for Frame 9.

a. ribbed fabric, [cor] _____

b. upper part of a dress, [bo] _____

c. clear soup, [bo] _____

d. frothy dessert, [mo] _____

12

Follow the instructions for Frame 9.

a. with cheese, [a] _____

b. cutout attached elsewhere, [ap] _____

c. light, fluffy, [ch] _____

d. light, fluffy egg dish, [s] _____

13

Follow the instructions for Frame 9.

a. frozen dessert, [sh] _____

b. to sterilize, as milk, [pa] _____

c. strained vegetables or fruit, [pu] _____

d. yarn-dyed cotton fabric, [gi] _____

8

In her zeal to *sterilize* everything, she even scalded *condiments* like pepper.

9

a. synthetic

b. condiment

c. canapé

d. fricassee

10

a. acetate

b. sterilize

c. meringue

d. croquette

11

a. corduroy

b. bodice

c. bouillon

d. mousse

12

a. au gratin

b. appliqué

c. chiffon

d. soufflé

14

Follow the instructions for Frame 9.

a. a stitch in knitting, [p] _____

b. Italian word for strings, [sp] _____

c. to make a yarn design on cloth, [em] _____

d. toasted bit, [cr] _____

e. to make with a hooked needle, [cr] _____

13

a. sherbe(r)t

b. pasteurize

c. puree (or purée)

d. gingham

15

Study each word that you misspelled in Frames 9–14. The information in Frames 1–8 may help you. Write each missed word correctly three times. Check your spellings against the list above Frame 1.

14

a. purl

b. spaghetti

c. embroider

d. crouton

e. crochet

UNIT 68 · Some troublesome words in carpentry, masonry, and plumbing

WORDS TREATED

abrasive	cement	furring	mortar	sewage
aggregate	chisel	gable	partition	spigot
asbestos	dowel	galvanize	plumb	trowel
batten	enamel	jamb	rabbet	upholstery
bibb	faucet	joist	scantling	veneer

---

1 dowel trowel chisel enamel

The words in this unit are not alike except that all are used in the building trades. We will observe some of their peculiarities.

Dowel generally means a round rod. It rhymes with *trowel*. Two other words ending in *el* are *chisel* and *enamel*.

Read aloud and then copy: I hit the *dowel* with the *trowel* and dropped the *chisel* into the *enamel*.

_____

_____

_____

2   aggregate   batten   rabbet   faucet

Note that in each of these words, the most difficult letter to remember is the *e*.

    To a mason, *aggregate* means the sand and gravel mixed with cement.

    To a carpenter, *batten* means a small strip of wood, and *rabbet* (not to be confused with *rabbit*, the animal) is a groove in wood.

a. Pronounce *aggregate*, *batten*, *rabbet*, and *faucet*, exaggerating the *e* sound.

b. Copy: While the mason mixed *aggregate*, the carpenter nailed on some *battens* and made some *rabbet* joints, and the plumber installed *faucets*.

_____

_____

_____

---

3   jamb   plumb

a. A *jamb* is the casing or sidepost of a doorway. Say aloud, "*Jamb* rhymes with *lamb*."

b. A wall or line is *plumb* if it is exactly vertical. Say aloud, "*Plumb* rhymes with *numb* and *dumb*."

c. Copy: The *jamb* wasn't *plumb*.

_____

---

4   joist   partition

a. A *joist* is a heavy timber used to support or frame. Say aloud, "Joist rhymes with *hoist* and *moist*."

b. A *partition* separates two rooms or other areas. Say aloud, "A *partition* keeps things *apart*."

c. Copy: A strong *joist* is necessary to support that heavy *partition*.

_____

_____

---

5   galvanize   mortar   sewage

Galvanize is spelled that way because the word honors an Italian scientist, Luigi *Galvani*.

    Mortar has its *a* because it comes from Latin *mortārium*.

    Sewage has its *a* because it combines *sew(er)* and the suffix *—age* (which means collectively).

Write the three words, capitalizing each *a* to emphasize it.

_____ , _____ , _____

1

I hit the *dowel* with the *trowel* and dropped the *chisel* into the *enamel*.

2

b. While the mason mixed *aggregate*, the carpenter nailed on some *battens* and made some *rabbet* joints, and the plumber installed *faucets*.

3

c. The *jamb* wasn't *plumb*.

4

c. A strong *joist* is necessary to support that heavy *partition*.

6 spigot bibb

Nobody knows for sure where *spigot* comes from, but it may have been from Old Provençal *espigot*, "little head of grain," which would explain the spelling if nothing else.

Bibb, also called *bibcock*, means a faucet or spigot with the nozzle threaded for a hose.

Copy: He put a hose on the *bibb* and opened the *spigot*.

_____

_____

---

7 abrasive asbestos cement furring

a. Something is *abrasive* if it is rough, like sandpaper. Say aloud, "*Abrasive* rhymes with *evasive*."

b. *Asbestos* (rarely *asbestus*) names a fiber that will not burn. Say aloud, "Inhaling *asbestos* dust can cause a disease called *asbestosis*."

c. *Cement* is a simplified spelling of Latin *caementum*. Say aloud, "Not a cent for *cement*!"

d. *Furring* strips are (usually) pieces of wood, fastened to a masonry wall before putting up paneling or the like. Say aloud,

> "The kitten was *purring*
> While I did the *furring*."

e. Write each of the four words three times.

_____ , _____ , _____
_____ , _____ , _____
_____ , _____ , _____
_____ , _____ , _____

---

8 gable scantling upholstery veneer

A *gable* is the triangular part of a roof or building end. Note the *le*.

Scantlings are lumber, usually two-by-fours or two-by-sixes. Note the *t* and the *g*.

In *upholstery*, note the *e*.

Veneer is a thin layer of decorative wood, formica, brick, or other material, fastened to a less costly base. Note that three out of six of the letters in *veneer* are *e*'s.

Write each of these four words twice.

_____ , _____
_____ , _____
_____ , _____
_____ , _____

5

gAlvAnize, mortʼAr, sewAge

6

He put a hose on the *bibb* and opened the *spigot*.

7

abrasive, abrasive, abrasive
asbestos, asbestos, asbestos
cement, cement, cement
furring, furring, furring

9

Match each definition with one of the words we looked at in this unit. The first letter or letters have been supplied. Write the complete word.

a. rough, like sandpaper, [ab] _____

b. heavy lumber or metal used for support, [j] _____

c. sturdy instrument for cutting, [ch] _____

d. faucet that can take a hose, [b] _____

e. fastening wood strips to masonry, [f] _____

10

Follow the instructions for Frame 9.

a. inverted v at end of a house, [g] _____

b. something that holds brick together, [m] _____

c. Your garbage is part of it. [s] _____

d. another name for faucet, [sp] _____

e. interior wall or divider, [p] _____

11

Follow the instructions for Frame 9.

a. fireproof material, [as] _____

b. material hard after it dries, [c] _____

c. sand and gravel to be mixed with *b*, [ag] _____

d. small board nailed over a crack, for example, [b] _____

e. frame for a door, [j] _____

12

Follow the instructions for Frame 9.

a. tool to spread plaster or cement, [tr] _____

b. immediate source of water, [f] _____

c. maybe a two-by-four, [sc] _____

d. something groovy, [ra] _____

e. thick, paintlike, substance, [en] _____

13

Follow the instructions for Frame 9.

a. rod, usually round, [d] _____

b. to coat with zinc, as a bucket or nail, [g] _____

c. exactly vertical, [pl] _____

d. decorative coating, often wood, [v] _____

e. soft covering for furniture, [up] _____

8

gable, gable
scantling, scantling
upholstery, upholstery
veneer, veneer

9

a. abrasive
b. joist
c. chisel
d. bibb
e. furring

10

a. gable
b. mortar
c. sewage
d. spigot
e. partition

11

a. asbestos (rarely −us)
b. cement
c. aggregate
d. batten
e. jamb

12

a. trowel
b. faucet
c. scantling
d. rabbet
e. enamel

14

Study each word that you misspelled in Frames 9–13. Review Frames 1–8 as necessary. Write each missed word correctly three times. Check your spellings against the list above Frame 1.

13

a. dowel
b. galvanize
c. plumb
d. veneer
e. upholstery

UNIT 69 · Business and secretarial words

WORDS TREATED

acquisition	director	invoice	quarterly	warranty
addressee	disbursement	lessee	remittance	
campaign	dismissal	manufacturer	requisition	
circular	financial	marketing	secretarial	
corporation	financing	percentage	subdivision	

---

1   acquisition   quarterly   requisition

The words in this unit are common ones in many business offices.

Acquisition and *requisition* are related to *acquire* and *require* respectively. Remembering that fact may help you to recall that the fifth letter in each is an *i*.

Quarterly is just *quarter* + *–ly*.

Copy: Our *quarterly requisition* resulted in the *acquisition* of a new typewriter.

---

2   addressee   lessee

The suffix *–ee* often means one who receives something. So an *addressee* is the one who will receive the mail and a *lessee* is one who receives a lease—one who rents. (One who does the addressing and the leasing is the *addresser* or *addressor* and the *lessor*.)

Copy: Each *addressee* was a *lessee* of company-owned land.

1

Our *quarterly requisition* resulted in the *acquisition* of a new typewriter.

---

3   financial   financing   corporation

Copy: *Financial* experts gave advice on *financing* the *corporation*.

2

Each *addressee* was a *lessee* of company-owned land.

---

4   director   marketing   campaign

Copy: The *director* of *marketing* planned the *campaign*.

_____

_____

5   disbursement   dismissal   warranty   subdivision

disburse + *–ment* = *disbursement* (Note the *burse*.)
dismiss + *–al* = *dismissal* (Note the *ss*.)
warrant + *–y* = *warranty* (Note the *ant*.)
sub + *division* = *subdivision*

Use each word in a short sentence: *disbursement, dismissal, warranty, subdivision.*

_____

_____

_____

_____

6   circular   invoice   secretarial

Copy: The *secretarial* staff prepares *circulars* and *invoices*.

_____

_____

7   manufacturer   percentage   remittance

Observe the *e* in *manufacturer*.

Note that *percentage* is written as one word, although *per cent* is generally two.

Note the doubled *t* in *remittance*.

Write a sentence with each word: *manufacturer, percentage, remittance.*

_____

_____

_____

3

Financial experts gave advice on *financing* the *corporation*.

4

The *director* of *marketing* planned the *campaign*.

5   Models:

The treasurer is responsible for *disbursement* of funds.
Theft led to her *dismissal*.
The calculator is still under *warranty*.
She manages a *subdivision* of the estate.

6

The *secretarial* staff prepares *circulars* and *invoices*.

8

Match each definition with one of the words studied in this unit. The first letter or letters have been given. Write each word in full.

a. assurance of quality, [wa] _____

b. pertaining to money, [fi] _____

c. payment, [rem] _____

d. something acquired, [acq] _____

e. person named on an envelope, [ad] _____

f. advertising leaflet, [c] _____

g. incorporated business, [cor] _____

9

Follow the instructions for Frame 8.

a. one way to increase sales, [cam] _____

b. part of a division, [sub] _____

c. one who directs, [d] _____

d. paying or arranging for payment, [fi] _____

e. proportion or share, [per] _____

f. selling, [mar] _____

g. one who leases from, [l] _____

10

Follow the instructions for Frame 8.

a. list of goods shipped, [in] _____

b. act of paying out, [dis] _____

c. discharge of an employee, [dis] _____

d. one who manufactures, [man] _____

e. four times a year, [qu] _____

f. request for required supplies, [re] _____

g. pertaining to a secretary, [sec] _____

11

Write in full each incomplete word, choosing the most suitable from those studied in this unit.

a. A large [per] _____ of the [dis] _____
_____s for the sales [cam] _____ came from
the profits of the first quarter.

b. For [fin] _____ reasons the [corp] _____
_____ decreased its work force.

12

Follow the instructions for Frame 11.

a. The advertising [cir] _____ referred to a [war] _____
_____ that would protect the buyer.

b. The [dir] _____ asked to see the list of [ad] _____
_____s.

He was a *manufacturer* of adult games.

A large *percentage* of her salary is withheld.

My *remittance* is enclosed.

8

a. warranty

b. financial

c. remittance

d. acquisition

e. addressee

f. circular

g. corporation

9

a. campaign

b. subdivision

c. director

d. financing

e. percentage

f. marketing

g. lessee

10

a. invoice

b. disbursement

c. dismissal

d. manufacturer

e. quarterly

f. requisition

g. secretarial

11

a. percentage, disbursements, campaign

b. financial, corporation

13

Follow the instructions for Frame 11.

a. The [ac] _____ of [sec] _____ skills is important.

b. The company had difficulty in [fin] _____ the [sub] _____ .

c. The [man] _____ always sends an [in] _____ promptly.

14

Follow the instructions for Frame 11.

a. I enclose our [re] _____ in payment for [req] _____ no. 72.

b. [Qu] _____ payments must be made by the [l] _____ .

c. [Dis] _____ of seven employees in the [mar] _____ department was necessary.

15

Study each word that you misspelled in Frames 8–14. Write each missed word correctly three times. Check your spelling against the list above Frame 1.

12

a. circular, warranty
b. director, addressees

13

a. acquisition, secretarial
b. financing, subdivision
c. manufacturer, invoice

14

a. remittance, requisition
b. Quarterly, lessee
c. Dismissal, marketing

UNIT 70 · Some troublesome words in mechanics and electricity

WORDS TREATED

ampere	diesel	electricity	mechanic	resistance	valve
capacitor	differential	electronics	ohm	rheostat	volt
carburetor	electrical	gasket	piston	soldering iron	watt
conduit	electrician	insulation	pliers	thermostat	wrench

1   ampere   diesel   ohm   volt   watt

The five words above have one thing in common. All are taken from persons' names, as follows:

ampere—André M. Ampere (French)
diesel—Rudolf Diesel (German)
ohm—George S. Ohm (German)
volt—Alessandro Volta (Italian)
watt—James Watt (Scottish)

Diesel, as in *Diesel engine*, is sometimes capitalized, but the others are not.

Copy: *Ampere*, *ohm*, *volt*, and *watt* represent electricial measurements, and *diesel* is a kind of engine.

_____

_____

_____

2   electrical   electrician   electricity   electronics   resistance

Greek *ēlectron* and Latin *ēlectrum* mean amber, which gives off sparks when rubbed. These words are the source of hundreds of English terms, including the first four above.

Resistance (note the *a*) is in this group because our electrical appliances are affected by resistance, defined as opposition to an electric current.

Make up a sentence with each word: *electrical*, *electrician*, *electricity*, *electronics*, *resistance*.

_____

_____

_____

_____

_____

3   carbUrEtOr   diFFerentIal   pistOn   vAlve

The four words above are familiar to all who have worked in automotive repair. The spelling trouble spots are shown in capitals.

Copy the four words, including the capitals.

_____ , _____ ,

_____ , _____

1

Ampere, *ohm*, *volt*, and *watt* represent electrical measurements, and *diesel* is a kind of engine.

2 Models:

Electrical current flows not only through wires.
I want to be an *electrician*.
Electricity is both useful and dangerous.
Electronics is a science dealing with movement of electrons.
Ohm's Law concerns *resistance*.

4 capacitor rheostat thermostat

In electricity a *capacitor* stores charge temporarily.

A *rheostat* is a resistor used to regulate current; note the *h*, which comes from Greek *rheos* "current, stream."

The familiar *thermostat* regulates temperature and is obviously related to *thermometer*.

Copy: The store had no *capacitor*, no *rheostat*, and only one suitable *thermostat*.

_____

_____

_____

5 conduit gasket insulation

One letter causes the common spelling trouble in each of these words. In *conduit* it is the *u*, in *gasket* the *e*, in *insulation* the *u*.
Write three times each: condUit, gaskEt, insUlation.

_____, _____, _____,

_____, _____, _____,

_____, _____,

_____

6 mechanic pliers soldering iron wrench

In *mechanic* the trouble spot is often the *e*, and in *pliers* it is the *i*.

The *l* in *soldering* and the *w* in *wrench* are silent. (Soldering makes things solid, and the spelling goes back to the Latin word for *solid*. The *w* in *wrench* was pronounced in Old English.)

Copy: Every *mechanic* needs *pliers*, a *soldering iron*, and a set of good *wrenches*.

_____

_____

7

Write in full each incomplete word, choosing the most suitable from those studied in this unit.

a. The *w* and *v* atop every light bulb stand for [w] _____ and [v] _____.

b. He heated his [s] _____ [i] _____ and joined the metal disks.

c. [El] _____ work is only my hobby now, but I want to become a full-time [el] _____.

3

carbUrEtOr, diFFerentIal, pistOn, vAlve

4

The store had no *capacitor*, no *rheostat*, and only one suitable *thermostat*.

5

condUit, condUit, condUit
gaskEt, gaskEt, gaskEt
insUlation, insUlation, insUlation

6

Every *mechanic* needs *pliers*, a *soldering iron*, and a set of good *wrenches*.

8

Follow the instructions for Frame 7.

a. In the garage one [m] _____ worked on the [dif] _____ and the other took the [car]_____ _____ apart.

b. A [d] _____ engine does not burn gasoline.

c. The [el] _____ics industry is still growing fast.

9

Follow the instructions for Frame 7.

a. The study of [re] _____ is important in [el] _____y.

b. Older cars had to have their [v] _____s ground frequently.

c. [Pl] _____ in one hand and [w] _____ in the other, she started to work on her ailing lawnmower.

10

Follow the instructions for Frame 7.

a. We used a [con] _____ to protect the wires.

b. The technician traced our trouble to a faulty [cap] _____ _____r.

c. With added [in] _____ and a new [gas] _____ she stopped the leak.

d. The [p] _____ moves back and forth inside the cylinder.

11

Follow the instructions for Frame 7.

a. "Amp" is short for [amp] _____.

b. An [o] _____ is a unit of electrical [re] _____.

c. Being cold, we turned up the [th] _____.

d. One use of a [r] _____ is to dim lights.

12

Match each definition or clue with a word studied in this unit. Write the word in full.

a. one type of engine, [d] _____

b. a gear in the rear axle, [dif] _____

c. electric current as source of power, [el] _____

d. pertaining to c, [el] _____

e. one who works with c, [el] _____

f. a tool with two basic parts, [pl] _____

g. used to prevent leaks, [ga] _____

h. It moves in a cylinder, [p] _____

7

a. watt, volt
b. soldering iron
c. Electrical, electrician

8

a. mechanic, differential, carburetor
b. diesel (or Diesel)
c. electronics

9

a. resistance, electricity
b. valves
c. Pliers, wrench

10

a. conduit
b. capacitor
c. insulation, gasket
d. piston

11

a. ampere
b. ohm, resistance
c. thermostat
d. rheostat

13

Follow the instructions for Frame 12.

a. often a metal pipe, [con] _____

b. science of the movement of electrons, [el] _____

c. used to prevent heat from escaping, [in] _____

d. He is often found in a garage, [m] _____

e. device to regulate flow, [v] _____

f. tool for turning, [w] _____

g. It gets hot, [s i] _____

h. It can control motor speed, [r] _____

14

Follow the instructions for Frame 12.

a. It controls temperature, [th] _____

b. It controls flow of fuel and air, [car] _____

c. It stores an electric charge, [cap] _____

d. unit of magnetomotive force, [amp] _____

e. unit of resistance, [o] _____

f. unit of electric potential, [v] _____

g. unit of power, [w] _____

15

Study each word that you misspelled in Frames 7–14. Write each missed word correctly three times. Check your spellings against the list above Frame 1.

12

a. diesel (or Diesel)
b. differential
c. electricity
d. electrical
e. electrician
f. pliers
g. gasket
h. piston

13

a. conduit
b. electronics
c. insulation
d. mechanic
e. valve
f. wrench
g. soldering iron
h. rheostat

14

a. thermostat
b. carburetor
c. capacitor
d. ampere
e. ohm
f. volt
g. watt

PART THREE

Spellings With Low Predictability

UNIT 71 · Avoiding extra letters

WORDS TREATED

allege	decision	exaltation	lose	prejudice	welfare
among	develop	exuberance	losing	regard	whether
college	development	laid	omit	said	
decide	enable	lightning	paid	sandwich	

---

1   develop   development

The twenty-one words in this unit have this in common: Many persons tend to write each of them with a letter or two more than necessary.

For instance, *develop* stops with the letter *p*; there is nothing more. *Development* has nothing between the *p* and the *m*.

Copy: To *develop* a housing *development* is expensive.

---

2   decide   decision

Note that each of the two words above starts with *dec*, not with a longer combination of letters.

Copy: It was decent of you to *decide* so soon. Thanks for your *decision*.

---

3   exuberance   exaltation

Note that a vowel comes right after the *ex* in each of the words above.

Copy: He spoke with *exuberance* in his voice; in his heart he felt *exaltation*.

---

4   omit   enable   lose   losing

Observe that there are no doubled letters in the words above.

Copy: If we *omit losing* money, it will *enable* us to *lose* little sleep.

1

To *develop* a housing *development* is expensive.

2

It was decent of you to *decide* so soon. Thanks for your *decision*.

3

He spoke with *exuberance* in his voice; in his heart he felt *exaltation*.

---

5 paid laid said

Although *paid* and *laid* do not rhyme with *said*, all three are spelled with the same last three letters.

Write *paid*, *laid*, and *said* twice each.

_____ , _____

_____ , _____

_____ , _____

6 among whether lightning regard

Be sure not to add an unnecessary vowel within any of the four words above.

Note that *lightning* (as in *thunder* and *lightning*) has only two syllables.

Write one or two sentences using *among*, *whether*, *lightning*, and *regard*.

_____

_____

_____

7 welfare college prejudice sandwich allege

Be sure not to add an unnecessary consonant within any of the five words above.

Copy: I *allege* that a *college* student on *welfare* cannot show *prejudice* against a cheap *sandwich*.

_____

_____

_____

8

Write in full a word studied in this unit that matches each definition. The first letters have been supplied.

a. to leave out, [o] _____

b. expended, [pa] _____

c. surrounded by, [amo] _____

d. to become bigger, [dev] _____

e. to look at, [re] _____

f. to misplace or be unable to find, [lo] _____

g. electrical discharge in the sky, [li] _____

4

If we *omit losing* money, it will *enable* us to *lose* little sleep.

5

paid, paid
laid, laid
said, said

6   Model:

In *regard* to your question, I don't know *whether lightning* struck *among* the soldiers.

7

I *allege* that a *college* student on *welfare* cannot show *prejudice* against a cheap *sandwich*.

9

Follow the instructions for Frame 8.

a. placed down, [la] _____

b. if, [whe] _____

c. bread with filling between slices, [sand] _____

d. institution of higher learning, [col] _____

e. to make possible, [en] _____

f. growth or filling out, [dev] _____

g. bias; insufficiently supported opinion, [pre] _____

h. to make a statement, [al] _____

10

Follow the instructions for Frame 8.

a. a feeling of intense joy, pride, or nobility, [ex] _____ [tion]

b. quality of existing in great abundance; happiness, [ex] _____ [ance]

c. did say, [sa] _____

d. health, happiness, and prosperity, [wel] _____

e. misplacing or being unable to find, [lo] _____

f. to make up one's mind, [de] _____

g. the result of making up one's mind, [de] _____

11

Write in full each unfinished word, choosing the most suitable from those studied in this unit.

a. I [sa] _____, "The money must be [pa] _____ at once."

b. The [san] _____ was invented by the Earl of Sandwich, who hated to [lo] _____ time from his gambling.

c. [Light] _____ struck somewhere [am] _____ the pines, causing a fire to [dev] _____ quickly.

12

Follow the instructions for Frame 11.

a. I have made a [de] _____ to go to [col] _____.

b. Let us [de] _____ quickly [whe] _____ or not to stop at the library.

c. "[Lo] _____ [pre] _____ is never easy, but we treated everyone equally," he [al] _____ d.

8

a. omit

b. paid

c. among

d. develop

e. regard

f. lose

g. lightning

9

a. laid

b. whether

c. sandwich

d. college

e. enable

f. development

g. prejudice

h. allege

10

a. exaltation

b. exuberance

c. said

d. welfare

e. losing

f. decide

g. decision

11

a. said, paid

b. sandwich, lose

c. Lightning, among, develop

13

Follow the instructions for Frame 11.

a. Suddenly a new [dev] _____ brought increased pleasure, amounting almost to [ex] _____ [tion].

b. "I [re] _____ a show of high spirits or [ex] _____ as unsuitable," Aunt Tabitha said stiffly.

c. If the scene of the play is [la] _____ in the Sahara Desert, it may [en] _____ us to [o] _____ construction of expensive scenery.

14

Study each word that you misspelled in Frames 8–13. Be especially careful not to include unnecessary letters in these words. Write each missed word correctly three times. Check your answers against the list above Frame 1.

12

a. decision, college
b. decide, whether
c. losing, prejudice, alleged

13

a. development, exaltation
b. regard, exuberance
c. laid, enable, omit

UNIT 72 · Words that change the spelling of the basic forms

WORDS TREATED

absorption	disastrous	forty	maintenance	shepherd
ancestry	entrance	hindrance	prevalent	wintry
curiosity	explanation	influential	pronunciation	wondrous
desperate	fiery	led	remembrance	

---

1   remembrance   wondrous

A number of English words are based upon other English words but make changes in the basic forms.

For example, *remembrance* drops an *e* from *remember,* and *wondrous* drops an *e* from *wonder.* The reason is that the sound of the *e* is lost in pronouncing each word.

Copy: That *wondrous* day will always live in my *remembrance.*

_____

_____

2   disastrous   wintry   entrance

a. *Disastrous* drops an _____ (What letter?) from *disaster*. Write *disastrous* in a sentence.

_____

b. *Wintry* drops an _____ (What letter?) from *winter*. Write *wintry* in a sentence.

_____

c. *Entrance* drops an _____ (What letter?) from *enter*. Write *entrance* in a sentence.

_____

3   hindrance   ancestry   explanation

a. *Hindrance* drops an _____ (What letter?) from *hinder*. Write *hindrance* in a sentence.

_____

b. *Ancestry* drops an _____ (What letter?) from *ancestor*. Write *ancestry* in a sentence.

_____

c. *Explanation* drops an _____ (What letter?) from *explain*. Write *explanation* in a sentence.

_____

4   pronunciation   curiosity   shepherd

a. *Pronunciation* drops an _____ (What letter?) from *pronounce*. Write *pronunciation* twice.

_____ , _____

b. *Curiosity* drops a _____ (What letter?) from *curious*. Write *curiosity* in a sentence.

_____

c. *Shepherd* drops an _____ (What letter?) from *sheep*. Write *shepherd* in a sentence.

_____

5   forty   maintenance   prevalent

a. *Forty* drops a _____ (What letter?) from *four*. Write *forty* twice.

_____ , _____

b. *Maintenance* changes the _____ (What two letters?) of *maintain* to _____ (What letter?). Write *maintenance* in a sentence.

_____

c. *Prevalent* drops an _____ (What letter?) from *prevail*. Write *prevalent* in a sentence.

_____

1

That *wondrous* day will always live in my *remembrance*.

2   Models:

a. *e.* The night was *disastrous*.
b. *e.* I like *wintry* weather.
c. *e.* The *entrance* was blocked.

3   Models:

a. *e.* Don't be a *hindrance*.
b. *o.* Her *ancestry* is Swedish.
c. *i.* The *explanation* is simple.

4

a. *o.* pronunciation, pronunciation
Models:
b. *u.* My *curiosity* is great.
c. *e.* The *shepherd* lost his dog.

6 led   influential   absorption

a. *Led* drops an _____ (What letter?) from *lead*.
Copy: I *led* the horse.

_____

b. *Influential* changes the *c* of *influence* to a _____ (What letter?).
Write *influential* in a sentence.

_____

c. *Absorption* changes the *b* of *absorb* to a _____ (What letter?). Write
absorption in a sentence.

_____

7 desperate   fiery

a. *Desperate* changes the _____ (What two letters?) of *despair* to _____
(What letter?). Write *desperate* in a sentence.

_____

b. *Fiery* reverses _____ (What two letters?) of *fire*. Write *fiery* in a
sentence.

_____

8

In Frames 8–13 write in full words we have studied in this unit.

a. a five-letter word meaning hot, flaming, _____
b. an eight-letter word meaning the opposite of exit, _____
c. an eleven-letter word meaning a token or memento, _____

_____

9

Follow the instructions for Frame 8.

a. a nine-letter word meaning something that interferes or gets in the
way, _____
b. a six-letter word meaning cold, snowy, _____
c. an eight-letter word meaning wonderful, _____

10

Follow the instructions for Frame 8.

a. a three-letter word meaning guided or went in front, _____
b. a ten-letter word meaning the process of soaking up, _____

_____

c. a nine-letter word meaning reckless or beyond hope, _____

5

a. *u.* forty, forty
Models:
b. *ai, e.* *Maintenance* of the status
quo will not be easy.
c. *i.* The *prevalent* winds are from
the west.

6

a. *a.* I *led* the horse.
Models:
b. *t.* The Queen was highly *influential*.
c. *p.* The *absorption* of the liquid
was slow.

7 **Models:**

a. *ai, e.* The killers were becoming
desperate.
b. *re.* He slipped toward the *fiery*
stairway.

8

a. fiery
b. entrance
c. remembrance

9

a. hindrance
b. wintry
c. wondrous

11

Follow the instructions for Frame 8.

a. an eleven-letter word starting with *in* and meaning powerful or exerting an effect upon, _____

b. an eleven-letter word meaning upkeep, _____

c. an eight-letter word meaning someone who takes care of sheep,

_____

12

Follow the instructions for Frame 8.

a. a nine-letter word starting with *pr* and meaning widespread,

_____

b. a five-letter word meaning four times ten, _____

c. a thirteen-letter word meaning the act of saying a word aloud,

_____

13

Follow the instructions for Frame 8.

a. a nine-letter word meaning a disposition to inquire about many things, _____

b. an eight-letter word referring to one's family tree, _____

c. an eleven-letter word meaning the act of making something clear,

_____

d. a ten-letter word meaning very unfortunate or calamitous, _____

_____

14

Choosing from words studied in this unit, write in full the incomplete words.

The [sh] _____ then [l] _____ the way from the [fi] _____ building into the [wint] _____ night. Our [cur] _____ had brought us to the [ent] _____, but we had not known that a [des] _____ maniac would bring us so close to a [dis] _____ end. For nearly [fo] _____ minutes he had held us prisoners. The [maint] _____ of calm was impossible. Our [remem] _____ of that night will never fade.

10

a. led
b. absorption
c. desperate

11

a. influential
b. maintenance
c. shepherd

12

a. prevalent
b. forty
c. pronunciation

13

a. curiosity
b. ancestry
c. explanation
d. disastrous

15

Study carefully each word you misspelled in Frames 8–14. If necessary, look back at Frames 1–7 to note the peculiar spellings of these words. Write each missed word correctly three times. Check your spellings against the list above Frame 1.

14

shepherd
led
fiery
wintry
curiosity
entrance
desperate
disastrous
forty
maintenance
remembrance

UNIT 73 · Those troublesome silent letters (I)

WORDS TREATED

chrome	doubt	indictment	rhetoric	sovereign
corps	foreign	khaki	rhythm	subtle
dealt	handsome	meant	schedule	
debt	indict	reign	source	

---

1   doubt   debt

As you know, many English words are borrowed from Latin. *Doubt* and *debt*, for example, go back to Latin *dubitare* and *debitus*, in which the *b*'s were pronounced distinctly. They are still pronounced in the English words *dubious* and *debit* but are silent in *doubt* and *debt*.

Write *doubt* and *debt* three times each.

——————, ——————, ——————

——————, ——————, ——————

---

2   subtle

Subtle is another modern word with a silent *b*. *Subtle* goes back to Latin *subtilis*, meaning woven fine. A subtle remark is "woven fine"; that is, it is not a coarse, obvious remark but one that merely hints.

Write *subtle* in a sentence.

————————————————————————

————————————————————————

1

doubt, doubt, doubt
debt, debt, debt

3   meant   dealt

Meant and *dealt* each have a silent *a*. It is there because the basic verbs *mean* and *deal* have *a*.

Copy: I *meant* that I *dealt* you the wrong cards.

_____

_____

4   indict   indictment

Indict and *indictment* are terms often used in law, as "The prisoner was indicted." The words are pronounced without the *c*, as if they were spelled *indite* and *inditement*. The reason for the *c* is that these two words go back to Latin *dictare,* meaning to say or to proclaim.

Copy: The grand jury *indicted* Jerry Rand. The *indictment* was long.

_____

_____

5   foreign   reign   sovereign

The silent *g* in *foreign* got in by mistake. *Foreign* comes from Latin *foris,* meaning out of doors or abroad, which as you see has no *g*. Someone, though, confused *foreign* with *reign* (from Latin *regnare*), and so the *g* crept in without a good reason. *Sovereign* got its *g* similarly. Make up a sentence with each word, *foreign*, *reign*, *sovereign*.

_____

_____

_____

6   corps   handsome   source

Printed above are three miscellaneous words with silent letters.
   Corps, as in "the Marine Corps," sounds like the center of an apple.
   In *handsome*, the *d* is silent.
   And in *source* the *u* really doesn't do any good.

Copy: A *handsome* recruit in the Marine *Corps* was the *source* of the rumor.

_____

_____

2   Model:

Your remarks are too *subtle* for me.

3

I *meant* that I *dealt* you the wrong cards.

4

The grand jury *indicted* Jerry Rand. The *indictment* was long.

5   Models:

Washington warned against *foreign* entanglements.
Queen Elizabeth I had a long *reign*.
She was *sovereign* from 1558 to 1603.

7   chrome   khaki   rhetoric   rhythm   schedule

An *h* is silent in a number of words. Here are some of them:

khaki (from Hindu *khaki*, meaning dust-colored)

rhythm (through French and Latin from Greek *rhythmos*, meaning measured motion)

chrome (from Greek *chroma*, meaning color)

schedule (through Latin from Greek *schide*, meaning a split piece of wood; the British say shĕd ūl)

rhetoric (through French and Latin from Greek *rhetorike*, related to the Greek word for orator)

Write each of the five words once.

_____, _____, _____, _____,

_____

8

In Frames 8–12, synonyms have been used for the eighteen words we have studied in this unit. You are to write the word that matches each synonym in brackets.

I cut gently through the [heavy brown cloth] _____. I [intended] _____ to find out how serious the wound was. Perhaps only I could save the life of our [good-looking] _____ [king] _____. I was glad that I was in the medical [branch of military service] _____.

9

Follow the instructions for Frame 8.

The attorney general prepared an [formal charge of violating a law] _____, claiming that Harper had [negotiated or been concerned with] _____ with a [alien] _____ power regarded as an enemy. To [charge] _____ a man on such a count was especially serious in time of war.

10

Follow the instructions for Frame 8.

The [cadence or regular sound] _____ of the drums followed us through the forest. Everywhere we went, the sound was in our ears, a [cunning, artful, half-hidden] _____ reminder that we were not really alone. It beat at us, [ruled] _____ed over us, hour after hour. What could its [origin, cause] _____ be?

6

A *handsome* recruit in the Marine *Corps* was the *source* of the rumor.

7

khaki
rhythm
chrome
schedule
rhetoric

8

khaki
meant
handsome
sovereign
corps

9

indictment
dealt
foreign
indict

11

Follow the instructions for Frame 8.

Don was a master of [skillful use of the language] _____. He could have made an automobile buyer believe that a heap of tortured metal was a beautiful [shiny alloy steel] _____ decorated mechanical marvel. I have no [hesitation in believing] _____ that he could have sold fur coats to Tahitians.

12

Follow the instructions for Frame 8.

Our [what we owe] _____ to Bell is indeed great. Without telephone contact, our business could hardly keep on [a planned arrangement of times] _____.

13

Choose two of the following words that may have been difficult for you to spell in the past. Make up and write a sentence that contains both of the words.

chrome dealt debt sovereign doubt foreign indict reign

_____

_____

14

Follow the instructions for Frame 13, using two of these words:

indictment khaki source meant rhetoric rhythm schedule
subtle

_____

_____

15

Study each word that you misspelled in Frames 8–14. Note especially the silent letters and any other trouble spots. Write each missed word correctly three times. Check your spellings against the list above Frame 1.

10

rhythm
subtle
reigned
source

11

rhetoric
chrome
doubt

12

debt
schedule

13

(Check your spelling by looking carefully at the words in Frame 13.)

14

(Check your spelling by looking carefully at the words in Frame 14.)

WORDS TREATED

answer	court	guard	pneumonia	solemn
circuit	courteous	guess	psychology	whole
column	courtesy	lieutenant	raspberry	yacht
condemn	guarantee	mortgage	rendezvous	

1   answer

Many English words have letters that are not now pronounced, although at some time in the past they probably were. The pronunciations have changed, but the spellings still keep the letters that have become silent.

For example, there was an Old English word *andswaru*, which came from two other words, *and* and *swerian*, meaning to swear against. If someone else made a statement and you said it was not true, you were swearing against him. From the Old English *andswaru* has come our word *answer*, in which the ____ (What letter?) is not now pronounced.

2   condemn   column   solemn

Our words *condemn*, *column*, and *solemn* each have a silent *n*. These words came from Latin words in which the *n* was pronounced: *condemnare, columna, solemnis.*

Copy: The words *condemn*, *column*, and *solemn* each have a silent *n*.

_____

_____

3   psychology   pneumonia   raspberry

The words *psychology*, *pneumonia*, and *raspberry* have silent *p*'s that were once pronounced. *Psychology* comes from Greek *psyche*, the soul. *Pneumonia* is from Greek *pneumones*, the lungs. *Raspberry* goes back to an English *raspis*, meaning raspberry, to which an unnecessary *berry* was later added.

Copy: While I was studying *psychology* in the *raspberry* patch, I caught *pneumonia*.

_____

_____

1

w

2

The words *condemn*, *column*, and *solemn* each have a silent *n*.

4   lieutenant   circuit

A *lieutenant* is an officer who may act in place of a higher officer. The word *lieutenant* is taken directly from French *lieu* (place) and *tenant* (holding). So a *lieutenant* holds the place. (You may know the expression *in lieu of*, meaning in place of.)

Circuit is spelled with a *u* and an *i* because the earlier Latin form was *circuitus*.

Write a sentence containing *lieutenant* and *circuit*.

_____

_____

---

5   court   courteous   courtesy   rendezvous

Courteous and *courtesy* are spelled as they are because they are related to *court*. Persons who lived in the royal court were supposed to have very good manners. The word *court* is from Old French.

French has also given us *rendezvous*, from *rendez-vous*, meaning you go to a certain place.

Copy: At the *court*, which stressed *courtesy*, it was not considered *courteous* to arrange a secret *rendezvous*.

_____

_____

_____

---

6   guard   guarantee   mortgage

French spelling also accounts for our spelling of *guard* (from Old French *guarder*) and *guarantee* (from Old French *guarantie*).

Mortgage, with its now silent *t*, comes from Old French *mort*, meaning dead, and *gage*, meaning pledge. If you mortgage your property, you pledge that the lender may have the property if you do not pay, but the pledge becomes dead when you do pay.

Copy: The *guard guaranteed* the payment of the *mortgage*.

_____

_____

---

7   yacht   guess   whole

The silent *ch* in *yacht* was not silent in the Dutch word, which was *jacht*, rhyming with *docked*.

We are not quite sure why *u* appears in *guess* or *w* in *whole*. Scandinavian or Low German influence appears in *guess*, and the *w* in *whole* may be akin to the *w* in such words as *who, what, why*.

Copy: I *guess* you can't charter less than a *whole yacht*.

_____

_____

3

While I was studying *psychology* in the *raspberry* patch, I caught *pneumonia*.

---

4   Model:

The *lieutenant* made a *circuit* of the camp.

5

At the *court*, which stressed *courtesy*, it was not considered *courteous* to arrange a secret *rendezvous*.

6

The *guard guaranteed* the payment of the *mortgage*.

8

In Frames 8–12, synonyms have been used for the nineteen words we have studied in this unit. You are to write the word that matches each synonym in brackets.

We [provide firm assurance] _____ that there will be no short [path of an electric current] _____ in this mechanism if it is properly installed. It is necessary, though, to [take precautions] _____ against careless installation.

9

Follow the instructions for Frame 8.

"I [suppose] _____ that we must be [polite] _____ to him," said the [junior officer] _____. "But he always looks so [serious] _____ in that comic opera outfit that I almost have to laugh."

10

Follow the instructions for Frame 8.

On board his [pleasure ship] _____, he suffered a severe attack of [inflammation of the lungs] _____. For one [entire] _____ day the crew hurried toward New York. The radio operator could send messages, but something was wrong with the set so that he could not receive any [reply] _____.

11

Follow the instructions for Frame 8.

A [feature article] _____ in a newspaper said that the [tribunal] _____ ought to [impose a sentence upon] _____ _____ the supposed murderer to the gas chamber. Obviously that writer, like much of the public, was in the grip of mob [feelings and actions of the mind] _____.

12

Follow the instructions for Frame 8.

If I am able to pay off the [debt secured by a property pledge] _____, I shall arrange a secret [meeting] _____ _____ with Claribelle, pay a [politeness] _____ call upon Monsieur Despoir, and return to live quietly forever in my [small red or black berry] _____ patch.

7

I *guess* you can't charter less than a *whole yacht.*

8

guarantee
circuit
guard

9

guess
courteous
lieutenant
solemn

10

yacht
pneumonia
whole
answer

11

column
court
condemn
psychology

13

Choose two or three of the following words that may have been difficult for you to spell in the past. Write a sentence in which you use the two or three words.

answer	courteous
circuit	courtesy
column	guarantee
condemn	guard
court	guess

_____

_____

14

Follow the instructions for Frame 13.

lieutenant	rendezvous
mortgage	solemn
pneumonia	whole
psychology	yacht
raspberry	

_____

_____

15

Study each word that you misspelled in Frames 8–14. Note especially the silent letters and any other trouble spots. Write each misspelled word correctly three times. Check your spellings against the list above Frame 1.

12

mortgage
rendezvous
courtesy
raspberry

13

(Check your spelling by looking carefully at the words in Frame 13.)

14

(Check your spelling by looking carefully at the words in Frame 14.)

UNIT 75 · Silent *k* or *w*

WORDS TREATED

awry	knave	knitting	knot	wreath	wriggle	wry
knack	knead	knob	knuckle	wrecker	wringer	
knackwurst	knife	knock	wrangle	wrestle	wrinkle	
knapsack	knight	knoll	wrapper	wretched	wrist	

1   wrist

Every language changes, slowly but steadily. Vocabulary grows, some words die out, grammar does not stay quite the same, and pronunciations may be altered so much that a word sounds very different.

Spelling always changes less than the spoken version of language, because print gives a permanence that speech does not have. In Old English, the language of about a thousand years ago, the word *wrist* was spelled just as we spell it. But King Alfred (849–899 A.D.) did not pronounce it as we do. He and his contemporaries said "wuh-rist." A *w* before *r* was always pronounced in Old and Middle English.

Copy: The now-silent *w* in words like *wrist* was once pronounced.

_____

_____

2   wrangle   wrapper   wreath   wrecker   wrestle

Listed above are five more words in which our spelling keeps a *w* that is no longer pronounced. (*Wrangle*, the least familiar, may mean either to argue or to herd horses.)

Write a short sentence with each word.

_____

_____

_____

_____

3   awry   wretched   wriggle   wringer   wrinkle   wry

Wry may be the least familiar of these words. It comes from Middle English *wrien* "to bend or twist" and means crooked. So a *wry* smile is a crooked smile. It is related to the adverb *awry* (pronounced "uh-rye"), which means twisted to one side: Our plans went *awry*.
Write a short sentence with each word.

_____

_____

_____

_____

_____

4   knot

In Old English *k* (generally written *c*) was pronounced before *n*. So *cnotta*, the old word for *knot*, was pronounced "kuh-nōt-tah." In Middle English the spelling became *knot* or *knotte*, and only gradually did the *k* become silent. The reason for the change was ease of pronunciation.

Copy: The now-silent *k* in words like *knot* was once pronounced.

_____

_____

1

The now-silent *w* in words like *wrist* was once pronounced.

2   Models:

The roommates *wrangled* for hours.
Don't tear the *wrapper*.
A Christmas *wreath* hung in the window.
The *wrecker* soon arrived.
I like to *wrestle* with serious problems.

3   Models:

The wind blew my clothes *awry*.
I felt *wretched*.
The snake *wriggled* convulsively.
I've been through the *wringer*.
Wrinkles are signs of age.
He gave me a *wry* look.

5 knack   knackwurst   knapsack   knave   knead   knife

Of these six words, *knack* is probably most often misspelled: People have a *knack* for leaving out the first *k*.

Germans still pronounce the *k* in words like *Knackwurst*: "kuh-nock voorst." (Our English dictionaries also record the spelling *knockwurst*.)

Knave now means a bad person, but once meant a boy, as the related German *Knabe* still does.

Some people still *knead* dough when they bake.

Copy: The *knave* had a *knack* for *kneading knackwurst*, which he sliced with a *knife* from his *knapsack*.

_____

_____

_____

6 knight   knitting   knob   knock   knoll   knuckle

A *knoll*, which in Old English was *cnoll* ("kuh-nōl"), is a small round hill. Use each word in a short sentence.

_____

_____

_____

_____

_____

7

Write the word studied in this unit that best matches each definition or clue. Since all these words except *awry* start with *kn* or *wr*, the first letters have not been supplied.

a. It pulls your car in. _____

b. Who's there? _____

c. Found on most doors, _____

d. tool for cutting, _____

e. Tie one. _____

f. It is above your hand. _____

g. squirm, _____

h. twisted to one side, _____

8

Follow the instructions for Frame 7.

a. to squeeze and stretch, as bread, _____

b. to quarrel; to herd horses, _____

c. one who makes packages, _____

d. in very poor condition, _____

e. a natural ability, _____

f. Carry this on your back. _____

g. crooked, _____

h. done with needles, _____

4

The now-silent *k* in words like *knot* was once pronounced.

5

The *knave* had a *knack* for *kneading knackwurst*, which he sliced with a *knife* from his *knapsack*.

6   Models:

The *knight* fell from his horse.
Stick to your *knitting*.
The *knob* fell off my drawer.
Don't bother to *knock*.
We sat on a *knoll*.
My *knuckles* were sore.

7

a. wrecker
b. knock
c. knob
d. knife
e. knot
f. wrist
g. wriggle
h. awry

9

Follow the instructions for Frame 7.

a. a German sausage, _____

b. villain, _____

c. grassy hill, _____

d. Count them on each hand. _____s

e. to grapple, struggle, _____

f. circular ornament, _____

g. that which wrings, _____

h. _____d as an uncooked prune.

i. He wore armor. _____

10

In Frames 10–12, the words we have studied are used in pairs or trios. Write each word where it fits best. Again, except for the *a* in *awry*, first letters are not given. Refer when necessary to the list above Frame 1.

a. She _____ed the bread and then resumed _____ a scarf.

b. The _____ was tied so tight that he had to cut it with his _____ _____.

c. Do not _____ on the door. Just turn the _____.

d. The car _____ed a telephone pole [a] _____ and had to be towed away by a _____.

11

Follow the instructions for Frame 10.

a. You _____, no-good _____!

b. At the top of a _____ he opened his _____ and ate some _____.

c. Some worms have a _____ for _____ off a hook.

d. A _____ wearing armor could fight with a sword, but he could not _____.

12

Follow the instructions for Frame 10.

a. He made a _____ face when he hurt his _____ and bruised several _____.

b. They started to _____ angrily about who had torn the _____ on the package and why the Christmas _____ _____ was misshaped.

d. The old man's face was as _____d as if the skin had been squeezed in folds by a _____.

8

a. knead

b. wrangle

c. wrapper

d. wretched

e. knack

f. knapsack

g. wry

h. knitting

9

a. knackwurst

b. knave

c. knoll

d. knuckles

e. wrestle

f. wreath

g. wringer

h. Wrinkled

i. knight

10

a. kneaded, knitting

b. knot, knife

c. knock, knob

d. knocked, awry, wrecker

11

a. wretched, knave

b. knoll, knapsack, knackwurst

c. knack, wriggling

d. knight, wrestle

13

Study each word that you missed in Frames 7–12. Write each misspelled word three times. Check your spellings against the list above Frame 1.

12

a. wry, wrist, knuckles
b. wrangle, wrapper, wreath
c. wrinkled, wringer

UNIT 76 · Some words that seem alike (I)

WORDS TREATED

accent	birth	formally	passed	principal	they're
ascent	decent	formerly	past	principle	your
assent	descent	loose	pedal	their	you're
berth	dissent	lose	peddle	there	

1   passed   past

This unit concerns homonyms (words like *passed* and *past*, which sound alike but have different meanings) and also other words that are somewhat alike without being homonyms.

Passed is a verb: She *passed* me the biscuits.

Past is an adjective, a noun, an adverb, or a preposition: The *past* (adjective) week already seems far in the *past* (noun). A car whizzed *past* (adverb). I walked *past* your house (preposition).

Write one original sentence using *passed* correctly and others using *past* correctly in each of the four ways.

_____

_____

_____

_____

2   their   they're   there

Their means belonging to them: *Their* heir is *their* son.

They're is a contraction of *they are*: *They're* going to the game.

There is the opposite of *here*. Note that *here* is in *there*.

Write an original sentence with each word: *their, they're, there*.

_____

_____

1   Models:

We *passed* another car.
The *past* winter was severe.
Don't live in the *past*.
They drove *past*.
Has he gone *past* Third Street?

3 loose lose

If something is *loose*, it is not fastened. If a goose escapes, you may say, "That goose is loose!"

If you *lose* something, you will probably try to find it again.

Write an original sentence with each word: *loose* and *lose*.

_____

_____

4 accent ascent assent

Your *accent* (pronounced *ak sent*) is the way you say words.

Ascent (pronounced *ă sent*) is the opposite of *descent*. It refers to a climb of some sort.

Assent (pronounced like *ascent*) means to consent to something or, as a noun, the act of consenting.

Write an original sentence with each word: *accent, ascent, assent*.

_____

_____

_____

5 decent descent dissent

Something is *decent* (pronounced *de′ sent*) if it is moral or kind.

Descent (pronounced *de sent′*) is the opposite of *ascent*. It refers to going down from somewhere.

Dissent (pronounced *dĭ sent′*) means to disagree or the act of disagreeing.

Write an original sentence with each word: *decent, descent, dissent*.

_____

_____

_____

6 berth birth

A *berth* is an allotted place, as a *berth* in a railway car.

Birth refers to being born: The cat gave *birth* to four kittens.

Write an original sentence with each word: *berth* and *birth*.

_____

_____

7 pedal peddle

Your bicycle has *pedals*, and you *pedal* to school.

To *peddle* is to sell, especially door to door.

Write an original sentence with each word: *pedal* and *peddle*.

_____

_____

2 Models:

They found *their* coats.
They're in the house.
There it is.

3 Models:

One of the bolts was *loose*.
Don't *lose* your hat.

4 Models:

He spoke with a British *accent*.
The *ascent* of the mountain was dangerous.
Will you *assent* to this proposal?

5 Models:

Paying his mother's bills was *decent* of him.
The *descent* in the elevator was rapid.
One justice *dissented* from the verdict.

6 Models:

I like to sleep in a lower *berth*.
What is the year of your *birth*?

8   formally   formerly

Formally means in a formal manner: Please do not dress *formally.*
   Formerly means at an earlier time: She was *formerly* Miss Wyoming.

Write an original sentence with each word: *formally* and *formerly.*

_____

_____

9   principal   principle

Principal has several meanings, as in *principal of a school,* the *principal parts,* and *principal* (money) that draws interest.
   Principle means a rule or law, or ethical conduct. (Some students associate the *le* of *rule* and the *le* of *principle.*)

Write one short sentence about the *principal* of a school, and another about a *principle* in mathematics.

_____

_____

10   your   you're

Your is a possessive form: *your* shirt, *your* typewriter.
   You're always means *you are: You're* early.

Write an original sentence with each word.

_____

_____

11

Match each definition with one of the words we studied in this unit. The first letter or letters have been supplied. Write each word in full.

a. went beyond, [pa] _____
b. belonging to them, [th] _____
c. opposite of tight, [lo] _____
d. way of pronouncing, [a] _____
e. moral or kind, [d] _____
f. an allotted place, [b] _____
g. most important, [prin] _____
h. in a dignified manner, [for] _____

7   Models:

One *pedal* was bent when my bicycle fell.
I tried to *peddle* apples in Springdale.

8

The ambassador was *formally* presented at court.
I *formerly* was an ice cream vendor.

9   Models:

The *principal* wanted to expel me.
I now understand this mathematical *principle.*

10   Models:

Your tie is crooked.
You're sure to get at least second place.

12

Follow the instructions for Frame 11.

a. device to be pushed with the foot, [pe] _____
b. the olden days, [pa] _____
c. contraction of *they are*, [th] _____
d. to misplace, [lo] _____
e. a climb, [a] _____
f. to disagree, [d] _____
g. belonging to you, [y] _____
h. Some time ago, [for] _____

11

a. passed   e. decent
b. their   f. berth
c. loose   g. principal
d. accent   h. formally

13

Follow the instructions for Frame 11.

a. act of being born, [b] _____
b. to sell from house to house, [pe] _____
c. in that place, [th] _____
d. to consent, [a] _____
e. a going down, [d] _____
f. you are, [y] _____
g. a rule, [prin] _____

12

a. pedal   e. ascent
b. past   f. dissent
c. they're   g. your
d. lose   h. formerly

14

Write in full each incomplete word, choosing the most suitable from those studied in this unit.

While I was going up the hill, a steep [as] _____, one [pe] _____ on my bicycle came [l] _____ and fell off. [Th] _____ was nothing to do except dismount and push my bicycle [pa] _____ the summit so that I could coast down the other side.

13

a. birth   e. descent
b. peddle   f. you're
c. there   g. principle
d. assent

15

Follow the instructions for Frame 14.

a. Since they have [pa] _____ [th] _____ final tests, [th] _____ sure to graduate.
b. Archie, who used to [pe] _____ fruit and vegetables, seemed to be a very [de] _____ man.
c. A sailor's [b] _____ is surprisingly comfortable.
d. The [prin] _____ said to me, "It's a matter of [prin] _____. You're able to understand that, aren't you?"

14

ascent
pedal
loose
There
past

254

16

Follow the instructions for Frame 14.

a. George continued to [d] _____ from the majority, as if he had nothing to [l] _____ .

b. Philip was a man of noble [b] _____ , or "noble [de] _____ _____ ," as history books might say.

c. I will never [as] _____ to speak with such a ridiculous, artificial [a] _____ .

d. Although we have never been [for] _____ introduced, we have met. I was [for] _____ employed by Keystone, and I remember that [y] _____ job was with Keystone too.

17

Select from the words we studied in this unit two or three that have given you trouble in the past. Write an original sentence with each (not the same sentence you wrote earlier in the unit).

_____

_____

18

Study each word you missed in Frames 11–16. Note its proper spelling and use in Frames 1–10. Write a phrase or a sentence illustrating the correct form and use of each missed word. Check your spellings against the list above Frame 1.

15

a. passed, their, they're
b. peddle, decent
c. berth
d. principal, principle

16

a. dissent, lose
b. birth, descent
c. assent, accent
d. formally, formerly, your

17

(Check Frames 1–7 to see whether you used each word correctly.)

UNIT 77 · Some words that seem alike (II)

WORDS TREATED

access	allusion	illusion	navel	prophesy
adapt	an	its	peer	to
adept	and	it's	pier	too
adopt	excess	naval	prophecy	two

1   its   it's

This unit concerns homonyms (words like *its* and *it's*, which sound alike but have different meanings) and also other words that are somewhat alike without being homonyms.

Its is a possessive form: The dog wagged *its* tail. Just as possessives like *his* and *my* have no apostrophe, neither does *its*.

It's is a contraction of *it is* or *it has: It's* warm today. *It's* been a long time.

Write one original sentence with each word: *its* and *it's*.

_____

_____

2   an   and

Probably *an* and *and* are misspelled chiefly through carelessness. Even children know that *an* is an article like *a* but is used before a vowel sound: *an* aspirin, *an* honor. They also know that *and* is a conjunction meaning in addition to.

Write an original sentence with each word: *an* and *and.*

_____

_____

3   access   excess

You have *access* to a place if you are able to go to it without being stopped: The cashier was the only person with *access* to the bank vault.

Excess is too great an amount: An *excess* of fatty foods harms some people.

Write an original sentence with each word: *access* and *excess.*

_____

_____

4   two   to   too

Two is a number: *two* fried eggs.

To, one of the most frequently used words in English, has its most common meanings illustrated in the nursery rhyme: *To* market, *to* market, *to* buy a fat pig.

Too means also, or refers to an excessive amount: Let me go, *too.* She is *too* thin.

Write an original sentence with each word: *two, to,* and *too.*

_____

_____

_____

1   Models:

Its fur was matted.
It's true that George saw me at the dance.

2   Models:

This is *an* easy sentence to write.
Pears *and* apples were lying on the ground.

3   Models:

I had *access* to the candy counter.
An *excess* of spending money may be dangerous.

5 adapt adopt adept

If you *adapt* something, you change it for a particular purpose: The book *Life with Father* was *adapted* for the stage.

To *adopt* is to make something your own: Mr. and Mrs. Smedley *adopted* two children.

Adept is an adjective meaning skillful: She is an *adept* actress.

Write an original sentence with each word: *adapt*, *adopt*, and *adept*.

_____

_____

_____

6 allusion illusion

An *allusion* is an indirect reference: The speaker made an *allusion* to the recent oil scandal.

An *illusion* may be a misconception or something that you only imagine you see: Some psychopaths have the *illusion* that they are Napoleon. A mirage is one kind of *illusion*.

Write an original sentence with each word: *allusion* and *illusion*.

_____

_____

7 naval navel

Naval means pertaining to the navy: *naval* warfare.

Navel means the depression in the middle of the abdomen: The baby's *navel* was infected.

Write an original sentence with each word: *naval* and *navel*.

_____

_____

8 peer pier

As a verb, to *peer* is to look at: I *peered* at the storm clouds. As a noun, a *peer* is an equal: Every accused person may be tried by a jury of his *peers*.

A *pier* is a dock. Some students associate the *ie* in *tie* and in *pier*: We *tied* the boat to the p*ier*.

Write an original sentence with each word: *peer* and *pier*.

_____

_____

4 Models:

I bought *two* cakes.
I went *to* the fair *to* see the races.
You are *too* careless, *too*.

5 Models:

The songwriter *adapted* an old tune.
Congress decided to *adopt* new rules.
John became *adept* with a fly rod.

6 Models:

I'll never make another *allusion* to his drinking.
Since Marley is dead, the figure before Scrooge must be an *illusion*.

7 Models:

My father is an expert in *naval* history.
A *navel* orange has one end that looks like a human *navel*.

9   prophecy   prophesy

These two words are alike except that *prophecy* (which ends in a sound like "see") is a noun and means something that is predicted, and *prophesy* (which ends in a sound like "sigh") is a verb and means to predict or foretell.

Read aloud: The long-bearded prophet spoke a *prophecy* of doom. Only a madman could *prophesy* so positively.

Write an original sentence with each word: *prophecy* and *prophesy*.

_____

_____

10

Match each definition with one of the words we studied in this unit. The first letter or letters have been supplied. Write each word in full.

a. contraction of *it is*, [i] _____
b. one plus one, [t] _____
c. also, [t] _____
d. pertaining to the navy, [na] _____
e. skillful, [ad] _____
f. to look carefully at, [p] _____
g. to predict, [pro] _____

11

Follow the instructions for Frame 10.

a. to make one's own, [ad] _____
b. too great an amount, [e] _____
c. in addition to, [a] _____
d. indirect reference, [al] _____
e. belonging to it, [i] _____
f. a prediction, [pro] _____
g. place where boats may be tied, [p] _____

12

Follow the instructions for Frame 10.

a. abdominal depression, [na] _____
b. permission to enter, [a] _____
c. one, [a] _____
d. toward, [t] _____
e. to change for a special purpose, [ad] _____
f. misconception, [il] _____

---

8   Models:

Why did she *peer* at me like that?
The *pier* was dark and lonely.

---

9   Models:

His *prophecy* came true.
I *prophesy* that the meek will inherit
    the earth.

10

a. it's
b. two
c. too
d. naval
e. adept
f. peer
g. prophesy

11

a. adopt
b. excess
c. and
d. allusion
e. its
f. prophecy
g. pier

13

Write in full each incomplete word, choosing the most suitable from those studied in this unit.

a. His [n] _____ was scratched in the accident.
b. They decided to [ad] _____ the baby.
c. [I] _____ ten o'clock.
d. Psychologists distinguish between a normal and an abnormal [il] _____.
e. You brought [t] _____ many buns.
f. Through their binoculars they [p] _____ed at the boat beside the [p] _____.

14

Follow the instructions for Frame 13.

a. You should [ad] _____ your storytelling to your audience.
b. Come [t] _____ my house.
c. May I have [a] _____ apple?
d. Do you have [a] _____ to the correspondence?
e. Admiral Nelson was a great [na] _____ hero.
f. I [pro] _____ that your [pro] _____ will never come true.

15

Follow the instructions for Frame 13.

a. Dogs [a] _____ cats sometimes are good friends.
b. Are you [ad] _____ at badminton?
c. Blue and green are my [t] _____ favorite colors.
d. The governor made no [al] _____ to his hopes for a Senate seat.
e. If there is an [ex] _____ of sand, the concrete will not last long.
f. The puppy was chasing [i] _____ tail.

16

Select from the words we studied in this unit two or three that have given you trouble in the past. Write an original sentence with each (not the same sentence you wrote earlier in the unit).

_____

_____

17

Study each word you missed in Frames 10–16. Note its proper spelling and use in Frames 1–9. Write a phrase or a sentence illustrating the correct form and use of each missed word. Check your spellings against the list above Frame 1.

12

a. navel
b. access
c. an
d. to
e. adapt
f. illusion

13

a. navel
b. adopt
c. It's
d. illusion
e. too
f. peered, pier

14

a. adapt
b. to
c. an
d. access
e. naval
f. prophesy, prophecy

15

a. and
b. adept
c. two
d. allusion
e. excess
f. its

16

(Check Frames 1–9 to see whether you used each word correctly.

WORDS TREATED

altar	carrot	counsel	here	statute
alter	complement	desert	rinse	waist
carat	compliment	dessert	statue	waste
caret	council	hear	stature	wrench

---

1   hear   here

This unit concerns homonyms (words like *hear* and *here* that sound alike but have different meanings) and also other words that are somewhat alike without being homonyms.

To *hear* is to receive sound. Associate it with *ear*: You *hear* with your *ear*.

Here means in this place. It is the opposite of *there*, which is the same in spelling except for the *t*: We wandered *here* and *there*.

Write one original sentence with each word: *hear* and *here*.

_____

_____

---

1   Models:

Did you *hear* what I said?
Here are the letters.

---

2   altar   alter

An *altar* is a table or other structure used in religious worship. It is spelled with -*ar* because it comes from Latin *altare*. The king placed his offering upon the *altar*.

Alter is a verb, meaning to change: Your arguments do not *alter* my opinion.

Write an original sentence with each word: *altar* and *alter*.

_____

_____

---

2   Models:

The children stood before the *altar*.
Mr. Gray decided to *alter* his will.

---

3   dessert   desert

A *dessert* is the last course of a meal: We had cake for *dessert*.

Desert (děz´ ert) as a noun means a large, desolate, sandy place: the Gobi *Desert*. *Desert* (dē zurt´) as a verb means to abandon: I will never *desert* my friends.

Write an original sentence with each word: *dessert* and *desert* (as a noun and as a verb).

_____

_____

4 compliment complement

You like to get a *compliment,* because it is something favorable said about you.

A *complement* is something that fills out or completes. Associate *complement* with *complete:* If an angle is 60°, its *complement,* which could be added to complete a right angle, is 30°. As a verb, *complement* means to add to in order to complete: Her work *complemented* her husband's.

Write an original sentence with each word: *compliment* and *complement.*

_____

_____

5 wrench rinse

A *wrench* is a tool: Please hand me that *wrench.* To *wrench* is to twist forcefully: He *wrenched* the stick from her hands.

To *rinse* is to wash lightly or to remove soap, etc., from something: *Rinse* the oil filter in gasoline.

Write an original sentence with each word: *wrench* and *rinse.*

_____

_____

6 counsel council

Counsel as a noun means advice: Her uncle was called upon for his *counsel.* As a verb, *counsel* means to give advice to: Will you *counsel* me?

A *council* is a governing or advisory group: Our Student *Council* meets weekly.

Write an original sentence with each word: *counsel* (as a noun and as a verb) and *council.*

_____

_____

_____

7 waist waste

Your *waist* is the small part of your body between your thorax and hips: Sylvia has a tiny *waist.*

To *waste* is to squander: Don't *waste* your money.

Write an original sentence with each word: *waist* and *waste.*

_____

_____

3 Models:

I enjoy fruit for *dessert.*
We found this tiny cactus in the *desert.*
Do not *desert* the cause!

4 Models:

What a delightful *compliment* you gave her!
Your answer *complements* Marcia's.

5 Models:

May I borrow your *wrench?*
Rinse the dirt from the pail.

6 Models:

We should have followed his wise *counsel.*
Counsel your friend well.
The chief assembled the members of his *council.*

8   carat   caret   carrot

Carat is a weight used by jewelers; a one-carat diamond weighs 200 milligrams. (*Carat* is also used for *karat* sometimes; 24-karat or 24-carat gold is pure gold.)

    Caret is a mark often used in editing to show an insertion: ∧ is a *caret*.

    A *carrot* is a vegetable.

Write an original sentence with each word: *carat, caret, carrot*.

_____

_____

_____

9   statue   stature   statute

These three words have quite different meanings. A *statue* is a sculpture, usually of a person: a *statue* in the park.

    Stature means height (literally or figuratively): a statesman of *stature*.

    A *statute* is a law or other official regulation: new *statutes* enacted by the legislature.

Write an original sentence with each word: *statue, stature, statute*.

_____

_____

_____

10

Match each definition with one of the words we studied in this unit. The first letter or letters have been supplied. Write the words in full.

a. rich food, usually sweet, [de] _____

b. table for worship, [al] _____

c. to receive sound, [he] _____

d. favorable comment, [com] _____

e. an orange vegetable, [c] _____

f. a piece of sculpture, [stat] _____

11

Follow the instructions for Frame 10.

a. part of body just above hips, [wa] _____

b. advice, [cou] _____

c. to change, [al] _____

d. a tool for turning, [w] _____

e. in this place, [he] _____

f. a law or ordinance, [stat] _____

g. a proofreader's mark, [c] _____

7   **Models:**

The corset pinched in her *waist*.
It is silly to *waste* time on some television programs.

8   **Models:**

This stone weighs three *carats*.
Too many *carets* make a page look messy.
Eat your *carrots*, children.

9   **Models:**

There is a *statue* of Lincoln.
Douglas was small in *stature* but big in heart.
A new *statute* regulates the permissible horsepower.

10

a. dessert
b. altar
c. hear
d. compliment
e. carrot
f. statue

12

Follow the instructions for Frame 10.

a. to squander, [wa] _____

b. dry, sandy region, [de] _____

c. that which completes, [com] _____

d. to wash lightly, [r] _____

e. advisory group, [cou] _____

f. a jeweler's weight, [c] _____

g. height, [stat] _____

11

a. waist

b. counsel

c. alter

d. wrench

e. here

f. statute

g. caret

13

Write in full each incomplete word, choosing the most suitable from those studied in this unit.

a. The accident made us [al] _____ our plans.

b. Did you ever [he] _____ such an eerie sound?

c. I should like to [com] _____ you on your informative speech.

d. In dry regions one should not [wa] _____ water.

e. Is it true that eating [c] _____s will add to one's [stat] _____?

12

a. waste

b. desert

c. complement

d. rinse

e. council

f. carat

g. stature

14

Follow the instructions for Frame 13.

a. A surprising number of animals live in the [de] _____.

b. Sir Kay tried to [w] _____ the sword from Sir Jay.

c. The old man's [co] _____ seemed sensible, although we could hardly hear his voice.

d. What is the [com] _____ of an angle of 57 degrees?

e. Place the flowers before the [al] _____.

f. It's too bad that we couldn't enforce a [stat] _____ saying that every diamond must weigh at least one [c] _____.

13

a. alter

b. hear

c. compliment

d. waste

e. carrots, stature

15

Follow the instructions for Frame 13.

a. The [de] _____ consisted of a tough, gelatinous, inedible gray mass.

b. Her [w] _____ measures twenty-four inches.

c. Stack the firewood over [he] _____.

d. Our teacher belongs to the National [Co] _____ of Teachers of English.

e. [R] _____ your hair thoroughly.

f. A [c] _____ looks like an upside-down v.

g. There are many jokes about what pigeons do to [stat] _____s.

14

a. desert

b. wrench

c. counsel

d. complement

e. altar

f. statute, carat

16

Select from the words we studied in this unit two or three that have given you trouble in the past. Write an original sentence with each (not the same sentence you wrote earlier in the unit).

_____

_____

17

Study each word that you missed in Frames 10–16. Note its proper spelling and use in Frames 1–9. Write a phrase or a sentence illustrating the correct form and use of each missed word. Check your spellings against the list above Frame 1.

15

a. dessert
b. waist
c. here
d. Council
e. Rinse
f. caret
g. statues

16

(Check Frames 1–9 to see whether you used each word correctly.)

UNIT 79 · Some old, old demons (I)

WORDS TREATED

alcohol	curriculum	sergeant	themselves
been	enough	strategy	together
benefited	knowledge	suppose	used to
brilliant	punctuation	tenant	whose

---

1 knowledge

The most often misspelled words are not rare words with many syllables. They are usually common words of one or two syllables.

Knowledge is an example—a word that you probably use every day. Note the –edge at the end. Each bit of knowledge brings you to the edge of a new discovery.

Copy: Each bit of knowledge brings one to the edge of a new discovery.

_____

_____

2 been

Been is so short and so frequently used that it should never be misspelled, but it is, perhaps because the standard American pronunciation and the spelling do not harmonize. Note the two e's.

Copy: I have been. Have you been? She has been. Have they been?

_____

_____

1

Each bit of knowledge brings one to the edge of a new discovery.

3 enough

Say *e nough*. Note that the last part of this word is like the last four letters of *tough*, both in pronunciation and spelling.

Copy: At the table it's *tough*
To stop with just *enough*.

_____

_____

4 together

Some persons remember *together* by noting that it happens to have in it the words *to, get,* and *her*. If such a device works for you, use it.

Write *to get her* once and *together* four times.

_____, _____, _____,

_____, _____

5 punctuation

Maybe sloppy pronouncing of *punctuation* leads to its misspelling. Say *punc tu a tion:* Don't forget to sound the *c*. The word comes from Latin *punctus*, point. The British refer to punctuation as "pointing."

Copy: *Punctuation* has a *c* because it comes from *punctus*.

_____

_____

6 whose suppose

Whose is a possessive: Tell me *whose* coat this is. *Whose* answer is best? (Don't confuse it with *who's*, which means *who is*.)

Suppose has two syllables: *sup pose*.

Write a sentence with *whose*, a sentence with *suppose*, and a third sentence with both *suppose* and *whose*.

_____

_____

_____

2

I have *been*. Have you *been*? She has *been*. Have they *been*?

3

At the table it's *tough*
To stop with just *enough*.

4

to get her
together
together
together
together

5

Punctuation has a *c* because it comes from *punctus*.

7 used to benefited

Used is most often misspelled in a sentence like *I used to like chocolate ice cream.* Note the *d* required in *used* in a sentence like that.

   Benefited is simply *benefit* + *–ed.* The *t* is not doubled, because the word *benefit* has the heavy accent on *ben*, not on *fit*. So *benefited* has only one *t*.

a. Write a sentence with *used to* similar to *I used to like chocolate ice cream.*

   _____

   _____

b. Write *benefited* three times.

   _____ , _____ , _____

---

8 alcOhol brillIant cUrriculum sErGEAnt straTEGy teNant theMselVEs

The letters capitalized above are the ones that cause most trouble in these words. Study each word, and in the spaces below write two or more times each that seems difficult to you.

   _____ _____ _____

   _____ _____ _____

9

Match each definition with one of the words studied in this unit. The first letter or letters have been supplied. Write the words in full.

a. information, [kn] _____

b. commas, periods, etc., [pu] _____

c. belonging to whom, [wh] _____

d. a noncommissioned officer, [s] _____

e. course of study, [c] _____

f. himself and herself, [th] _____

10

Follow the instructions for Frame 9.

a. the third principal part of *be*, [be] _____

b. did formerly, [us] _____ ___

c. helped, [ben] _____

d. an intoxicant, [al] _____

e. a long-range plan, [str] _____

---

6 Models:

Whose tie do you like best?
I *suppose* you will decide soon.
I *suppose* you know now *whose* tie you like best.

---

7 Model:

a. She *used to* attend many dances.
b. benefited, benefited, benefited

8

(Answers will vary. Check yours carefully.)

9

a. knowledge
b. punctuation
c. whose
d. sergeant
e. curriculum
f. themselves

11

Follow the instructions for Frame 9.

a. sufficient, [e] _____
b. in a group, [to] _____
c. to assume or believe on slight grounds, [s] _____
d. shining; intelligent, [bri] _____
e. one who rents, [t] _____

10

a. been
b. used to
c. benefited
d. alcohol
e. strategy

12

Write in full each incomplete word, choosing the most suitable from those studied in this unit.

a. The medicine [ben] _____ my mother last year.
b. [Wh] _____ pen is this?
c. Include only necessary [pu] _____ marks.
d. The [s] _____ told the privates to behave [th] _____ _____ away from the base, and to avoid drinking any of the local [al] _____ .

11

a. enough
b. together
c. suppose
d. brilliant
e. tenant

13

Follow the instructions for Frame 12.

a. I [s] _____ you'll go to the West for your vacation.
b. I had [be] _____ washing the car.
c. His [kn] _____ of foreign languages astounded me.
d. The [c] _____ at West Point of course includes military [str] _____ .

12

a. benefited
b. Whose
c. punctuation
d. sergeant, themselves, alcohol

14

Follow the instructions for Frame 12.

a. Maybe all four of us can go [to] _____ .
b. We [u] _____ _____ live in Madison.
c. Have you [e] _____ money to pay for the suit?
d. The [t] _____ thought he had a [bril] _____ scheme to avoid paying the rent.

13

a. suppose
b. been
c. knowledge
d. curriculum, strategy

15

Select from the words we studied in this unit one or two that have given you trouble in the past. Write an original sentence with each word.

_____

_____

14

a. together
b. used to
c. enough
d. tenant, brilliant

16

Study each word you misspelled in Frames 9–15. Write each missed word correctly three times. Check your spellings against the list above Frame 1.

15

(Check Frames 1–8 to see whether you have spelled each word correctly.)

UNIT 80 · Some old, old demons (II)

WORDS TREATED

almost	choose	friend	remember	warrior
already	expense	huge	suspense	
anxious	fascinating	interrupt	until	
attach	forward	pleasant	volume	

1   choose

The most often misspelled words are not rare words with many syllables. They are usually common words of one or two syllables.

Choose is an example. This is the simple form of the verb; the past tense is spelled differently. *Choose* your partner. Did you *choose* your partner? I'll *choose* you.

Write two original sentences with *choose*.

_____

_____

2   friend

Some persons remember the spelling of *friend* by thinking of this rhyme:

> It would be a sad *end*
> To *die* without a *friend*.

Copy: *End* is the end of *friend*.

_____

1   Models:

I *choose* Jacqueline.
Shall I *choose* again?

3   until

There is only one *l* in *until*.

Copy the above sentence three times.

_____

_____

_____

2

End is the end of *friend*.

268

4 fascinating

Fascinating goes back to Latin *fascinum*, meaning a spell. A fascinating person seems to put you under a spell. In Latin both the *s* and the *c* were pronounced. We have changed the pronunciation but not the *fascin* spelling.

Write *fascinum* once and *fascinating* three times.

_____ , _____

_____ , _____

---

5 remember

Carelessness is probably the chief reason why many persons misspell *remember*. You need only *re mem ber* that it has three syllables.

Copy: *Remember* November, *remember* December,
     Remember one part of *remember* is *member.*

_____

_____

---

6 volume

The last letter of *volume* is *e*. It comes from the Latin *volumen*. We simply dropped the *n*.

Copy: *fume, flume, plume, volume.*

_____ , _____ , _____ , _____

---

7 already   almost

Already means at this unexpectedly early time: Johann has *already* come.

   Almost means nearly: The work was *almost* done.

Write an original sentence with *already*, one with *almost*, and a third with both *almost* and *already*.

_____

_____

_____

---

8 expense   suspense

Copy: Both *expense* and *suspense* end in *pense.*

_____

_____

---

9 pleasant   forward

Copy: A *pleasant* peasant brought *forward* a pheasant.

_____

_____

3

There is only one *l* in *until.*
There is only one *l* in *until.*
There is only one *l* in *until.*

4

fascinum
fascinating
fascinating
fascinating

5

Remember November, *remember* December,
Remember one part of *remember* is *member.*

6

fume
flume
plume
volume

---

7 Models:

Already I'm half through.
It is *almost* noon.
I am *almost* finished *already.*

8

Both *expense* and *suspense* end in *pense.*

10　　　interrupt　　warrior

Copy: *Interrupt* and *warrior* each have two *r*'s together.

_____

_____

11　　　anxious　　attach　　huge

Copy: We were *anxious* to *attach* the *huge* rudder.

_____

_____

12

Match each definition with one of the words we studied in this unit. Write each word in full. The first letter or letters have been supplied as a clue.

a. charming, [fa] _____

b. up to this time, [un] _____

c. very large, [h] _____

d. cost, [ex] _____

e. toward the front, [for] _____

13

Follow the instructions for Frame 12.

a. a book, [v] _____

b. to recall, [rem] _____

c. opposite of an enemy, [fr] _____

d. fasten, [at] _____

e. break in upon, [inter] _____

f. full of anxiety, [an] _____

14

Follow the instructions for Frame 12.

a. at this unexpectedly early time, [al] _____

b. to select, [ch] _____

c. nearly, [al] _____

d. fighter, [war] _____

e. agreeable, giving pleasure, [pl] _____

f. anxiety caused by uncertainty, [sus] _____

9

A *pleasant* peasant brought *forward* a pheasant.

10

Interrupt and *warrior* each have two *r*'s together.

11

We were *anxious* to *attach* the *huge* rudder.

12

a. fascinating

b. until

c. huge

d. expense

e. forward

13

a. volume

b. remember

c. friend

d. attach

e. interrupt

f. anxious

15

Write in full each incomplete word, choosing the most suitable from those studied in this unit.

a. My best [fr] _____ is going to college next year.
b. Pour water into the pipe [un] _____ it overflows.
c. Take one step [for] _____.
d. An elephant is [h] _____.
e. Please don't [inter] _____ when I'm talking.

16

Follow the instructions for Frame 15.

a. Did you [ch] _____ the blue or the green?
b. I've spent [al] _____ all my money.
c. Do you [re] _____ the song "Juanita"?
d. I'm [an] _____ to get the examination results.
e. The [ex] _____ was greater than we could afford.
f. The movie keeps the audience in constant [sus] _____.

17

Follow the instructions for Frame 15.

a. She is the most [fa] _____ blonde I've ever met.
b. The librarian said that this [vo] _____ is very rare.
c. Have you [al] _____ voted?
d. Her voice is low and [pl] _____.
e. [At] _____ the lid with a screwdriver.
f. In battle Siegfried was a valiant [war] _____.

18

Select from the words we studied in this unit one or two that have given you trouble in the past. Write an original sentence with each word.

_____

_____

19

Study each word you misspelled in Frames 12–18. Write each missed word correctly three times. Check your spellings against the list above Frame 1.

14

a. already
b. choose
c. almost
d. warrior
e. pleasant
f. suspense

15

a. friend
b. until
c. forward
d. huge
e. interrupt

16

a. choose
b. almost
c. remember
d. anxious
e. expense
f. suspense

17

a. fascinating
b. volume
c. already
d. pleasant
e. Attach
f. warrior

18

(Check Frames 1–11 to see whether you have spelled each word correctly.)

UNIT 81 · Spelling oddities (I)

WORDS TREATED

ache	banana	buoyant	ecstasy
aisle	biscuit	camouflage	marriage
all right	breadth	carriage	pursue
awkward	buoy	colonel	survey

---

1   colonel

It will help you to remember rather strange spellings if you know something about why the oddities exist.

Colonel, for instance, is pronounced like *kernel*, as if it has an *r* in it. The French word from which it was borrowed does have an *r*, but *colonel* goes back further to Old Italian *colonello*, which meant column of soldiers. (Our word *column* is a relative.)

Copy: The lieutenant *colonel* reported to the *colonel*.

---

2   aisle

The Middle English spelling of *aisle* (as in a church) was much simpler: *ile*. The word goes back further to French *aile* and Latin *ala*, meaning wing. The *s* crept in because of confusion with *isle*, meaning island.

Write a sentence in which you refer to the *aisle* in a theater.

1

The lieutenant *colonel* reported to the *colonel*.

---

3   camouflage

In time of war, ships or other military equipment may be painted or covered in some way to hide them or to disguise what they really are. They are then said to be *camouflaged*. The *ou* is explained by the fact that the word comes from French *camoufler*, meaning to disguise.

Write a sentence using *camouflage* or *camouflaged*.

---

2   Model:

The usher took us down the *aisle* of the theater.

4 biscuit

The *ui* in *biscuit* also is attributable to the French. In Middle French, from which we borrowed the word, the spelling was *bescuit*. When the English took it over, the *e* became an *i*, but the *ui* remained.

Write *biscuit* three times.

_____, _____, _____

5 banana

The Spanish and the Portuguese centuries ago found growing in Africa a long yellow fruit. They borrowed the African name for it, *banana*. The English then borrowed the word from the Spanish and Portuguese. Thus *banana* is one of a small number of African words that have come to us with little or no change.

Write a sentence including *banana*.

_____

_____

6 buoy buoyant

Buoy used to be spelled *boie*, and *buoyant* may come from the same source or from a Spanish *boyante*, floating. No one is sure how the *u* crept in, but it probably did so because the sound of *u* is present in the pronunciation.

Pronounce *buoy* and *buoyant*, exaggerating the sound of *u*. Then write each word three times.

_____, _____, _____

_____, _____ . _____

7 ecstasy

Ecstasy may be traced to Greek *ekstasis*, meaning deranged. A person in ecstasy is so overwhelmed by emotion that he is temporarily almost out of his mind.

Write a sentence including *ecstasy*.

_____

_____

8 all right

Although some modern dictionaries list *alright* as acceptable, some people insist that *all right* must be two words. They argue that nobody would write *alwrong*. In writing for school or college or for publication, you will probably find it wise to spell it *all right*.

Write a sentence using *all right* as the first two words.

_____

3 Model:

The *camouflage* was so excellent that the cannon was invisible from fifty feet away.

4

biscuit
biscuit
biscuit

5 Model:

My little brother peeled the entire *banana*.

6

buoy, buoy, buoy
buoyant, buoyant, buoyant

7 Model:

Joan's *ecstasy* when she received the fur coat was indescribable.

9 **breadth**

Breadth is related to *broad*, meaning wide. The Old English spelling of *broad* was *brad*. Another word meaning width was *brede*. *Brad* and *brede* became confused in spelling, and the *th* was added by analogy with *width* and *length*. As a final result, we have *breadth*. Write *breadth* three times.

_____, _____, _____

---

10 **ache** **awkward**

If you look in the dictionary, you will see that no other common English word uses either *ache* or *awk* as its beginning. Both these spellings go back to the Middle Ages.

Copy: My feet *ache* and I run in an *awkward*, gawky way.

_____

_____

---

11 **carriage** **marriage**

If you can spell either *carriage* or *marriage*, you can spell the other. Both spellings are from Old French.

Copy: "It won't be a stylish *marriage*,
     I can't afford a *carriage*." [Old song]

_____

_____

---

12 **pursue** **survey**

The first *u* in *pursue* goes back to Old French, and the *sur* in *survey* goes back ultimately to Latin *super*, meaning over: to survey is to look over.

Copy: pUrsue, pUrsue, pUrsue
     sUrvey, sUrvey, sUrvey

_____, _____, _____

_____, _____, _____

13

To match the definitions below, choose words we studied in this unit. The beginning letter or letters have been supplied. Write the words in full.

a. military officer outranking a major, [c] _____
b. yes, certainly; entirely correct, [a] _____
c. width, [br] _____
d. an anchored floating object serving as a marker, [b] _____
e. a long yellow fruit, [ba] _____
f. to chase, [p] _____
g. a wedding, [m] _____
h. to feel pain, [a] _____

---

8 **Model:**

All right, you may go.

9

breadth
breadth
breadth

10

My feet *ache* and I run in an *awk-ward*, gawky way.

11

"It won't be a stylish *marriage*,
I can't afford a *carriage*."

12

pUrsue, pUrsue, pUrsue
sUrvey, sUrvey, sUrvey

14

Follow the instructions for Frame 13.

a. able to float, [b] _____

b. narrow passageway, usually in a building, [a] _____

c. to conceal or disguise, [cam] _____

d. small kind of bread, [bis] _____

e. state of great joy, [e] _____

f. to look over; to measure, [s] _____

g. horse-drawn vehicle, [c] _____

h. clumsy, [a] _____

13

a. colonel

b. all right

c. breadth

d. buoy

e. banana

f. pursue

g. marriage

h. ache

15

Write in full the word that best fits each sentence below, choosing from those studied in this unit.

a. Some swimmers are more [b] _____ than others.

b. The length is twelve feet, and the [br] _____ is four feet.

c. [A] _____, I agree to your terms.

d. The major and the [c] _____ discussed strategy.

e. In England a cracker is called a [bis] _____.

f. A giraffe is an [a] _____ beast.

g. We hired a surveyor to [s] _____ our land.

h. A wedding between an old and a young person is called a December–May [m] _____.

14

a. buoyant

b. aisle

c. camouflage

d. biscuit

e. ecstasy

f. survey

g. carriage

h. awkward

16

Follow the instructions for Frame 15.

a. Henry ate an orange and a [b] _____.

b. The men tried to [cam] _____ the ship by painting zigzag lines on it.

c. A red and white [b] _____ helped to mark the channel.

d. When Quintus finally proposed to her, she thought that she had never felt such [e] _____.

e. The members of the wedding party marched solemnly down the [a] _____.

f. Arthritis makes bodily joints [a] _____.

g. The dog started to [p] _____ the cat.

h. The ornate [c] _____ was pulled by two white horses.

15

a. buoyant

b. breadth

c. All right

d. colonel

e. biscuit

f. awkward

g. survey

h. marriage

Study each word that you misspelled in Frames 13–16. Review the appropriate explanation in Frames 1–12 to help you remember why the word is spelled in such an odd way. Write each missed word correctly three times. Check your spellings against the list above Frame 1.

a. banana
b. camouflage
c. buoy
d. ecstasy
e. aisle
f. ache
g. pursue
h. carriage

UNIT 82 · Spelling oddities (II)

WORDS TREATED

absurd	hearse
against	hearth
coarse	hoarse
etc.	hypocrisy
exhilarate	inoculate

1   coarse

It will help you to remember rather strange spellings if you know something about why the oddities exist.

    Coarse, for instance, was spelled either *corse* or *course* until the eighteenth century. It means rough, or in large pieces, or vulgar. In the eighteenth century the spelling *coarse* developed to distinguish the word from *course,* a word with several different meanings.

Write a sentence using *coarse.*

2   hoarse

Hoarse, as in *a hoarse voice,* was spelled *hors* in Middle English. Then, possibly influenced by *harsk,* meaning harsh, the present spelling with an *a* developed. Perhaps the wish to distinguish *hoarse* from *horse* encouraged the change.

Write a sentence using *hoarse.*

3   absurd

Absurd is spelled with a *u* because it comes from the Latin *absurdus,* meaning ridiculous or incongruous.

Copy: *Absurd! Absurd! A true absurdity!*

1   Model:

The *coarse* salt quickly melted the ice.

2   Model:

A crow's caws sound *hoarse.*

4   against

Against is related to *again*. Both words go back to Old English *ongean*, and an early meaning for each was "in the opposite direction." The two forms gradually separated in meaning, so that *again* now most often means once more, and *against* means in opposition to.

Write a sentence using *against*.

_____

_____

5   exhilarate

Exhilarate is simply the English spelling of Latin *exhilaratus*, meaning cheered or gladdened. *Exhilaratus* is based on *hilarus*, cheerful, from which our word *hilarious* also comes. If someone is *exhilarated* he is made extremely cheerful.

Write a sentence using *exhilarate* or *exhilarated*.

_____

_____

6   etc.

In Latin *et cetera* means and others, or and so on. (*Et* means and.) In English we use the abbreviation much more often than the two words. Since it is an abbreviation, it requires a period.

Copy: *et cetera, etc.*

_____ _____, _____

7   hypocrisy

Hypocrisy owes its spelling, including the *y* and the *is*, to the fact that it goes back to Greek *hypocrisis*, which meant the act of playing a part on the stage or any other kind of false pretense or outward show. The latter meaning still exists: a person is guilty of *hypocrisy* if he pretends to be something that he is not or to believe something that he does not.

Copy: A *hypocrite* is guilty of *hypocrisy*.

_____

_____

8   hearse

Hearse now usually means a vehicle for carrying a dead person. The older spelling is *herse*, which usually meant a harrow or something shaped like a harrow. The *a* perhaps was put into *hearse* because of this relationship to *harrow*.

Copy: He hears the *hearse* approaching.

_____

_____

3

Absurd! Absurd! A true *absurdity!*

4   Model:

The fight *against* cancer goes on and on.

5   Model:

The news of our father's recovery *exhilarated* all of us.

6

et cetera, etc.

7

A *hypocrite* is guilty of *hypocrisy*.

9   hearth

The Old English spelling of *hearth* was *heorth,* and *heart* was spelled *heorte.* The *eo* in several such Old English words changed to *ea* in later spelling.

Copy: The crude *hearth* was made of earth.

_____

_____

---

10   inoculate

An earlier meaning of *inoculate* was to put a bud into a tree by grafting. That meaning came logically from the Latin words *in,* which means in, and *oculus,* which means bud. The present meaning of *inoculate,* to put bacteria or serums into a body to prevent disease, is related, although the idea of the bud has been lost. *Inoculate* has only one *n* and one *c* because the Latin *in* and *oculus* have only one of each.

Copy: *Inoculate* comes from *in* plus *oculus.*

_____

_____

11

To match the definitions below, choose words we studied in this unit. The beginning letter or letters have been supplied. Write the words in full.

a. in opposition to, [ag] _____
b. not fine, [co] _____
c. vehicle for carrying the dead, [h] _____
d. insert bacteria or serums into, [in] _____
e. and so forth (abbreviation), [e] _____

12

Follow the instructions for Frame 11.

a. fireside, [h] _____
b. rough; grating; harsh, [h] _____
c. ridiculous, [ab] _____
d. to make extremely cheerful, [ex] _____
e. undesirable kind of pretending, [hyp] _____

8

He hears the *hearse* approaching.

9

The crude *hearth* was made of earth.

10

Inoculate comes from *in* plus *oculus.*

11

a. against
b. coarse
c. hearse
d. inoculate
e. etc.

13

Write the word in full that best fits each sentence below, choosing from those studied in this unit.

a. We numbered the exhibits A, AA, B, BB, [e] _____.
b. His struggles [ag] _____ temptation were never very strong.
c. The body was taken to the grave in a black [h] _____.
d. This fresh air is enough to [ex] _____ me.
e. The doctor decided to [in] _____ us all against typhoid fever.

14

Follow the instructions for Frame 13.

a. Our ancestors cooked their meals at an open [h] _____.
b. My father told me, "Gentlemen never make [c] _____ remarks in the presence of ladies."
c. I first suspected his [hyp] _____ when he began boasting about his patriotism.
d. To say that snow will not melt at fifty degrees seems [ab] _____.
e. We cheered so much that we became [h] _____.

15

Study each word that you misspelled in Frames 11–14. Review the appropriate explanation in Frames 1–10 to help you remember why the word is spelled in such an odd way. Write each missed word correctly three times. Check your spellings against the list above Frame 1.

12

a. hearth
b. hoarse
c. absurd
d. exhilarate
e. hypocrisy

13

a. etc.
b. against
c. hearse
d. exhilarate
e. inoculate

14

a. hearth
b. coarse
c. hypocrisy
d. absurd
e. hoarse

UNIT 83 · Spelling oddities (III)

WORDS TREATED

dying	mediocre	persuade	restaurant
impromptu	nowadays	plebeian	tying
kindergarten	parliament	prairie	
lying	pastime	reminisce	

1 kindergarten

It will help you to remember rather strange spellings if you know something about why the oddities exist.

For instance, *kindergarten* is spelled as it is because it is taken over exactly from German. *Kinder* in German means children, and *garten* is the German spelling of *garden*.

Copy: Kids often *smarten*
      In *kindergarten*.

---

2 mediocre

Something is *mediocre* if it is neither very good nor very bad. The Latin words from which it comes are *medi* and *ocris*, meaning halfway up a stony mountain. (Probably that is a situation that is neither good nor bad!)

Write a sentence using *mediocre*.

---

3 pastime

If English spelling were entirely logical, *pastime* should have a double *s*, because a *pastime* is something that one engages in to pass the time. However, *pass* apparently became confused with *past*, perhaps because of the *t* in *time*. So we write *pastime*.

Write a sentence using *pastime*.

---

4 parliament

The exact reason for the *ia* in *parliament* is difficult to discover. The word goes back to French *parler*, Old French *parlier*, meaning to speak. The word *parley*, meaning a conference, is related. The French refer to *parlement*, but the British have used the spelling *parliament* since the Middle Ages.

Copy: Imagine a liar in *parliament*.

1

Kids often *smarten*
In *kindergarten*.

---

2 Model:

My grades this year are only *mediocre*.

---

3 Model:

My favorite *pastime* is playing badminton.

5 persuade

It is rather unusual in English for *ua* to be pronounced like *way*, as it is in *persuade*. The explanation of this word is simple. *Persuade* is only a shortened form of the Latin *persuadere*, which has the same meaning.

Write a sentence using *persuade*.

_____

_____

6 plebeian

Three consecutive vowels like the *eia* of *plebeian* are also rather rare in English. In Latin, *plebs* meant the common people, and the adjective *plebeius* meant of the common people. *Plebeian* is the latter word, with English *–an* substituted for Latin *–us*.

Copy: He is a *plebeian*, not a patrician.

_____

7 prairie

Old French had a word *praerie*, which probably was derived from Latin *pratum*, meaning a meadow. In English the *aer* of the French word became the *air* of *prairie*, possibly by confusion with *air* or possibly because the *aer* spelling is rare in English.

Write a sentence using *prairie*.

_____

8 restaurant

Restaurant has an *au* because it is derived from French *restaurer*, to restore. The name is appropriate because in a restaurant one restores his strength.

Write *restaurant* three times.

_____, _____, _____

9 reminisce

The noun *reminiscence*, meaning a remembrance or recollection, was taken from the French without change in the sixteenth century. Our verb *reminisce*, to recollect, is a shortened form of *reminiscence* (called a back-formation). It seems to have been used first only a little more than a century ago.

Copy: *reminisce, reminiscence, reminiscent.*

_____, _____,

_____

4

Imagine a liar in *parliament*.

5 Model:

I tried to *persuade* him to report the theft to the police.

6

He is a *plebeian*, not a patrician.

7 Model:

The oxen stolidly pulled the covered wagon across the *prairie*.

8

restaurant
restaurant
restaurant

10   nowadays

Pronounce all three syllables of *nowadays*, not forgetting the first *a*. *Nowadays* is the word *now* plus *a* (which in Middle English meant *in*) plus *days*, so that the full meaning of *nowadays* is now in (these) days. (The useful word *nowanights* also exists but is rarely heard.)

Write a sentence using *nowadays*.

_____

_____

11   dying   lying   tying

The verbs *die*, *lie*, and *tie* would look strange if we dropped the *e* before *–ing*: *diing*, etc. And not dropping the *e* would result in three vowels in a row. To avoid those problems, we substitute *y* for the *ie*.

Copy: The *dying* man was *lying* there, *tying* his shoes.

_____

_____

12   impromptu

Something is done *impromptu* if it is done without much previous planning: an *impromptu* speech. Some persons think of *prompt* in this word.

Write *impromptu* three times.

_____ , _____ , _____

13

To match the definitions below, choose words we studied in this unit. The beginning letters have been supplied.

a. way to amuse oneself, [pa] _____
b. British legislative body, [Par] _____
c. school for small children, [kin] _____
d. between good and bad, [med] _____
e. an eating place, [res] _____
f. unplanned, [im] _____
g. fastening with rope, [t] _____

14

Follow the instructions for Frame 13.

a. in these days, [now] _____
b. recollect; remember, [rem] _____
c. pertaining to the common people, especially of Rome, [pl] _____

_____
d. convince; win over to do, [per] _____
e. flat and grassy country, [pr] _____
f. reclining, [l] _____
g. passing away, [d] _____

9

reminisce
reminiscence
reminiscent

10   Model:

People *nowadays* are much interested in outer space.

11

The *dying* man was *lying* there, *tying* his shoes.

12

impromptu
impromptu
impromptu

13

a. pastime
b. Parliament
c. kindergarten
d. mediocre
e. restaurant
f. impromptu
g. tying

15

Write the complete word that best fits each sentence below, choosing from those studied in this unit.

a. The House of Lords and the House of Commons are the two parts of the British [Par] _____ .

b. We ate frog legs in a French [res] _____ .

c. Do you enjoy playing cards as a [pas] _____ ?

d. The Republicans tried to [per] _____ my father to run for the City Council.

e. Today some children learn to read in [kin] _____ .

f. While [l] _____ in bed, I wrote an [im] _____ composition.

16

Follow the instructions for Frame 15.

a. The heavy wind flattened the tall grass on the [pr] _____ .

b. A person of [pl] _____ birth had little chance to rise to high position in ancient Rome.

c. Old men like to [rem] _____ concerning their childhood.

d. I have had only [med] _____ success as a basketball player.

e. Our hopes of [t] _____ the score were [d] _____ .

17

Study each word that you misspelled in Frames 13–16. Review the appropriate explanation in Frames 1–12 to help you remember why the word is spelled in such an odd way. Write each missed word correctly three times. Check your spellings against the list above Frame 1.

14

a. nowadays
b. reminisce
c. plebeian
d. persuade
e. prairie
f. lying
g. dying

15

a. Parliament
b. restaurant
c. pastime
d. persuade
e. kindergarten
f. lying, impromptu

16

a. prairie
b. plebeian
c. reminisce
d. mediocre
e. tying, dying

UNIT 84 · Spelling oddities (IV)

WORDS TREATED

muscle	vegetable
rehearsal	vilify
souvenir	weather
sure	woman
tawdry	women
tortoise	

1   tawdry

It will help you to remember rather strange spellings if you know something about why the oddities exist.

Etheldreda, also known as St. Audrey, was an early medieval queen of Northumbria who was very fond of showy necklaces. *Tawdry*, which means tastelessly showy, is based upon her religious name. The *s* and *e* have been dropped and the *u* changed to *w*.

Copy: Though she was accused of *bawdry*,
        Her clothes were never *tawdry*.

_____

_____

2   woman   women

Some persons have trouble in remembering that *woman* is singular and that *women* is plural. These words are derived in part from *man* and *men*.

$$Singulars \begin{cases} man \\ woman \end{cases} \qquad Plurals \begin{cases} men \\ women \end{cases}$$

Remembering them in this way is easy.

Copy twice: one *man*, one *woman*, two *men*, two *women*.

_____ _____, _____ _____, _____ _____,

_____ _____, _____ _____, _____ _____,

_____ _____

3   rehearsal

Rehearsal comes from *re*, meaning again, and *hercier*, to harrow. A farmer sometimes had to harrow his field again; hence the word came to mean repeating of any kind, such as the repetition of the words of a play or an opera. The *a* may have come in by association with *harrow*.

Write a sentence using *rehearsal*.

_____

_____

4   sure

Sure, an innocent-looking four-letter word, is among the spelling demons. It sounds as if it should be spelled with an *sh*, but it is not because it comes from a French word now spelled *sur* but formerly spelled *sure*. The *sh* sound in the English pronunciation of *sure* is probably due to the fact that the earlier French form was pronounced in a way that sounded a little like *sh*. (If this word bothers you, think of the two four-letter words *sure cure*.)

Copy this sentence: Are you *sure* that this is a *sure cure*?

_____

_____

1

Though she was accused of *bawdry*,
Her clothes were never *tawdry*.

2

one *man*, one *woman*, two *men*,
    two *women*
one *man*, one *woman*, two *men*,
    two *women*

3   Model:

The next *rehearsal* of our play will
    be held tonight.

5   vegetable

The second *e* in *vegetable* is the chief trouble spot. That letter is there because *vegetable* goes back to Latin *vegetare*, which means to make lively. Vegetables, being nutritious, should make one lively. (If you forget the last part of the word, remember a vege*table* on the *table*.) Write *vegetable* three times.

_____ , _____ , _____

6   tortoise

The feet of South European tortoises are crooked. Hence these creatures were called by the Latin word for crooked or twisted, *tortus*. The word has been spelled in a half-dozen ways in English, with *tortoise* becoming the accepted spelling after the nineteenth century, for no apparent reason.

Copy: A *tortoise* makes little *noise*.

_____

7   vilify

Vilify has only one *l* because it is related to *vile*. The suffix *–ify* means to make. You vilify someone if you say things about him that make him seem vile.

Use *vilify* in a sentence.

_____

_____

8   souvenir

Latin *sub* means under, and *venire* means to come. *Subvenire* means to come under consideration or to come up. In French, Latin *sub* becomes *sous*, pronounced like *soo*. Latin *subvenire* led to a French noun *souvenir*, something that comes up as a memory or that brings memories. The English borrowed the French word without changing the spelling or the meaning. Notice that *ir* appears in both the Latin and the French.

Write *souvenir* three times.

_____ , _____ , _____

9   muscle

The ancient Romans had a sense of humor. When one of them bent his arm to show his muscle, his friends would tease him by saying *"Musculus."* *Musculus* means little mouse; they were saying that his muscle was no bigger than a mouse. Because of the Latin *musculus* we have a *c* in our word *muscle*.

Write a sentence using the word *muscle* or *muscles*.

_____

_____

4

Are you *sure* that this is a *sure cure*?

5

vegetable
vegetable
vegetable

6

A *tortoise* makes little *noise*.

7   Model:

I did not mean to *vilify* him, but I really believed that he was a liar and a cheat.

8

souvenir
souvenir
souvenir

10   weather

A small boy wrote *whafhir* for *weather*. His teacher said, "Henry, that's the worst spell of *weather* we've ever had!"

Write the word *weather* three times in the way that Henry should have spelled it.

_____, _____, _____

11

To match the definitions below, choose words we studied in this unit. The beginning letter or letters have been supplied. Write the words in full.

a. a female human being, [w] _____
b. cheap and showy, [ta] _____
c. certain, [s] _____
d. keepsake or remembrance, [so] _____
e. land-based turtle, [to] _____

12

Follow the instructions for Frame 11.

a. two or more female human beings, [w] _____
b. repetition, as of a play practice, [re] _____
c. a food plant, [veg] _____
d. to say bad things of a person, [vi] _____
e. rain, snow, sunshine, [w] _____
f. bundle of tissue in a body, [mu] _____

13

Write in full the word that best fits each sentence, choosing from those studied in this unit.

a. The [w] _____ this year has been unusually cold.
b. A man and a [w] _____ were walking along the road.
c. I was [s] _____ that I could succeed.
d. We bought a [so] _____ at a roadside stand.
e. Those huge earrings look [ta] _____ to me.

14

Follow the instructions for Frame 13.

a. Do you prefer a flower garden or a [veg] _____ garden?
b. To call a man a thief is to [vi] _____ him.
c. "Let's start the [re] _____," the director said.
d. The two [w] _____ began quarreling violently.
e. Stand perfectly still. Don't move a [m] _____.
f. Someone had carved initials on the shell of the [tor] _____.

---

9   **Model:**

The little boy's *muscles* grew stronger.

10

weather
weather
weather

11

a. woman
b. tawdry
c. sure
d. souvenir
e. tortoise

12

a. women
b. rehearsal
c. vegetable
d. vilify
e. weather
f. muscle

13

a. weather
b. woman
c. sure
d. souvenir
e. tawdry

15

Study each word that you misspelled in Frames 11–14. Review the appropriate explanation in Frames 1–10 to help you remember why the word is spelled in such an odd way. Write each missed word correctly three times. Check your spellings against the list above Frame 1.

14

a. vegetable
b. vilify
c. rehearsal
d. women
e. muscle
f. tortoise

UNIT 85 · Names of the months and days

WORDS TREATED

April	Friday	March	October	Thursday
August	January	May	Saturday	Tuesday
December	July	Monday	September	Wednesday
February	June	November	Sunday	

---

1   January

A few of the names of months and days offer spelling difficulties. Knowledge of where these names came from is interesting in itself and also may help you to remember a troublesome spelling or two.

January, for instance, came from Latin *Januarius*, a month named for the god *Janus*. Janus had two faces, one looking in each direction. Tell why the name *January* is appropriate for the first month of the year.

_____

_____

---

2   February   March   April   May

February, from Latin *Februarius*, is named for *Februa*, a Roman feast of purification.

   March is named for *Mars*, the Roman god of war.
   April is derived from the Latin name for that month, *Aprilis*.
   May is named for the Roman goddess of spring, *Maia*.

Copy: *January, February, March, April,* and *May* are the first five months.

_____

_____

1   Model:

Like Janus, January "looks both ways," toward the past year and toward the coming year.

3   **June**   **July**   **August**

June is based on a common Roman name, *Junius.*
    July is named in honor of *Julius* Caesar.
    August is named for another Roman ruler, *Augustus* Caesar.

Copy: *June, July,* and *August* are my favorite months.

_____

_____

4   **September**   **October**   **November**   **December**

If you have studied Latin, you have learned to count *septem, octo, novem,* and *decem* for *seven, eight, nine,* and *ten.* The months that we call *September, October, November,* and *December* were the seventh, eighth, ninth, and tenth months in the ancient Roman calendar.

Copy: *September, October, November,* and *December* come from *septem, octo, novem,* and *decem.*

_____

_____

5   **Sunday**   **Monday**

The names of the days of the week come from three sources.
    Sunday and *Monday* (which almost no one misspells) go back to the Old English words for *sun (sunne)* and *moon (mona).*

Write a sentence using *Sunday* and *Monday.*

_____

_____

6   **Tuesday**   **Wednesday**

Tuesday, Wednesday, Thursday, and *Friday* are all named for old Norse or Germanic gods.
    Tuesday comes from *Tiw,* god of war.
    The *d* in *Wednesday* precedes the *n* because *Wednesday* comes from *Woden,* the chief of the gods in Germanic mythology.

Write *Tuesday* and *Wednesday* three times each.

_____, _____, _____

_____, _____, _____

7   **Thursday**   **Friday**

Thursday is derived from *Thor,* Norse god of thunder.
    Friday comes from the Old High German *Fria,* the goddess of love.

Write a sentence using *Thursday* and *Friday.*

_____

_____

2

January, February, March, April, and *May* are the first five months.

3

June, July, and *August* are my favorite months.

4

September, October, November, and *December* come from *septem, octo, novem,* and *decem.*

5   **Model:**

Sunday and *Monday* are his days off.

6

Tuesday, Tuesday, Tuesday
Wednesday, Wednesday, Wednesday

8 Saturday

Unlike names of other days, *Saturday* comes from Latin. *Saturnus* was an ancient Roman god of agriculture. (The planet *Saturn* is also named for him.)

Copy: *Saturday* and *Saturn* are related.

_____

9

Write the names of the months in the correct order, *January* through *December*.

_____, _____, _____, _____,
_____, _____, _____, _____, _____,
_____, _____, _____

10

Write the names of the months in reverse order, *December* through *January*.

_____, _____, _____,
_____, _____, _____, _____,
_____, _____, _____, _____,
_____

11

Write the names of the days in correct order, *Sunday* through *Saturday*.

_____, _____, _____, _____,
_____, _____, _____

12

Write the names of the days in reverse order, *Saturday* through *Sunday*.

_____, _____, _____,
_____, _____, _____, _____

13

Study carefully each word that you misspelled in Frames 9–12. Write each missed word correctly three times. Check your spellings against the list above Frame 1.

---

7 Model:

Can you come on *Thursday* or *Friday?*

8

Saturday and *Saturn* are related.

9

January	July
February	August
March	September
April	October
May	November
June	December

10

December	June
November	May
October	April
September	March
August	February
July	January

11

Sunday	Thursday
Monday	Friday
Tuesday	Saturday
Wednesday	

12

Saturday	Tuesday
Friday	Monday
Thursday	Sunday
Wednesday	

Word List

The **boldface** numbers indicate the units in which the words are treated; the numbers in parentheses indicate the pages on which the units begin.

297

plumb **68** (219)
pneumonia **74** (244)
poem **17, 62** (54, 195)
polar **35** (109)
political **48** (150)
politicked **13** (41)
politicking **13** (41)
poll **65** (207)
portray **47** (147)
possess **34** (106)
possession **34** (106)
possessive **34** (106)
possible **46** (144)
potatoes **31** (97)
practical **12** (37)
practically **17** (54)
prairie **83** (279)
preamble **65** (207)
precarious **53** (166)
precede **25** (78)
precinct **65** (207)
predicate **61** (192)
predominance **39** (121)
predominant **39** (121)
prefer **18** (57)
preference **26** (81)
preferred **22** (70)
prejudice **71** (233)
prelude **63** (190)
prepare **18** (57)
preposition **61** (192)
presence **28** (88)
present **28** (88)
pretentious **53** (166)
prettier **6** (18)
prettily **6** (18)
prevalent **72** (236)
priest **9** (28)
primitive **45** (140)
principal **48, 76** (150, 251)
principally **10** (31)
principle **76** (251)
privilege **45** (140)
probable **51** (160)
probably **16** (51)
procedure **25** (78)
proceed **25** (78)
profession **49** (154)
professor **49** (154)
prominence **28** (88)
prominent **28** (88)
pronoun **61** (192)
pronunciation **72** (236)
propaganda **52** (163)
propeller **22** (70)
prophecy **77** (255)

prophesy **77** (255)
prospective **19** (60)
protoplasm **64** (203)
psychology **74** (244)
pumpkin **17** (54)
punctuation **79** (264)
puree (purée) **67** (215)
purl **67** (215)
pursue **81** (272)

quadratic **66** (211)
quality **1** (3)
quantitative **44** (137)
quantity **16** (51)
quarter **15** (47)
quarterly **69** (223)
quatrain **62** (195)
question **1** (3)
questionnaire **1** (3)
quiet **1** (3)
quit **1** (3)
quite **1** (3)
quiz **1** (3)
quizzed **21** (68)
quizzes **32** (100)
quotation **1** (3)
quote **1** (3)

rabbet **68** (219)
radiance **39** (121)
radiant **39** (121)
radioactive **64** (203)
radius **66** (211)
rarity **44** (137)
raspberry **74** (244)
readily **45** (140)
realize **36** (112)
really **2** (6)
recede **25** (78)
receipt **9** (28)
receive **9** (28)
receptacle **50** (157)
recognize **16** (51)
recommend **2, 49** (6, 154)
rectangle **66** (211)
recurrence **26** (81)
recurrent **26** (81)
reference **26** (81)
referred **22** (70)
referring **22** (70)
reforestation **14** (43)
refrain **54** (170)
regard **71** (233)
regular **35** (109)
rehearsal **84** (283)
reign **73** (240)

relative **52** (163)
reliability **6** (18)
reliable **6** (18)
relieve **9** (28)
religion **20** (64)
religious **53** (166)
remember **80** (268)
remembrance **72** (236)
reminisce **83** (279)
remittance **69** (223)
rendezvous **74** (244)
repellent **22** (70)
repentance **39** (121)
repentant **39** (121)
repetition **58** (183)
repetitious **53** (166)
represent **58** (183)
requisition **69** (223)
residence **28** (88)
resident **28** (88)
resistance **39, 70** (121, 226)
resistant **39** (121)
resourceful **5** (15)
respiration **64** (203)
response **20** (64)
responsible **46** (144)
restaurant **83** (279)
retriever **9** (28)
reverence **26** (81)
reverent **26** (81)
revise **23** (73)
rheostat **70** (226)
rhetoric **73** (240)
rhyme **62** (195)
rhythm **73** (240)
ridicule **50** (157)
ridiculous **30** (95)
righteous **24** (76)
rinse **78** (260)
roommate **2** (6)
rubbing **21** (68)
runner **21** (68)

sacrifice **45** (140)
sacrilegious **53** (166)
safety **5** (15)
said **71** (233)
sandwich **71** (233)
Saturday **85** (287)
saxophone **63** (199)
scandalous **30** (95)
scantling **68** (219)
scarcely **5** (15)
scarcity **44** (137)
schedule **73** (240)

scholar **35** (109)
scissors **47** (147)
scraping **12** (37)
scratches **32** (100)
screeches **32** (100)
secede **25** (78)
second **42** (129)
secretarial **69** (223)
secretary **52** (163)
seize **9** (28)
senator **47** (147)
sense **19** (60)
sensible **46** (144)
sensitive **45** (140)
sentence **29** (91)
sentinel **59** (186)
separate **35** (109)
September **85** (287)
sequel **1** (3)
serenade **63** (199)
sergeant **79** (264)
series **20** (64)
several **48** (150)
severely **5** (15)
sewage **68** (219)
shan't **40** (124)
she'd **40** (124)
she'll **40** (124)
shellacked **13** (41)
shellacking **13** (41)
shepherd **72** (236)
sherbe(r)t **67** (215)
shield **9** (28)
shining **11** (33)
shipping **21** (68)
shoeing **11** (33)
shriek **9** (28)
siege **9** (28)
significance **39** (121)
significant **39** (121)
silence **28** (88)
silent **28** (88)
similar **35** (109)
simile **62** (195)
simple **50** (157)
simply **11** (33)
simultaneous **24** (76)
since **19** (60)
sincerely **5** (15)
singeing **11** (33)
sinner **12** (68)
sipped **21** (68)
sitting **21** (68)
skies **7** (22)
slimmest **21** (68)
slimy **12** (37)

B 7
C 8
D 9
E 0
F 1
G 2
H 3
I 4
J 5